Plural World Interpretations
The Case of the South-Siberian Tyvans

Plural World Interpretations are part of our everyday lives, even if we are not aware of the fact. They result from the simultaneous existence of different but equal models for interpreting the world we live in. These models are the product of human constructivity and co-exist as parallel realities, complementing and contradicting each other. Based on fieldwork among the Tyva of southern Siberia, this book discusses practices of dealing with this multiplicity of world interpretations and shows how individual actors oscillate flexibly between two of many possible models for interpreting specific situations and act on them. The author analyses the rules Tyvans apply in varying contexts, the reasons behind their choices and the consequences they have to deal with. The result is an account of contemporary culture that explores the flexibility and plurality of human interpretation, action and behaviour.

Halle Studies in the Anthropology of Eurasia

General Editors:

Christoph Brumann, Kirsten Endres, Chris Hann, Thomas Hauschild,
Burkhard Schnepel, Dittmar Schorkowitz, Lale Yalçın-Heckmann

Volume 32

LIT

Anett C. Oelschlaegel

Plural World Interpretations
The Case of the South-Siberian Tyvans

LIT

Cover Image: Collage by Ullrich Wannhoff, Berlin, *Deer and Woman* (Courtesy of the artist).

Bibliographic information published by the Deutsche Nationalbibliothek
The Deutsche Nationalbibliothek lists this publication in the Deutsche Nationalbibliografie; detailed bibliographic data are available on the Internet at http://dnb.d-nb.de.

ISBN 978-3-643-90788-2

A catalogue record for this book is available from the British Library

©LIT VERLAG Dr. W. Hopf
Berlin 2016
Fresnostr. 2
D-48159 Münster
Tel. +49 (0) 2 51-62 03 20
Fax +49 (0) 2 51-23 19 72
E-Mail: lit@lit-verlag.de
http://www.lit-verlag.de

LIT VERLAG GmbH & Co. KG Wien,
Zweigniederlassung Zürich 2016
Klosbachstr. 107
CH-8032 Zürich
Tel. +41 (0) 44-251 75 05
Fax +41 (0) 44-251 75 06
E-Mail: zuerich@lit-verlag.ch
http://www.lit-verlag.ch

Distribution:
In the UK: Global Book Marketing, e-mail: mo@centralbooks.com
In North America: International Specialized Book Services, e-mail: orders@isbs.com
In Germany: LIT Verlag Fresnostr. 2, D-48159 Münster
Tel. +49 (0) 2 51-620 32 22, Fax +49 (0) 2 51-922 60 99, e-mail: vertrieb@lit-verlag.de

In Austria: Medienlogistik Pichler-ÖBZ, e-mail: mlo@medien-logistik.at
e-books are available at www.litwebshop.de

Contents

	List of Illustrations	vii
	Preface	ix
	Acknowledgements	xi
	Note on Transliteration	xiii
	Prologue: Progress and Stability, the Quest for Balance	**1**
	Introduction: The Tyvans, a Turk Language-Speaking People in South Siberia	**7**
	Research Problem	16
	Data Collection	18
Plates	Social Life: Festivals and Life in the Taiga (1-35)	23
Part I	**The Theory of Plural World Interpretations**	**39**
	From Tradition and Modernity to Plural World Interpretations	40
	Multiple Realities	44
	Transdifference	47
	Two Models of World Interpretation	48
	Terms and Definitions	53
	Change in Perspective	57
	Summary	58
Plates	Religious Life (36-62)	61
Part II	**Ethnography of the Tyvan Interaction Model**	**77**
	Non-Human Interaction Partners and Religious Forms of Interaction	78
	Respectful Interaction and its Violation	98
	Fortune and Misfortune in Response to Human Behaviour	103
	Talent and Gifts as Obligations in the Interaction Model	108
	Misfortune, Illness, and Death as Punishment by Evil Spirits	120

	The Pursuit of Stability in the Interaction Model	124
	Wilderness and Pure Ground	136
	Summary	140
Plates	Local Economy (63-104)	145
Part III	**Tyvan Plural World Interpretations**	**165**
	Two Models of World Interpretation and their Parallel Existence	167
	The Conflict between These Models in their Extreme Forms	171
	The Spontaneous Switch and its Most Common Trajectory	176
	The Spontaneous Switch to the Interaction Model and its Consequences	182
	Situational and Contextual Complementation and Substitution	184
	Context, Place, Time, and Counterpart as Reasons for Switching	189
	Hardship Resulting from the Spontaneous Switch to the Interaction Model	198
	The Strategic Switch between the Models by Laypersons	201
	The Professional Switch as a Tool for Shamans	203
	Dealing with Change in the Interaction Model	211
	Summary	214
	Epilogue: Plural World Interpretations, a Diversity of Views	**217**
	Appendices	227
	Краткое содержание	227
	Notes on the Author	240
	Bibliography	241
	Index	255

List of Illustrations

Map

1	Administrative units of the Republic of Tyva	5

Plates

Social Life: Festivals and Life in the Taiga
1	Sculpture of the White Bearded Old Man
2-4	Participants in the Naadym festival
5-9	Activities at the Naadym festival
10	Winner of a wrestling match
11	Wrestling to entertain the spirits
12-16	Horse races for the spirits
17	Wooden saddle
18-21	Musicians and dancers
22	Summer yurt camp
23	Yurt interior
24-27	Dismantling and transporting a yurt
28	Winter camp in Toolajlyg
29	Winter camp at Ak Bashtyg
30	Children on holiday
31	Preparing winter reserves
32-33	Driving in the taiga
34	Mugur River
35	Hospitality

Religious Life
36	Ancestor worship
37	Stone *ovaa*
38	Stone *ovaa* at Nine Heavens
39	Wooden *ovaa*
40-41	*Ovaa* at Ak Bashtyg Mountain
42	Stupa with *ovaa*
43	'The Arat' monument
44	Stupa near Kyzyl
45	Sacred spring near Kyzyl
46-48	Shamans light a sacrificial fire
49	A shamaness
50	Another shamaness
51-53	Consecration of an *ovaa*

54	*Khuvaanak* divination
55-56	Shamanic trees
57	Horse cranium in a tree
58	Sacred trees
59	Buddhist monks and temple
60-61	Interior of a Buddhist temple and monk
62	A yurt

Local Economy

63	Sheep and goats
64	'Two Larches' settlement
65-66	Stock animals
67	Girl milking goats
68	Milking yaks
69	Yaks grazing
70	Yaks carrying equipment
71-74	Riding horses
75	Bactrian camel
76	A herd of camels in Ėrzin
77	A herd of camels in Ulug Khem
78	Cows
79	A rare pig
80-81	Tozhu-Tyva reindeer herders
82	Castrating yearlings
83	Processing milk
84	Milking pails
85-86	Boiling, filtering, and skimming milk
87	Fermenting *khoitpak*
88	Making cheese
89	Goat nibbling curds
90-92	Making flour
93	Hunters making ammunition
94	Luring deer and maral
95-96	Entertainment and rituals during hunting
97	A hunter's knife
98-99	The 'Great Hunter' and his son
100	Stream refrigeration
101	A slaughtered sheep in a yurt
102	Fishing on the Yenisei River
103	The 'Great Hunter's' trophies
104	Russian hunter

Preface

The phrase 'plural world interpretations' denotes the plurality of world interpretation models to be observed in the world today and the human ability to handle them in a flexible manner. By analysing the plurality of world interpretations among the South-Siberian Tyvans, the present book demonstrates the co-existence and cooperation of 'traditional' and 'modern' elements of culture.[1] The concept of plural world interpretations may help to meet the challenge of adopting a broader perspective that shows tradition and modernity as equal, co-existing side by side.

Using the practice of individual actors as a frame of reference, the concept of plural world interpretations enables us to describe contemporary culture as comprising many parallel models of world interpretation, which are both co-existent and equally valued as well as complementary and contradictory. Based on field data collected in the Republic of Tyva (Russian Federation) during 2004-2005, I demonstrate how individual local actors deal with the choices between different models of world interpretation, and how they flexibly use these models to respond to events and to act in daily life situations. In doing so, I propose to study the actual plurality of world interpretation models as well as the human ability to handle them flexibly in everyday life.

In this case study, two of many different models of world interpretation are identified. Both exist as equally valued realities but can be differentiated structurally as a 'model of human dominance' and a 'model of interaction between human and non-human subjects'. The first stresses the human dominance over the environment, seen as a series of more or less passive objects of human agency, the second emphasises interaction in a world that encloses humans but consists of both human and non-human subjects. Both models are coherent systems and are part of the repertoire of knowledge, behaviour, and action of Tyvan agents. To them, these models count as equal and mutually contradictory. The models compete and oppose each other. But they form a continuum within which a human actor constantly repositions him- or her-self depending on situation and context. The empirical material shows that Tyvans use these models in various ways – replacing, complementing, and mixing them according to their individual needs in specific contexts.

The material assembled in this case study shows how local actors deal with the plurality of world interpretation models in their daily lives, how they switch from one to another, and how they mix the models in different situations and contexts. The rules of their flexible handling of plural world

---

[1] This volume is a revised version and translation of Oelschlägel 2013a.

interpretations, the reasons behind their choice for one or for a specific mix of models, as well as the consequences of these choices, will be analysed.

Acknowledgements

I thank my research partners in Tyva for the invitation to participate in their lives, for many experiences I no longer want to miss, for their generous hospitality, for food and drink, for the bivouacs, for memorable conversations, and for the rich treasure of contemporary legends that I could take home. The daily life in their yurt camps remains unforgettable.

For practical contributions during the work on this project – especially for discussions, reviews, and editing – I thank Dmitrij Anatol'evich Funk, Antonina Saar-oolovna Dongak, Urana Aldyn-oolovna Dongak, Ojumaa Maadyr-oolovna Saaja, Chajzat Donahoe, Birgit Huber, Michael Schetsche, Katharina Gernet, Stephan Dudeck, Jutta Turner (cartography), Christian Bogen, and Hans Szédeli. Han F. Vermeulen, Andreas Hemming, Jennifer Cash and Berit Westwood were invaluable for language and copy editing and for preparing the manuscript for print. Mariya Petrova (M.P.) provided the Russian translation of the final summary. Christine Oelschlägel edited the photographs. All colleagues and friends enriched my work with their scholarly and human qualities.

For supervision, guidance, and support I thank Bernhard Streck, Erika Taube, Joachim Otto Habeck, Hubert Seiwert, Chris Hann, and Günther Schlee.

My work was supported by many colleagues and guests of the Max Planck Institute for Social Anthropology in Halle (Saale). The project could reach its present quality only as result of the fruitful discussions and inspiring exchanges in the context of this institute.

I am also grateful to my relatives, parents, grandparents, and sister, who supported me with great commitment. My daughter Erato was born in the writing phase of this project. Ever since she has brought both structure and turbulence, and is the sunshine of our lives. This book is also dedicated to her.

For financial support of the research, the book, and its translation, I thank the German Academic Exchange Service (DAAD) in Bonn, the German Research Council (DFG) in Bonn, and the Siberian Studies Centre (SSC) of the Max Planck Institute for Social Anthropology in Halle (Saale).

Note on Transliteration

For the Russian and Tyvan terms included in this work, I have used the system that was in use by the Russian government from 1997-2010 for transliterating Russian names in international passports. This system corresponds closely to the British (Oxford) standard, but has no diacritics. The Tyvan alphabet, also written in Cyrillic, contains three additional letters to the Russian alphabet. I have transliterated these (ң, ө, and ү) respectively as ng, ö, and ü. Certain exceptions apply for the names of authors and other individuals who are well-known by other spellings of their names.

*I dedicate this book to all those
looking for a good compromise*

Prologue: Progress and Stability, the Quest for Balance

The story of this book has been told from time immemorial. It describes both the human pursuit of progress in and domination over the mundane world and divine attempts to preserve creation by limiting humans' impact and their claims to power. Even if humans invent their gods themselves, they overcome their own pursuit of dominance by serving their gods, and in this way reduce the dangers for their environment and their own lives produced by strivings for dominance. Human beings need their material and immaterial, natural and artificial environments for their survival. That is why they exploit it. To use it more effectively and efficiently, humans adapt their environment to their own benefit and work incessantly on its remodelling, reshaping, and irretrievable destruction. Religions, however, show that all earthly things arise from the work of non-human beings more powerful than humans, and are therefore under the protection of these powerful beings. The people who exploit the world for their own purposes are also committed by their creators to safeguard it. That humankind will perish should they damage their environment is thus a warning that is additionally underlined.

Be it gods, ancestors, spirits, dwarves, giants, or other charismatic beings of intelligence who oppose the human drive to dominate the earthly world, the conflict is found in myths, legends, and folk tales around the world.[1] To this day, the battle is handed down orally and has for thousands of years been fixed in writing, recomposed again and again in allegoric narratives.

Such a narrative is that of Prometheus. Prometheus gave human beings more power over the forces of nature than the gods were prepared to accept. When he taught them to domesticate and use fire, Prometheus and human beings were severely punished. Prometheus was bound to a rock, and an eagle was sent to hack out and eat his liver each day, while at night his liver grew back again. Prometheus's punishment carried an allegory for the

---

[1] That humans offend the property of non-human intelligent beings and have to fear punishment is a typical theme in contemporary Tyvan legends.

eternal damnation of the human soul that came into the world together with fire: 'From the flaming forge came the weapons for war and all the ills that disturb a peaceful life' (Cotterell 1999: 75).

The idea that knowledge and suffering are mutually dependent was part of the thinking that the Enlightenment wanted to discard.[2] This idea asserts that cognition arises from suffering just as suffering emerges from cognition. The opposition between progress and development on the one hand and religiously motivated stagnation on the other played an important role in Enlightenment thought. Many eighteenth-century philosophers rejected the idea that the God-given and God-willed world is the only sure framework for human existence and should therefore be accepted unquestioned. For proponents of the Enlightenment, this was an ideology that obstructed the emerging bourgeoisie's emancipation. Instead, the use of rationality by all people and of objective scientific knowledge was at the basis of the Enlightenment's pursuit of progress and development.

Goethe's *Faust*, written in 1808, shows that the unconditional belief in rationalism and empiricism raised doubt as well. In Goethe's version, Faust aspired to insight and self-fulfilment to such an extent that he concluded a blood-contract with Mephisto to abstain from abidance in personal joy[3], not only to his own misfortune but also to that of other participants.

Whatever form the narrative of the search for balance has taken, it has always faced two contradictory insights. Progress provides for increasing security and a comfortable life in an environment that is increasingly adapted to human needs. This development consistently creates new possibilities for altering the world dominated by human beings according to their interests. But the integrity of creation, and thus of human beings, is ensured only when humans (who are part of the world) do not become too powerful. The consideration of both insights alludes to the necessity for balance and to the equality of all interested parties, human and non-human.

The quest for balance is a human mission rooted deeply in mental culture as well as in all other cultural elements. With balance, the possibility emerges to save creation and at the same time provide humans with sufficient space for self-fulfilment. Wherever religious integrity of creation, the protection of nature (i.e. human representations of nature's interests), or stability-endowing social mechanisms (e.g. protection of one's own,

---

[2] The following allegories for 'knowledge and suffering' from ancient mythology are based on Schwab (1977), Burn (1993), and Cotterell (1999). The interpretation is mine.

[3] Following the example of Faust, 'abidance' can be interpreted as a stability that rejects further developments. Mephisto did not refuse Faust the spontaneous short-lived joy of an idea or experience. Instead, it was Faust's willingness to give up the ability to abide in an enduring state of joy that proved to be Mephisto's victory over Faust's ambition.

inheritance) can be observed beside the human impulse for change and pursuit of progress – there we can also observe the human quest for balance between both addictions.

The human pursuit of progress is the motor of development. The idea of conservation, whether religiously or rationally motivated, causes a deceleration of change within cultural, economic, or social developments, thus their stabilisation. The plural world interpretations that emerge when considering both, and the observation of human practice in handling them, demonstrate the human willingness to find meaningful compromises. This often happens only when it is necessary to keep the world and the environment in a well-balanced state between progress and stability.

The description of plural world interpretations entered the humanities early, but only received slow recognition. William James's ground-breaking work, *The Principles of Psychology* (1890), in which he used the example of the human mind to speak about endless contradictory but also intersecting 'sub-universa', is now more than 120 years old. Human beings can attend to these universes consecutively, but can also withdraw their attention. In so doing, people shift the accent of reality from one 'sub-universum' to another and accept interpretations from whichever 'sub-universum' that they are presently attending as true.

Some examples of the practice, if not the use of the actual concept, of plural world interpretations can be found in Edward Evans-Pritchard's *Witchcraft, Oracles and Magic among the Azande* (1937) and Maurice Leenhardt's *Do Kamo: Die Person und der Mythos in der melanesischen Welt* (1984 [1947]). Both works were among the earliest anthropological studies to deal with simultaneously existing and mutually contradictory ways of thinking. Both authors objected to the widespread evolutionary idea of a linear development from mythical to rational thinking. Instead, they acknowledged that the mythical and rational are two ways of thinking that exist parallel to each other and are common to all human beings. As Leenhardt formulated it: 'Each mentality includes a rational and a mythical aspect', and 'rationality is as inherent in the history of thinking as much as is myth' (1984 [1947]: 241). Evans-Pritchard declared that rational and mythical thinking co-exist and can be combined in explaining the causes of accidents. He wrote: 'The belief in death as a consequence of natural causes and the belief in death as a consequence of witchcraft do not exclude each other. To the contrary, the one explains what the other does not explain' (Evans-Pritchard 1984: 68). He showed that accidents among the Azande cause a shift from daily rational thinking to the mythical. The reports of accidents and their causes collected in the present work reveal this same fundamental relation. In the view of both Evans-Pritchard and Leenhardt, people are capable of switching flexibly between at least two modes of thinking according to their needs, combining them, and substituting them.

What Leenhardt and Evans-Pritchard recognised independently as rational and mythical thinking has not lost its importance in the early twenty-first century. The present study attempts to outline the concept and potential of plural world interpretations by analysing the case of the South-Siberian Tyvans. It shows that the search for a meaningful balance between progress-accelerating human dominance over the environment and the stabilising interaction model in which non-human subjects have a much-needed say in all human interventions into the environment is a permanent balancing act of human existence and the quality of human life in the world.

Halle (Saale), Spring 2016
Anett C. Oelschlaegel

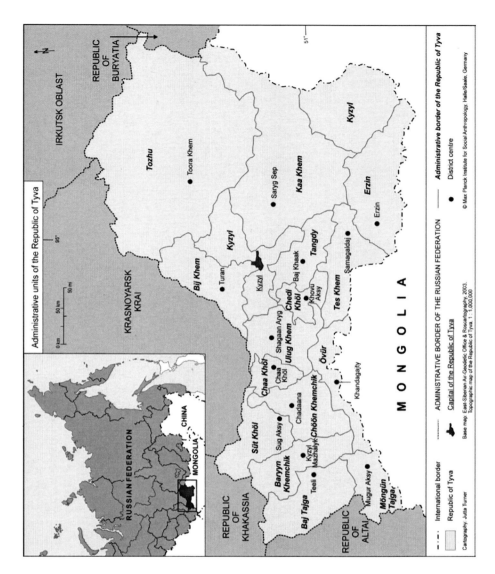

Map 1. Administrative units of the Republic of Tyva.

Introduction: The Tyvans, a Turk Language-Speaking People in South Siberia

The Tyvans are a Turk language-speaking people composed of several linguistic[7], economic, and cultural groups whose settlement area is divided between three modern states: the Russian Federation (in South Siberia's border regions with north-western Mongolia between the Altai Mountains and Lake Baikal), in northern and north-western Mongolia[8], and in the Altai Mountains in the People's Republic of China.[9] In their contemporary and historical culture Tyvans combine characteristics of nomad stockbreeders of northern Central Asia (Mongolia, Kazakhstan, and Kyrgyzstan) and South Siberia (Russia's republics of Altai and Buryatia) with those of reindeer nomads of Siberia. The members of these ethnic groups are often referred to as Tuvan or Tuva in the literature, but call themselves as *Tyva kizhi* in South Siberia or as *Dyva gizhi* in the Mongolian and Chinese Altai Mountains. I prefer to use the correct transliteration of their names: Tyva or Tyvans.

The present study is based on 18 months of fieldwork conducted in the Russian Federation's Republic of Tyva in 1995, 1997, 2004, and 2005. This is where the majority of Tyvans live. The republic (168,600 square

---

[7] In western Mongolia live the Khalkh-Uriankhai or Uriankhan; in northern Mongolia (around Lake Khoevsgoel Nuur) – the Darkhat. Both groups are linguistically and culturally Mongolised to some degree. Other groups, in northern Mongolia (i.e. the Soyon Uriankhai) and in the Altai Mountains of north-western Mongolia (i.e. the Dyva), continue to speak the Tyvan language (Tyv. *tyva dyl*), a Turk language that belongs to the Altaic language family. The close relation between the Darkhat and the Tyvans was first pointed out by Gregory Nikolaevich Potanin (1883), who wrote that at that time the shamans of the Mongolised Darkhat used the Tyvan language in their séances (Ottinger 1993; Taube, E. 1994a).

[8] Before 1996 altogether ca. 6,000 Dyva and Soyon Uriankhai lived in Mongolia, making up about 1.1 per cent of the total population. They settled among other groups in the territories of the Bajan-Oelgij-Aimak and the Khovd-Aimak, both bordering on the South Siberian Republic of Tyva (Ottinger 1993; Taube, E. 1994a).

[9] In 1999, 2,400 speakers of Dyva (the Altai dialect of the Tyvan language) were living in the Chinese part of the Altai Mountains, in Xinjiang's A-erh-tai district (Mongush 1994; Taube, E. 1996b; Hoppe 1998: 450-68).

kilometres) counted 307,930 inhabitants in 2010, an increase of just under 2,000 people since 2002. The Tyvans are the majority and the largest non-Russian group, representing about 81 per cent of the total population and (in 2010) numbered 249,299 individuals.[10] Apart from the Tyvans, 16.1 per cent ethnic Russians (2010: 49,434 individuals) and 3 per cent members of other ethnic groups (2010: 9,197 individuals) live in the republic. The non-Tyvan population lives in the capital Kyzyl and a few other urban centres together with fewer than half of the Tyvans (2002: 107,850). More than half of the Tyvans (2002: 135,592) make up the rural population of the republic.[11]

In economic terms the Tyvans perceive themselves as stockbreeders and nomads. It must be noted, however, that there exist two nomadic breeding cultures in the Republic of Tyva: the stockbreeders of the mountain steppes and taiga, and the hunters and reindeer holders of the taiga (see Taube, E. 1981b). The former make up the majority of South-Siberian Tyvans[12], with the exception of those living in Tozhu, in the north-east of the republic (see below). Their economic basis is nomadic or semi-nomadic stockbreeding, and they own five varieties of gregarious animal typical for Mongolia and South Siberia: the yak, horse, camel, sheep, and goat. However, depending on geographical circumstances, the constitution of the stock varies. In the western Silver Taiga, close to the Altai Mountains, the stocks are predominantly made up of yaks. By contrast, some camels can be found in the stocks of southern and northern Tyvan nomads. However, in the republic as a whole, all stockbreeders have sheep and goats and use horses for their daily work. Today, the stocks are usually supplemented by cattle. Pigs and poultry are rare, but can be found in some nomadic households. From the milk of the animals, Tyvans produce a manifold of staple food products, especially during the summer (see Oelschlägel 2000). In seasons when the animals produce less milk, meat comes to the fore in the diet. Furthermore, wild onions, roots, and fruits offer a welcome diversity in the nomads' diet. Hunting plays only a secondary role in providing Tyvan stockbreeders with meat.

The Tozhu-Tyva, living in the Tozhu territory in the north-east of the Republic of Tyva, belong to the hunter and reindeer nomads of the taiga zone (see Vajnshtejn 1961).[13] Today, the Tozhu-Tyva form an ethnic group that is legally independent, being a member of the 'small numbered

---

[10] In 1989 it numbered 198,446; in 2002 there were 243,442 individuals.
[11] http://www.gks.ru/free_doc/new_site/population/demo/per-itog/tab7.xls
[12] The nomadic stockbreeders also include the Dyva of the Mongolian and Chinese Altai Mountains.
[13] The reindeer breeders of the taiga zone further include the Soyon Uriankhai (see Ottinger 1993).

indigenous peoples of the North, Siberia and the Far East' (see Funk and Sillanpaa 1999; Donahoe 2002, 2003a, 2003b, 2004, 2005, 2006a, 2006b, 2008, 2009). For the hunter and reindeer breeders of the taiga zone, hunting is more important than it is for the stockbreeders of the steppes. Especially during the winter, meat is mainly provided by hunting various cervids such as maral deer, wild reindeer, and roe deer. Fish occasionally complements the menu. Similarly important is the hunting of fur-bearing animals. The Tozhu-Tyvans hunt squirrels, sables, minks, silver foxes, and wolves, as well as various deer. Popular for trading with China are deer antlers, which rise in value if they are almost full-grown but not yet rubbed off, as well as the musk of musk deer (Ottinger 1993: 92ff). Furs are an important source of income for all reindeer breeders, who have few possibilities for selling their own products or earning money otherwise. Therefore, the sale of furs is almost the only way of acquiring essential consumer products like food, tools, equipment, clothing, or articles of daily use.

The wide range of Tyvan subsistence strategies and modes of life are dependent on the geographical and climatological conditions of the territories they inhabit. The eastern part of the republic, covered by larch and Siberian yellow pine mountain forests, stands in marked contrast to the smaller western part dominated by steppes. Paleoarctic reindeer appear mainly in the north-eastern parts of the republic. In central, northern, and southern Tyva, the stockbreeders also raise camels and in the mountains of south-western Tyva, the yak dominates the nomads' stocks.

The history of the Republic of Tyva is characterised by a high degree of independence. Prior to its incorporation into the Soviet Union in 1944, Tannu Tuva was an independent people's republic. In 1944 the republic joined the Soviet Union voluntary, initially as the Tuvinian Autonomous Territory; from 1961 it was known as the Republic of Tuva; and since 1993 as the Republic of Tyva. Although the People's Republic of Tannu Tuva was already socialist before 1944, a fundamental socialist reform was enforced after the republic's incorporation into the Soviet Union. The term 'Sovietisation' subsumes the following economic changes in Tyva: (1) the installation of a state-directed and state-controlled, centrally-planned economy; (1.1) the concomitant collectivisation of animal husbandry in which the stockbreeders continued to care for now collective stocks in nomadic and semi-nomadic modes of life; (1.2) the development of state-directed and state-controlled trade of animal husbandry products; (1.3) the exploitation of natural resources under state management; (1.4) the development of agriculture, especially in the southern parts of the republic, to a small degree; (1.5) the beginnings of industrialisation, especially in the capital Kyzyl; and (1.6) the electrification of cities, villages and kolkhoz centres as a Soviet prestige project. In addition to the economic reforms, several further transformations determined the lives of Tyvans since 1944. The changes of a political nature were: (2) the development of a political awareness of 'socialist progress' by means of political education; (3) the concomitant prosecution, imprisonment and even murder of religiously active people, such as shamans and Buddhist lamas; (4) 'dekulakisation' or prosecution, imprisonment, and murder of prosperous stockbreeders; as well as (5) the repression of political dissidents or people with different political ideas.

However, there were also several positive developments since 1944 that Tyvans today count as socialism's accomplishments: (6) the implementation of a system of welfare and pension entitlements; (7) the development of a comprehensive medical care system; (8) the alphabetisation of the population[14]; (9) the implementation of an education system with several levels, with instruction in either the Russian or Tyvan language[15], that included elementary schools (Russ.: *nachalnoye*), secondary schools (Russ.: *nepolnoye sredneye obrazavaniye*), and eventually the 'middle' or 'complete secondary education' (Russ.: *sredneye obrazavaniye*), as well as professional and university levels; and, finally, (10) compulsory school attendance and equal education opportunities for all citizens, including inhabitants of economically underdeveloped areas.

The restructuring of society and economy after years of dictatorship and mismanagement that came in the course of the perestroika and glasnost initiated by Mikhail Gorbachev in 1986, the dissolution of the Soviet Union under Boris Yeltsin (on 31 December 1991), and the formation of the Russian Federation (in 1992), resulted in the Russian economic crisis of the 1990s. The Republic of Tyva was hit hard by this development. As in Russia as a whole, the economy of Tyva was partially privatised and democratic reforms were initiated. Instead of taking a positive turn, the Tyvan economy collapsed, a catastrophe from which the Republic of Tyva has not yet recovered.

The Republic of Tyva has always been an economically poor region, lacking industry almost completely. At the same time, the rights for the use of land and natural resources continue, according to Russian law, to belong to the state. Profits from mineral extraction, like asbestos in western Tyva

---

[14] In the 1930s, scholars developed an alphabet for the Tyvan language using Latin letters. The philologist Aleksandr Adol'fovich Pal'mbach performed this task, building on preliminary studies by Wilhelm Radloff (Radloff 1960 [1893-1911]; Ischakov und Pal'mbach 1961). In the 1940s the Latin script was replaced by Cyrillic, which is used to date.

[15] The ability to choose between a Russian or a Tyvan language school is normal practice in the Republic of Tyva since Soviet times.

and gold in the north-eastern parts of the republic, as well as those from the wood industry, flow directly to central Russia. In this way, the strong financial dependency of the Republic of Tyva on Moscow has been consolidated.

In the 1990s, the Tyvan population became impoverished from the high rate of inflation, temporary cessation of cash flowing from Moscow into the republic, extremely high unemployment, and very low salaries that were not paid for months at a time. Simultaneously, a thin upper class emerged, accumulating a prosperity above average, whose members in Russia are called *Novye Russkiye* (New Russians). Due to chronic underfinancing of the republic, among other causes, nearly all forms of social security were terminated. Many Tyvans today perceive their lives and their struggle for survival as fundamentally harder than before 1986. Most Tyvans long for their previous regular earnings and social security, a well-functioning and free health care system, and fair education opportunities. At the same time, many Tyvans condemn all kinds of daily repression and the persecution of differently-minded or religiously-engaged people during the socialist era. The discussions about the developments of the past 25 years and how they are to be evaluated are multifaceted. But on several issues many Tyvans agree: The daily struggle for life has become much harder. To save money or to ensure the financial support of one's own family for a longer stretch of time is nearly impossible. Both the people of urban areas and those of rural areas live hand-to-mouth. There are moments in their lives in which people are unable to provide the necessary means and depend on food from relatives or acquaintances. Many desires exceeding daily alimentation remain unrealistic fantasies. The future of the family, and the answer to the question of how to feed one's own children in the coming year, is always open. The public social networks of benefits have long been replaced by family ties and clan connections. Among their own kin, Tyvans mutually help each other by obtaining food, jobs, money, or necessary goods. But despite this mutual assistance among many Tyvans, the general living conditions in Tyvan society are alarming, as expressed in endemic unemployment, poverty, alcoholism, crime, and suicide, especially in urban contexts.

It is probably a blessing in disguise that the collectivisation of animal husbandry was not completely reversed after 1991. After the abolishment of collective farms[16], most Tyvan breeders voluntarily organised themselves into cooperatives that may be seen as follow-up organisations of the former collective farms. These cooperatives are associations of stockbreeders who

---

[16] Humphrey (1998) described a Soviet kolkhoz in detail, using the example of the Karl Marx kolkhoz in Buryatia.

predominantly operate privately. This means that the stockbreeders mainly care for their own stocks and for those of the cooperative, but share the grazing land with other members of the cooperative, jointly organise the marketing of their products, and finance the cooperative's centre as a base and contact zone for all stockbreeders in the cooperative. Compared with the socialist kolkhoz, the current cooperatives – as reduced versions of cooperation – have lost many advantages. Nevertheless, there are good reasons for breeders to align with each other, including fixed cooperative centres (Russ. *baza*) where the nomads have at their disposal a shopping facility, medical care (Russ. *medpunkt*), a boarding house, a sauna (Russ. *banya*) and sometimes even a basic primary school for their children. In addition, the cooperatives provide nomads with the possibility to more successfully market the products of their animal husbandry, a market itself, and the rotating distribution of grazing lands and mutual support. However, the nomads also perceive negative social consequences from decollectivisation in the loss of regular salaries, annuity, and social security, and the drastic financial insecurities produced by these losses. Moreover, deficient governmental regulation and lack of assistance in the marketing of the stockbreeders' products unfavourably affect their economic situation. The meat and milk products produced by Tyvan nomads are rarely sold in Tyvan shops, neither in the villages nor in the few urban centres. Tyvan retailers sell comparable goods such as pork and beef, milk, and cheese from other Siberian regions, mainly from Krasnoyarsk District. Thus, Tyvan stockbreeders fail to find a market that would ensure them of vitally needed regular financial earnings. This is one of the basic problems of the Tyvan economy and one of the causes of the current poverty of Tyvans living as nomads and stockbreeders in both steppes and taiga.

    The incomes of stockbreeders are unsteady and very low. Their capital consists exclusively of the animals they raise in their flocks. But the nomads fail to sell them with profit. At the same time, this capital is permanently at risk of adverse weather conditions or epidemics. In this way, stockbreeding protects from hunger, but does not produce sufficient means to cover further expenses. Financial means for the purchase of clothing, school materials, additional food, articles of daily use, or tools are mainly provided by the small pensions of the generation of grandparents, paid for their work during the Soviet period. By contrast, the stockbreeders working today do not have any chance to save or provide for their old age. Even stockbreeders, who constitute the economic backbone of the republic, remain uninsured. To make matters worse, the generation of Soviet-era pension recipients is dying out. Thus, sooner or later the nomads' families will have to relinquish this minimal inflow of funds and trust almost exclusively on the subsistence economy, a condition that will make it difficult to send their children to school or provide them with the necessary paraphernalia for school attendance.

Many stockbreeders attempt to balance this financial situation by strengthening their bonds to members of their extended family groups. The stockbreeders supply their relatives in villages and urban centres with food. Because the meat and milk products available in Tyvan shops are expensive and delivered from other areas of Siberia, this mode of support is most welcome. In exchange, the stockbreeders receive home-cultivated vegetables, in particular potatoes, cabbage, and carrots, from their village relatives and financial support from their relatives in Kyzyl. Apart from agricultural commodities and money, Tyvans also exchange labour with their relatives. A well-developed net of kinship relations is currently indispensable for ensuring the livelihood of all members of the extended family, who all depend on one another. However, such transfer benefits within family groups cannot belie the conspicuous social downward slope between the wealthier working city dwellers and the stockbreeders in the steppes and taiga who live on a shoestring budget. High unemployment rates and minimal prospects for finding a job in the capital lead Tyvans who were previously settled to return to the steppes and taiga as stockbreeders and hunters to at least ensure themselves with sufficient food.

Another conspicuous trait of Tyvan society is to be found in differing life ambitions of men and women. On the one hand, the possibilities of an ambitious professional education within the Russian Federation can be evaluated as good. Many Tyvans send their children for education to other areas of Siberia (particular Krasnoyarsk, Novosibirsk, or Omsk) or to the European part of Russia (Moscow or St. Petersburg). Women especially use opportunities to educate themselves. On the other hand, unemployment in the cities of Tyva is high. The limited employment market is dominated by positions in public administration. While women may comparatively often find jobs in the professional sectors of the republic – as physicians, teachers, childcare workers, scholars, journalists, and administration officials – the men, who are generally less educated, lag behind. A large part of the urban male population work for the police and the army; a smaller and socially privileged number work in public administration. In rural areas, some men find jobs in the extraction industry. However, members of European ethnic groups, mainly Russians, are preferred as employees. Low-paid workers also produce resources like timber and furs. The limited employment market is supplemented by a little handicraft production sector and by a booming private retail trade.

The high unemployment rates result in many problems, albeit mainly among men. This includes a shocking number of cases of suicide, alcoholism, and crime. It is disturbing that nearly every family with which I was acquainted in Tyva lamented that several male members were victims of alcohol abuse, murder, manslaughter (often knifings in states of drunkenness), or accidents. The average life expectancy in Tyva of 54 years counts among the lowest in Russia, and the life expectancy of men (in 1994 less than 50 years) lies far below that of women. Among the adult population, men are noticeably lacking; many single mothers raise their children alone.

The high degree of independence of Tyvan women is rooted in history. Even before the incorporation of the republic into the Soviet Union, Tyvan families were characterised by gender relations ranging from equality to female dominance. Therefore, until the present day, women are central in providing support to their families and plan and execute strategic steps to safeguard their survival.

Considering this dramatic socio-economic and political environment, I ask how the population of Tyva copes. The answer to this question includes a vital factor that I would like to call 'social warmth'. This factor, which is characteristic for the Siberian and Central Asian regions, concerns social and kinship networks as well as reciprocal support that is not state decreed. Such networks and support are indispensable to life for all Tyvans and therefore lived by most Tyvans in a most impressive manner. Kinship and neighbourhood assistance play a key role in generating social warmth. Tyvans in steppe and taiga regions practise hospitality, help each other with money or food, support each other with animal husbandry or childcare or – more dubiously – carouse together around the clock. In doing so, the kinship and social context of a family in Tyva becomes absolutely obligatory and at the same time secures their existence. Especially during the Russian financial crisis (1998), the lead-up to which I witnessed during my fieldwork in 1995 and 1997, kinship and social networks became essential for survival. In that period, when people did not receive their salaries for months and their financial reserves were depleted, and when they suffered pronouncedly from bitter poverty and hunger, the pastoral nomads supported their relatives and acquaintances in the cities and villages without any compensation. After the turn of the millennium, during my fieldwork in 2004-05, the dependencies were reversed. While those who had found work in the cities and villages were prospering, the nomads were affected by epizootics and extremely cold winter months, forcing them to draw on the financial support of their relatives and acquaintances, especially those in towns, for their subsistence. Intensive networking and a skilful positioning of relatives in three living spaces (taiga, village, and city) were indispensable for all Tyvans during the crisis-ridden 1990s and 2000s, not only to achieve minimal prosperity, but even to satisfy basic needs.[17]

However, positive developments can also be observed since the beginning of the 2000s. Especially South-Siberian Tyvans have become well known due to an increasing interest in their traditional culture by Western media. In the centre of numerous, often romantically idealised reports are the pastoralists: nomadic to the present day, their everyday lives spent in yurts, practising (neo-)shamanism and the traditional art of throat and overtone singing. These are not moribund relics, but elements of a vibrant Tyvan culture. With the increasing international publicity of the South-Siberian Tyvans comes an active exchange between people from the republic and those from other parts of the world. Herewith are connected incentives for the development of the region for tourism and the consolidation of Tyvan cultural self-confidence. Today, many Tyvans proudly stand by their culture and facilitate and cultivate it in public and private spaces.

Not only in Europe, but also in the United States and Canada, Tyvan shamanism is now well known to the wider public. Exhibitions in museums and newspaper, magazine, and televised reports regularly offer information and background stories about shamanism in the small South Siberian republic. In the last two decades alone, an esoteric scene has developed that attends to and practises a kind of modern- or neo-shamanism, mainly modelled on Tyvan shamanism (e.g. Denaeghel 1998; Grünwedel 2008, 2010, 2012; Voss 2011). Western shamans and laypeople interested in shamanism regularly meet Tyvan shamans at conferences in Europe, the Americas, and in the Republic of Tyva. Tyvan shamans often travel to Europe and the Americas, while Western friends of shamanism visit the Republic of Tyva to exchange experiences and together perform rituals or hold séances. The strong influence of Tyvan shamanism can be observed in Western shamanism today, while contemporary Tyvan shamanism is influenced by Western esotericism.

The shamans of the Republic of Tyva have integrated themselves into several shamans' associations in a modern way. They practise for local and foreign clients in special houses, mainly in Kyzyl, and for high fees. Not only for this reason, critical voices have become louder in Tyva, warning against the increasing commercialisation of shamanism and the development of 'show shamanism'. From this point of view the shamans are losing their credibility. Discussions about 'proper' and 'false' shamans determine the discourse about skills and merits of contemporary shamans among

---

[17] For further information see Arakchaa (2009).

laypeople. Connected to these discussions are contemporary legends about historical shamans (see Oelschlägel 2013b) that were all told from the desire to provide an example and a model of 'proper' shamans, as they lived and acted among the Tyvans in the past.

Similar developments of intercultural exchange and increasing worldwide publicity of Tyvan culture can be observed in the world music scene. Throat and overtone singing (Tyv. *kargyraa* and *khöömej*), for which the Tyvans are now known worldwide, finds its maximum dissemination and most of its practitioners in the Republic of Tyva (e.g. Deusen 2004; Levin and Süzükei 2006). There are now many Tyvan bands that tour Europe and North America. Tyvan music has become an important element in Western ethnic and folklore festivals, and increasing numbers of Europeans, North Americans, and Japanese travel to Tyva to learn this special vocal art.

Western enthusiasm for such elements of Tyvan culture and the efflorescent cultural self-confidence of many Tyvans outshine the problems outlined above. They are a positive impulse and a point of departure for a better future. In turn, the special characteristics and increasing popularity of Tyvan culture since the beginning of the twenty-first century facilitate the formation of environmentally sensitive tourism in the region. The increasing touristic development of the republic opens up a new and profitable employment market for the local population.

Also interested in Tyvan culture are scholars from the humanities. The Republic of Tyva facilitates two centres of research in the humanities, both located in Kyzyl. The first is the Tyvan Research Institute for the Humanities, in which local scholars investigate the archaeology, geography, history, language, and culture almost exclusively of the Republic of Tyva and adjacent areas. The second is the Khöömej International Scientific Centre. The Tyvan State University and the Aldan Maadyr (Sixty Warriors) National Museum of the Republic of Tyva complete the scientific community in the republic. In addition, increasing numbers of Western scholars visit the Republic of Tyva for fieldwork. As a result, both inside and outside the small South Siberian republic, numerous works about the history, language, and literature of the Republic of Tyva have been published in the past few decades. I will cite some of them in the following section on research methods.

Research Problem

The initial data collection on the specific Tyvan interaction model presented in this book was carried out by means of narrative and subject-centred interviews from July 2004 to January 2005. In the course of these interviews I suggested particular terms in Tyvan to my interview partners and asked them to explain them in their own words, among them 'nature' (Tyv. *bojdus*), 'sacred'/'consecrated' (Tyv. *ydyk*), 'pure ground'/'wilderness' (Tyv. *aryg cher*), 'sacred place or ground' (Tyv. s. *ydyktyg cher*, pl. *ydyk cher*), or various spirits (Tyv. *ee, eeren, albys, shulbus, aza, puk, diireng, chetker*). Depending on their affections or preferences, my interview partners could add poems, songs, blessings, or invocations (Tyv. *algyshtar*) to my data. In addition, I recorded numerous contemporary legends, the so-called true occurrences (Tyv. *bolgan tavarylgalar*).[18] These allowed me greater access to the Tyvan interaction model and the intellectual world of religiously active Tyvans, who base their actions and thinking on this model of world interpretation.

During the second stage of my research, from May to October 2005, I collected additional data for my description of what I call 'plural world interpretations'. I focused my research on the flexibility and changeability of what Tyvans communicate as 'true' and what they express in their actions and behaviour. Initially I observed and analysed many discrepancies between self-expressions and behaviour. My aim was to compare the ideal self-expressions with the observable behaviour. In doing so, it soon became clear that self-expression and observable behaviour were far from analogous. Most Tyvans I met did not act in the way they pretended to act or claimed they should act. While the statements of any specific research partner were almost always focused on one particular model of world interpretation, in practice, it could be observed that several models of world interpretation were mixed and complemented.

I therefore focused my research on the parallel existence of several models of world interpretation and questioned how Tyvans make use of them in a flexible way, how they switch from one model to another, and how they combine models in their everyday lives. I looked for explanations and interpretations of events as well as for actions and behaviour in characteristic situations and tried to determine when a mix of both models was applied or when a switch from one model to another took place. My research partners were only rudimentarily aware of their plural world interpretations, of their switching from one to another, and their mixing of models – and then only in a limited number of characteristic situations. Because of this, it soon became clear that the flexible use of different models of world interpretation could

---

[18] Throughout this work, I use interchangeably the English phrases 'contemporary legends', 'true occurrences', and 'true events' for what the Tyvans call *bolgan tavarylgalar* (lit. true occurrences or true events). I recorded these legends in the Republic of Tyva between 1995 and 2005. They can be defined as religiously motivated, wondrous, or awesome short narratives that are orally transmitted. The Tyvans regard them as true reports that are based on religiously interpreted events that could have taken place or did take place (see also Oelschlägel 2013b).

not be explored by asking directly about them, but only through observation. The second stage of research therefore required me to take a distant view of events and to reflect retrospectively and repeatedly analyse the occurrences I had witnessed with my research partners.

After bringing together numerous characteristic situations that showed both models in action or the switch from one to another model, I was able to summarise regularities that form the basis of the parallel existence and the flexible use of the two models of world interpretation presented here. The exact observation and systematic retrospective analysis of many occurrences that I witnessed together with my Tyvan research partners, revealed step-by-step the rules of the specific Tyvan plural world interpretations described in the present study.

One of the main aims of my research was the collection and description of a model of world interpretation that I will characterise as an 'interaction model' in the following chapters. For that purpose I collected and evaluated three kinds of sources: information from religious laypeople, information from religious specialists, and numerous written sources published as scholarly works, mainly in Russian or Tyvan, since the incorporation of the Republic of Tyva into the Soviet Union.

Data Collection

My experience during initial fieldwork in the 1990s was that many Tyvans preferred to remain silent about their tradition to foreigners, or admitted adherence only to Buddhism or to atheism. The silence of many Tyvans was based on their experience during the Soviet era and even after the collapse of the Soviet Union. At least since the incorporation of Tyva into the Soviet Union, the official propaganda branded their belief system, associated with magic and superstition, as backward. This negative stereotyping took place in further education seminars and political education. However, visible symbols of the liveliness of traditional religious culture could be found in many places. Ritual sites (Tyv. s. *ovaa*, pl. *ovaalar*), sacred trees, and sacred springs could be found easily in the Tyvan landscape. They could be identified as distinct sacred places, marked by colourful ribbons, and visible from a long distance. The large number of such places indicated already in 1995 and 1997 that the traditional Tyvan kind of animism was coming alive again.

During my stays in Tyva in 2004 to 2005, many Tyvans discussed their traditional animism much more openly and intensively than before. With the beginning of the 2000s, it was no longer a problem to find sufficient numbers of respondents to willingly discuss the contents of Tyvan animism. I then found many occasions to observe how Tyvans practise their religion, not only by means of interviews but also by actively participating in their rituals. It soon became apparent that not only the shamans but also laypersons functioned as religious specialists who consciously and deliberately complement shamans in their religious abilities. These people provided one another with religious expertise and used the competence of acquaintances to accomplish a maximum of religious protection in everyday life, as well as during celebrations and rituals. Whether in the city, in the villages, or in the yurts of the pastoral nomads, everywhere there were Tyvans who were known for collecting or composing songs, adages, invocations, and blessings. In practice it made no difference whether they were handed-down or new.

Some research partners were acquainted with numerous true occurrences or contemporary legends that focused on encounters between humans and non-human subjects. This narrative genre is characterised by the incorporation of religious interpretations into the narration of an event and a way that enables the narrator to convey the impression of a permanent interaction between humans and non-human subjects to his audience.

The narration of such true occurrences keeps the interaction model alive in the minds of the audience. The narrator achieves this by repeatedly transmitting a permanent reminder of how to deal respectfully with non-human subjects in the Tyvan world. Other interview partners were acquainted with methods of divination and fortune telling. They served the community as advisers and interpreted the intentions of spirits and natural subjects. Special mention must be made of interview partners who were able to systematise their knowledge of traditional Tyvan world interpretation. Together with them I discussed difficult and complex connections in the 'traditional' reality of Tyvan society.

Since the 1990s, the blossoming of so-called neo-shamanism can be observed in Tyva (see Johansen 1992, 2001, 2004; Zorbas 2007; Grünwedel 2008, 2010, 2012). Closely connected to this movement is the Tyvan scholar Mongush Kenin-Lopsan, who founded the first shamans' association Düngür (Drum) in the early 1990s. During the Soviet period, Kenin-Lopsan collected material about what he called 'traditional religious conceptions', but he was only able to publish these with the beginning of perestroika.[19] He published his work with the ambition to hand back to his own people the traditions that were repressed during the decades of religious and cultural oppression. With the help of the data he collected and published, he succeeded in reanimating shamanism in Tyva and educating new shamans.

---

[19] His work *Ritual Praxis and Folklore of Tyvan Shamans* appeared in Russian in 1987.

There were many more shamans in Kyzyl in 2004 and 2005 than in the 1990s. In 1995, they had begun to organise themselves as shamanistic clinics. In 1997 there were already two such clinics in Kyzyl; in 2004, there were three of them: the above-mentioned Düngür, Tos Deer (Nine Heavens), and Adyg Eeren (Bear Spirit). Furthermore, after the collapse of the Soviet Union, many shamans visited western Europe and North America to be inspired by the esoteric and New Age movements, which they adapted and spread to Tyva (see Grünwedel 2008, 2010, 2012). I could thus observe among several Tyvan shamans ideas, phrased in Western languages, about 'cosmic powers' or 'extraterrestrial beings' that they mixed with older religious beliefs.

The tradition of the ethnographic study of Tyvan culture goes back to the years prior to the incorporation of the republic into the Soviet Union in 1944 (e.g. Potanin 1883). In that time a considerable number of ethnographic works by Russian and Tyvan scholars emerged.[20] They can be studied in two important libraries in Kyzyl: the library of the Sixty Warriors National Museum and the library of the Tyvan Research Institute for the Humanities. Studies by Western scholars[21] and several chapters in older monographs (Mänchen-Helfen 1931; Leimbach 1936; Harva 1938) complement the Tyvan and Russian publications. My first impulse to study world interpretations in Tyva and the subsequent daily and ritual action was given by the numerous articles of Erika Taube.[22] During several expeditions to Mongolia's Altai Mountains, Erika Taube studied the oral traditions, customs, religious conceptions, and religious behaviour of the Dyva. Her extensive field data provided rich material for comparison between the Dyva of the Altai and South-Siberian Tyvans, and also formed the first basis for a content analysis of the Tyvan interaction model of world interpretation described in the present survey.

---

[20] Some of the most important studies are: Kuular (1959); Potapov (1960, 1963, 1969, 1975, 1996); Vajnshtejn (1961, 1963, 1964, 1972, 1977, 1980, 1984, 1996a, 1996b, 2005); D'yakonova (1975, 1976, 1977, 1981, 1996, 2005); Kenin-Lopsan (1987, 1993, 1994a, 1994b, 1994c, 1995, 1996, 1997, 1998, 1999, 2002, 2003, 2005, 2009, 2011); Budegechi (1994); Mongush (1994); Arakchaa (1995); Donahoe et al. 2008.

[21] Johansen (1961, 1992, 1998, 2001, 2003, 2004); Diószegi (1962, 1963, 1978); Humphrey (1980, 1989, 1999); Humphrey, Mongush and Telengit (1993); Peters (1993); Kim and Hoppál (1995); Diószegi and Hoppál (1996); Alphen (1998); Devlet (1998); Oelschlägel (2000, 2004a, 2004b, 2005a, 2005b, 2006, 2010); Tryjarski (2001); Donahoe (2002, 2003a, 2003b, 2004, 2006a, 2006b, 2008, 2009); Deusen (2004); Grünwedel (2008, 2010, 2012); and Purzycki (2010).

[22] Taube, E. (1972, 1974a, 1974b, 1977a, 1978, 1981a, 1981b, 1981c, 1992, 1994a, 1994b, 1995, 1996a, 1996b, 1997, 2000, 2004, 2007, 2008).

On the following pages are reproduced several texts I recorded, transcribed, and translated from Tyvan or Russian during my fieldwork in 2004 and 2005. These texts include excerpts and analyses of interviews, contemporary legends, poems, songs, blessings, invocations, myths, and fairy tales. An almost complete collection of these texts, including the original texts in Tyvan or Russian, has already been published in a separate volume (Oelschlägel 2013b).

Social Life: Festivals and Life in the Taiga

Plate 1. The White Bearded Old Man grants fertility and wealth. As a sculpture in the central park of Kyzyl, he is a popular site for photo sessions with children (2004).

Plates 2-4. Many Tyvans participate in the Naadym festival on horseback and in traditional dress (Kyzyl, 2-3: 2004, 4: 1997).

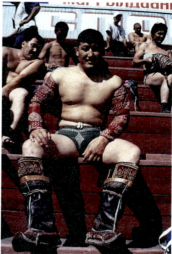
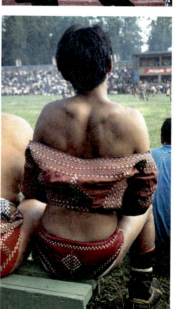

Plates 5-9. Festival activities include wrestling, riding and archery (Kyzyl, 1997).

Plate 10. The winner of a wrestling match dances the eagle dance around the Tyvan flag (Mugur Aksy, 2004).

Plate 11. Wrestling matches are popular not only among the people. During many festivities and rituals they are also carried out to entertain the spirits. The best wrestlers owe their talent to the spirit masters of this sport (Mugur Aksy, 2004).

Plates 12-16. Entertainment for the spirits includes numerous horse races (Kyzyl, 1997).

Plate 17. Tyvan saddle made of wood (Kyzyl, 1997).

Plates 18-21. The annual Naadym festival is accompanied by music and dance. Many artists presenting their crafts enjoy international renown (Kyzyl, 1997).

Plate 22. Summer yurt camp in the Baj Taiga (2005).

Plate 23. View inside a yurt (2005).

Plates 24-27. Dismantling and transporting a yurt in the Toolajlyg cooperative (24: 2004, 25-27: 2005).

Plate 28. Winter camp in the old baza of the Toolajlyg cooperative (2004).

Plate 29. Winter camp with a house and a yurt at Ak Bashtyg near Mugur Aksy (2005).

Plate 30. Many children from villages and towns spend their holidays in the yurts of their relatives (Toolajlyg, 2005).

Plate 31. In the fall the nomads begin to prepare meat for their winter reserves (Kyzyl, 1995).

Plates 32-33. In the rough terrain of the taiga, nomads need to be good drivers and are often able to repair their cars themselves (Süt Khöl, 2004).

Plate 34. The Mugur River near Mugur Aksy in the Möŋgün Taiga (2005).

Plate 35. Hospitality necessarily includes freshly slaughtered meat (Toolajlyg, 2005).

Part I
The Theory of Plural World Interpretations

The present study draws inspiration from two theories which claim that alternative worldviews can be found next to the modern worldview not only in the non-European context, but also in the Western world, and which recommend taking these alternative worldviews seriously. The first is the actor-network theory (ANT) developed by Michel Callon, Bruno Latour, and John Law in the 1980s (Latour 1987; Law and Hassard 1999; Belliger and Krieger 2006); the second is Gerd Spittler's 'interactive work' (Spittler 1998, 2003). While ANT could itself be understood as an argument for a new, alternative worldview, the present study makes no such claims. The aim is not to show whether a particular worldview or a model of world interpretation is 'realistic'. Instead, I will show which models of world interpretation an individual actor has at his or her disposal for interpreting the world, and moreover, how he or she flexibly applies them. The aim for such a demonstration is to observe and identify several models of world interpretation, not only in different societies and not only among different agents in one particular society, but rather by focusing on individual agents in one and the same society. Using the example of the Tyvans, I will describe and define two of many models of world interpretation, which I propose to call the 'interaction' and the 'dominance' models. Their abstract form will make it possible to order a confusing reality and render it describable. In order to understand the plurality of world interpretations, Alfred Schütz's theory of multiple realities, developed in the tradition of William James (1890), will prove to be very helpful (Schütz 1945, 1955, 1971a, 1971b and Schütz and Luckmann 2003 [1975], translated into English [1973-89]). Following James, the multiple realities described by Schütz and Luckmann make it possible to formulate an account of plural world interpretations based on several, simultaneous models of world interpretation that belong to the human repertoire of knowledge, behaviour, and action as coherent systems of content and structure, both equally valued and mutually contradictory. According to the concept of 'transdifference'

(Allolio-Näcke, Kalscheuer and Manzeschke 2005), these models of world interpretation exist not only in mutual competition, but form in one person a network of continua in which the human medium continually needs to position him or herself. Thus the actor applies several models of world interpretation by replacing, complementing, and mixing them depending on the situation and context. In the following section, I will introduce and discuss the studies most important for this study.

From Tradition and Modernity to Plural World Interpretations

The problems inspiring this study were the omnipresent simultaneity of tradition and modernity in Tyva as well as their contradictions, which were openly discussed by many Tyvans. Terms like 'modern conceptions' (Russ. *sovremennye predstavleniya*) or 'modern worldview' (Russ. *sovremennoe mirovozzrenie*) as well as 'traditional conceptions' (Russ. *tradicionnye predstavleniya*) or 'traditional worldview' (Russ. *tradicionnoe mirovozzrenie*) are used here as emic categories, that is as terms that Tyvans themselves employ regularly. In the following, I will first discuss the terms 'tradition' and 'modernity', as used by most Tyvans and by several Russian ethnographers.[20] On the basis of the Tyvan understanding of 'tradition' and 'modernity', I then explain why I abstain from using both terms as central categories in the present work. My most important aim is to represent a living complex of world interpretations that is not limited to only one model of world interpretation and that does not leave out alternative models within the same society. Instead, the present book will demonstrate the plurality of models of world interpretation within one society on the basis of the interpretations, behaviour, and action of individual persons. I will then illustrate the concepts that the extended perspective I adopted requires and explain how I came to define them.

(1) In Tyvan society, 'tradition' (Russ. *tradiciya*) is used in the conventional meaning of the term as an unbroken continuity of cultural essences. 'The prevailing conception of tradition, both in common sense and in social theory, has envisioned an isolable body or core of unchanging traits handed down from the past' (Handler and Linnekin 1984: 286). Against this naturalistic view on tradition, which presumes boundedness and essence, Handler and Linnekin argued 'that tradition is a symbolic process' and 'that traditional is not an objective property of phenomena but an assigned meaning' (ibid.). The latter understanding of the term is based on the insight 'that the past is always constructed in the present' (ibid.). In this sense, my

---

[20] The Tyvan language does not have terms for 'tradition' and 'modernity', so Tyvan speakers use the indicated Russian words and phrases.

own observations in Tyva suggest that tradition can be seen as 'invention' (Hobsbawm and Ranger 1992). It thus becomes clear that what we generally call 'tradition' is permanently changing, and that it is difficult to distinguish historical cultural elements from more recent inventions.

(2) The concepts 'tradition' and 'modernity' as they are used not only in Russian everyday speech but partly also in Russian scientific terminology tend to ignore the fact that components of both 'traditional' and 'modern' culture develop continuously and are subject to external and internal influences. As Bernard Cullen (2003: 218) commented, 'traditions are at their core not static by their very nature.... Traditions are dynamic cultural entities in a state of constant change. They are exposed to a continuous hail of changing influences, both from within and without, from which the current generation adopts some to integrate them in their own version of tradition'.

(3) The vibrance of what Tyvans call their 'tradition' is clearly visible. It includes, for example, the figure of the traditionally living pastoral nomad or herdsman (Tyv. *malchyn*) with livestock (Tyv. *mal*) and a yurt (Tyv. *ög*); traditional tools used in the subsistence economy and religious artefacts; traditional food (e.g. white food, i.e. milk products [Tyv. *ak chem*] or the rump of Tyvan sheep [Tyv. *uzha*]; traditional clothing for festive occasions or, more rarely, for everyday use (e.g. the Tyvan coat [Tyv. *ton*], cap [Tyv. *bört*], and boots with high-bent top [Tyv. *kadyg idik*]); features of the landscape with religious importance (e.g. a healing spring [Tyv. *arzhaan*], a sacred tree [Tyv. *ydyktyg yjash*], a mountain [Tyv. *dag*], a mountain pass [Tyv. *art*], a river [Tyv. *khem*], and ritual sites for the cult spirit masters). Nevertheless, such visible cultural traits do not in themselves guarantee the claim of completeness that we have with the concept of a 'culture'. Any search for *the* traditional culture of the Tyvans will soon reveal that such a complex does not appear as a bounded whole. 'Tyvan tradition' presents itself as an incomplete conglomeration of artefacts, behavioural norms, patterns of explanation, and practices that do not include all areas of Tyvan life. In order to describe the traditional culture of the Tyvans as a whole, it would have been necessary to reconstruct the 'primary' or 'original' tradition and to complement contemporary traditions. By contrast, my goal has been to study and to describe the present situation of Tyvan world interpretations.

(4) I started my work with intensive literature studies of international[21], German[22], and Russian[23] publications. But I soon discovered a

---

[21] Diószegi (1962, 1963, 1978); Humphrey (1980, 1989, 1999); Peters (1993); Diószegi and Hoppál (1996); Alphen (1998); Devlet (1998); Furst (1998); Donahoe (2002, 2003a, 2003b,

contradiction between my goal to describe contemporary Tyvan world interpretations and the historical-comparative approach of above all German and Russian publications that had initially shown me the way to the Tyvans of South Siberia. To explain current empirical data on the culture of a particular society, the comparative method includes historical data that can no longer be verified today, as well as data from neighbouring or culturally related ethnic groups that cannot or can no longer be found among the Tyvans. Especially when the meaning of so-called traditional actions and traditional interpretations of the world cannot be understood through direct observation, the comparative approach tries to clarify them by including data from other eras and other societies.

While the historical-comparative approach is valuable for exploring traditional cultural elements, for a study of contemporary Tyvan culture, like I had in mind, it was less suitable.

On the one hand, I did not intend to examine the patterns of interpretation, behaviour, and action of Tyvan actors through an intuitive and necessarily subjective filter in order to 'cleanse' so-called Tyvan traditions of modern Russian and other influences.

On the other hand, it did not seem justifiable to fill in the gaps in the description of present everyday life with cultural elements described in older works that today can no longer be observed among Tyvans, or that might still be found among neighbouring peoples but are no longer present in Tyvan culture. To do so would be create an artificial and unrealistic patchwork of 'contemporary traditions'. Both approaches would have forced me to separate sets of cultural knowledge that actually merge, and to merge historically or geographically separate cultural elements. Both would have prevented me from describing and analysing the contemporary complexity of Tyvan world interpretations.

(5) Furthermore 'tradition' and 'modernity' are not value-free terms in Tyva. On the one hand, they stand for an implicit time reference. The term 'traditional' refers to the past and to subsequent continuity. The term

---

2004, 2005, 2006a, 2006b, 2008, 2009); Deusen (2004); Zorbas (2007); Pimenova (2009); Chevalier (2010); Purzycki (2010).

[22] Harva (1938); Johansen (1961, 1967, 1992, 1998, 2001, 2003, 2004); E. Taube (1972, 1974a, 1974b, 1977a, 1977b, 1981a, 1981b, 1981c, 1990, 1992, 1994a, 1994b, 1995, 1996a, 1996b, 1997, 2000, 2004, 2007, 2008); Grünwedel (2008, 2010).

[23] The most important studies are: Kuular (1959); Potapov (1960, 1963, 1969, 1975, 1996); Vajnshtejn (1964, 1972, 1977, 1980, 1984, 1996a, 1996b, 2001, 2005); Potapov et al. (1966); D'yakonova (1975, 1976, 1977, 1981, 1996, 2005); Kenin-Lopsan (1987, 1993, 1994a, 1994b, 1994c, 1995, 1996, 1997, 1998, 1999, 2002, 2003, 2005, 2009, 2011); Mongush (1992, 1994, 2001); Budegechi (1994); Arakchaa (1995); Arapchor (1995); Kurbatskij (2001); Tryjarski (2001); Mannaj-ool (2004).

'modern', by contrast, is commonly used synonymously with the Russian words *novyj* (new), *zapadnyj* (Western), or *russkoe vlianie* (Russian influence). On the other hand, Tyvans often evaluate one model from the point of view of the other. The so-called modern position defines itself as enlightened or rational, and looks down on 'tradition' as associated with irrational religious customs, or looks up to it romantically as primordial and pristine. By contrast, the traditional position looks at modernity as human presumption against all non-human elements of the environment that co-determine the lives of human beings.

(6) Several scholars tend to assign 'traditional' or 'modern' lifestyles to individual persons or social groups. Such an identification of a person with a particular lifestyle does not correspond to reality because, as in my observations, there is no tradition comprising all areas of life in contemporary Tyva. Rather, it often appears that Tyvans find themselves in a situation of having to choose from a plurality of alternatives in order to adequately master an actual situation.

(7) A study of traditional perceptions of the environment today soon proved to be impossible because of their incompleteness in everyday use and the typical inconsequence that many Tyvans show in their interpretations, actions, and behaviour. Despite a good deal of knowledge of their own traditions, those Tyvans with whom I worked proved unwilling to always and consistently follow the norms, values, and patterns of action prescribed by their 'traditional culture' in social interaction and communication.

The question of why people were so inconsistent in following the codified traditions (oral or written) and social norms (expectations for individual behaviour) prescribed by tradition (i.e. why in many cases their behaviour (practice) differed from the normative standards) can only be answered, in my mind, by allowing for the possibility of plurality in the scientific description of human behaviour in, and human interpretations of, the world. Anomalies between rule and practice indicate the existence not only of *one* normative model of world interpretation, but of several, possibly mutually contradictory models (i.e. different ideal states) in one and the same human society. Social practice (i.e. the factual state) would then emerge situationally and contextually from a mixing or replacing of several normative models that are applied in making decisions on proper interpretation, behaviour, and action.[24]

(8) These considerations directed my attention to the observation of connections. The present study looks to examine plural world interpretations

---

[24] As Seiwert (2005) shows on the basis of material from the Vinaya of China, the existence of intersubjectively codified and social norms within a culture (ideal state) is not a sufficient precondition for their observation in practice (factual state).

as flexible arrangements of several, strikingly different models. Only in this way can 'tradition' and 'modernity' be reconciled as equally valued and an intuitive and subjective selection of daily observations and collected data be avoided.

(9) In realising this goal a number of further developments in my research were decisive. In identifying several co-existent and equally valued models of world interpretation, the central question of my research shifted from an exclusive description of Tyvan tradition to a detailed presentation of plural world interpretations. The temporal frame of the research project (36 months) only allowed for a focus on two such models of world interpretation. These can be identified as subsets of Schütz's 'world of daily life' (Schütz 1945: 533; 1971b: 394). The world of daily life, according to Schütz, is that reality which forms the basis of all other realities. It represents normality and is basic to other realities, such as the reality of natural science, religion, dreams, insanity, theatre, and art.

In the following I will describe two models of world interpretation. Based on their most essential structural characteristics, I will call them the model of human dominance (dominance model) and the model of interactions between human and non-human subjects (interaction model). The first stresses the human dominance over the environment, seen as a series of more or less passive objects of human agency; the second emphasises interaction in a world encompassing humans and consisting of both human and non-human subjects. These models are equivalent neither to the terms 'tradition' and 'modernity', nor to 'Tyvan tradition' and 'Tyvan modernity'. Rather, they are to be understood as models of world interpretation that are common to all people and from which traditional and modern models of world interpretation emanate worldwide. The specific Tyvan form of modernity takes its routines (i.e. 'recipes for the mastery of routine problems' [Berger and Luckmann 1966: 43]) mainly from the dominance model, while Tyvan tradition mainly evolves from the interaction model. For this reason, it seems legitimate to speak about the existence of a *specific* Tyvan dominance model and a *specific* Tyvan interaction model. As a heuristic tool for my data acquisition, I drew an artificial but permeable line between both models that might be considered intuitive and subjective. It is not meant to select or exclude but rather to allow us to differentiate between both models, enabling us to describe the whole as plural world interpretations.

Multiple Realities

The notion of one individual applying a plurality of world interpretations is closely related to Alfred Schütz's theory of multiple realities. Studying the psychological work of William James (1890), Schütz concluded that human beings possess 'several, probably an infinite number of various orders of realities' (Schütz 1971a: 237, 263; 1971b: 392; James 1890: 290ff). 'James calls them "sub-universes" and mentions the world of senses or physical objects (as paramount reality); the world of sciences; the world of ideal relations; the world of "tribal idols"; various supernatural worlds of mythology and religion; the various worlds of individual opinions; the worlds of sheer madness and of vagaries as examples' (Schütz 1945: 1, citing James 1890: 291ff). Basic to all these 'realities' is that they have, when we face them, their 'own special and separate style of existence' (James 1890: 290ff). That is, 'each world whilst it is attended to is real after its own fashion; only the reality lapses with the attention' (James 1890: 293, 533 and Schütz 1945: 1). 'In order to free this important insight from its psychologistic setting', Schütz (1945: 16) prefers 'to speak instead of many sub-universes of reality of finite provinces of meaning upon each of which we may bestow the accent of reality'.

Therefore, human beings are able to interpret directly tangible events and artefacts in distinct and contradictory ways. James asserts 'first, that we are liable to think differently of the same; and second that, when we have done so, we can choose which way of thinking to adhere to and which to disregard' (cited in Schütz 1945: 16, 551).

Despite the possibility of switching between the different provinces of meaning (Gmn. *Sinnbereiche*), Schütz considers the borders of each province of meaning to be finite. 'Hence we call a certain set of our experiences a finite province of meaning' (1945: 16, 551). Thus, the

> consistency and compatibility of experiences with respect to their peculiar cognitive style subsists merely within the borders of the particular province of meaning to which those experiences belong. By no means will that which is compatible within the province of meaning P be also compatible within the province of meaning Q. On the contrary, seen from P, supposed to be real, Q and all the experiences belonging to it would appear as merely fictitious, inconsistent and incompatible and vice versa (Schütz 1945: 18).

In Schütz's assessment, James correctly sees the 'world of sense or physical things' as 'the paramount reality' (Schütz 1945: 1f., 8ff). But Schütz prefers to describe this paramount reality as the world of daily life:

> We begin with an analysis of the world of daily life which the wide-awake, grown-up man who acts in it and upon it amidst his fellow-men experiences with the natural attitude as a reality. 'World of daily life' shall mean the intersubjective world which existed long before our birth, experienced and interpreted by others, our

predecessors, as an organized world. Now it is given to our experience and interpretation. All interpretation of this world is based upon a stock of previous experiences of it, our own experiences and those handed down to us by our parents and teachers, which in the form of 'knowledge at hand' functions as a scheme of reference. To this stock of experiences at hand belongs our knowledge that the world we live in is a world of well circumscribed objects with definite qualities, objects among which we move, which resist us and upon which we may act. To the natural attitude the world is not and never has been a mere aggregate of colored spots, incoherent noises, centers of warmth and cold (Schütz 1945: 1f).

The world of daily life is perceived by us to be 'the natural one, and we are not ready to abandon our attitude toward it without having experienced a specific shock which compels us to break through the limits of this "finite" province of meaning and to shift the accent of reality to another one' (Schütz 1945: 17; see also Schütz 1971a: 265; Schütz and Luckmann 2003 [1975]: 69). These shocks lead us to realise that the world of daily life 'is not the sole finite province of meaning but only one of many others accessible to my intentional life' (Schütz 1945: 17; Schütz 1971a: 266). 'There are as many innumerable kinds of different shock experiences as there are different finite provinces of meaning upon which I may bestow the accent of reality. Some instances are: the shock of falling asleep as the leap into the world of dreams [or] the inner transformation we endure if the curtain in the theater rises as the transition into the world of the stage-play' (Schütz 1945: 17).

Therefore, humans are able to switch between these several finite provinces of meaning. As mentioned above, 'the passing from one to the other can only be performed by a "leap", as Kierkegaard calls it, which manifests itself in the subjective experience of a shock.... What has just been called a "leap" or a "shock" is nothing else than a radical modification in the tension of our consciousness, founded in a different attention *à la vie*' (Schütz 1945: 18, my emphasis). Schütz (1971a: 267) also pointed out that on a single day we may successively 'bestow the accent of reality' to all kinds of provinces of meaning. The frequency of this switching between such provinces of meaning is unlimited.

The 'symbolic meanings' of finite provinces of meaning are 'intersubjectively' fixed (Schütz 1971b: 395). This means that they are the collective interpretative patterns of a group of people that connect the group members with one another and at the same time distinguish the group from other groups with other 'intersubjective symbolic meanings'. Forming historical and social connections, these meanings are what ethnographic studies describe as cultural specifics. Schütz and Luckmann expressed it in this way: 'historically seen, the intersubjective agreement of symbolic meanings leads to an exceedingly large diversity of socio-historical forms' (2003 [1975]: 658).

Transdifference

The concept of transdifference, as developed by the Erlangen Graduate School 'Cultural Hermeneutics: Reflections of Difference and Transdifference' presents itself as a possibility to describe the space between the extremes of two Tyvan models of world interpretation.[25] This graduate school set itself the goal to develop a model that would reconcile 'the orientational function of distinctive (binary) thinking with moments of uncertainty, impurity and the figure of the "third"' (Allolio-Näcke and Kalscheuer 2005: 16; see also Breinig and Lösch 2006). The orientational, binary, or dichotomous way of thinking in terms of differences should be maintained and complemented by the often ignored space of transdifference. 'Heuristically speaking, transdifference is an *umbrella concept* that allows us to inspect phenomena that do not neatly fit models of clear-cut difference, thus defying – at least to a certain extent – explanation on the basis of binary logic.... Transdifference can be seen as a part of the wide range of phenomena of non-linearity that has come increasingly under investigation in recent times' (Breinig and Lösch 2002: 22, original emphasis).

Transdifference does not abolish difference but complements it. Transdifference 'does not do away with the originary binary inscription of difference, but rather causes it to oscillate' (Breinig and Lösch 2002: 23). 'We do not intend to overcome difference in favour of a higher unity, but to preserve and appreciate it as a genuinely necessary condition for orientation. Rejecting an exclusive focusing on difference and its radical deconstruction as insufficient approaches, we understand transdifference as a thus far neglected supplement of difference' (Allolio-Näcke und Kalscheuer 2005: 17). 'Transdifference ... denotes all that which resists the construction of meaning based on an exclusionary and conclusional binary model. While there can be no transdifference without difference – transdifference does not mean indifference – the term refers to whatever runs "through" the line of demarcation drawn by binary difference' (Breinig und Lösch 2002: 23).

Christoph Keitel and Lars Allolio-Näcke (2005: 105) see the reduction of complexity as 'the basic problem of Western thinking.... We predominantly reduce dichotomously'. In this way arise the conceptions of

---

[25] Theses and publications of the Erlangen Graduate School can be found under: http://www.kulturhermeneutik.uni-erlangen.de, last accessed on 22 September 2014.

'pure differences' or of 'polar differences'. Klaus Lösch (2005: 27) understands differences to be mainly 'binary oppositions as ordering categories'. The concept of transdifference allows us to constitute and describe 'moments of ambiguity, indecision and contradiction that we blend out while constructing difference on the basis of a binary logic of order' (Lösch 2005: 27). This includes considering the possibility of crossing a border. The border, which separates oppositions, such as the own and the other, on the one hand creates a difference, but on the other hand also includes the possibility of transdifference, by being surmountable under certain conditions: 'a border is only a border if it allows the possibility to pass it: border [difference] and passing [transdifference] therefore make up an inseparable unity' (Keitel and Allolio-Näcke 2005: 108).

Thus the term 'transdifference' stands for a perspective that allows for differences and represents and describes the space between them. Transdifference does not abolish differences but complements them. There is no transdifference without difference and 'pure differences' cannot exist either.

Two Models of World Interpretation: The Interaction and the Dominance Model

In the observable everyday lives of many Tyvans, they do not apply an exclusive canon of interpretation, action, and behaviour, and they do not decide explicitly between a life based on traditional or modern models. Both modern and traditional components of Tyvan culture are equally available for application. They are each accepted to a similar degree and each has its own value for dealing with a current life situation. It seems as if Tyvans can always, in accordance to their needs, grab into a box filled to the brim with traditional and modern components of culture in order to select that sample of interpretation, behaviour, or action that at that moment appears suitable for use in their actual situation. At first sight, a colourful mix of interpretations, behaviours, and actions emerge that can often only be correlated with great difficulty as long as the scholar tries to order them according to her own (i.e. etic) terms and models.

The introduction and definition of the terms 'dominance model' and 'interaction model' constitute such an attempt at a clarifying order.

The dominance model is in line with Cartesian thinking, and more specifically with Cartesian dualism (Bargatzky 2007: 61f). Following René Descartes (1596–1650), Cartesian dualism separates the 'mind' (*res cogitans*, i.e. mental substance), and the 'body' (*res extensa*, i.e. material substance), declaring the latter to be a mere passive object of human agency.

The juxtaposition of human beings imbued with rationality and intelligence with all merely existing 'things' reveals the following characteristics: (1) It separates human beings from their non-human environment and opposes them. (2) It differentiates between active subjects (humans) and passive objects of human agency as the constituent parts of the non-human environment; the act takes place from the subject to the object. (3) The non-human components of the environment follow natural principles. Humans are able to understand the principles and use them to their own advantage. (4) Interaction is possible only between subjects (i.e. human beings). Animal instincts are a border case: they appear to modern humans as an interaction between humans and animals, but are not regarded as equal to the rationality and intelligence of humans. (5) Non-human components of the environment have no rationality or intelligence. Humans alone have the ability to consciously and deliberately create human lives, even if the possibilities for doing so are limited by natural principles. (6) While human beings shape their own lives, they create their environment too. Only a false understanding of natural connections curbs the human ambitions to create their own world to live in.

In the specific ways in which Tyvans shape their lives, the 'dominance model' is a mode for interpreting the world that to a large extent co-determines Tyvan everyday life.

In addition to the dominance model, Tyvans orient themselves in many situations on a model I call the 'interaction model'. In this model of world interpretation, all norms of proper behaviour in the traditional Tyvan world point to an obligatory, respectful interaction between human and non-human components of the Tyvan world. This model of world interpretations, and the actions and behaviour patterned on it, requires Tyvan actors to interact with the different components of the Tyvan world, such as stones, trees, fire, cars, or even spirit masters. The Tyvan conviction that they are part of a world consisting of human and non-human subjects or 'actors' implies that they are in permanent interaction with all non-human components of the Tyvan world. According to this model for interpreting the world, humans participate in the power of non-human elements of the Tyvan world, experience the influence and will power of non-human subjects, and perceive the reasons for which they are controlled, dominated, and afflicted by non-human subjects (e.g. spirits) which they may fear. The model described is a specific Tyvan version of the interaction model that I want to define as a model of interactions in a world encompassing both human and non-human subjects. It has the following attributes: (1) Humans are integral components of the world. (2) In addition to humans, the world includes non-human subjects. (3) Interactions take place not only between humans but also between human and non-human partners and actors. The phrase 'interactions between subjects' is not only related to humans. In the specific Tyvan case, (3.1) articles of daily use, tools and machinery, spirits, gods, landscapes, animals and plants are seen as subjects that interact with humans. (4) A self-awareness similar to human awareness is not ascribed to all subjects. In the specific Tyvan case, (4.1) spirits and gods without a will, intelligence, rationality, and intention are unthinkable. The same is thought of animals and plants. For example, a hunter apologises to an animal that he has killed and a woodcutter apologises to a felled tree, both to avoid the negative consequences of their acts. However, energies, for example, do not have a will or intelligence but anyway act upon humans. (4.2) The subjects of the interaction model are hierarchically ordered. The gods and spirits are at the top of the hierarchy, the second place is taken by humans. Placed parallel to humans are energies and powers without self-awareness that can act on all components of the world. Wild and domestic animals, plants, parts of the landscape, tools and articles of daily use are subordinated to humans and spirits, energies, and powers. (4.3) This hierarchy is not universally valid. According to the specific situation in which an interaction takes place, different subjects can be superior, equal, or inferior to one another. For example, a tree cannot consent to being felled and a wild animal cannot avoid being killed.

The core difference in the definition of both models of world interpretation is in the role of 'subjects' and 'objects'. While humans are identified as subjects in both models of world interpretation, non-human components of the world are perceived as 'objects' in the dominance model but as 'subjects' in the interaction model. Here I define 'subjects' as actors who are capable of deliberately acting upon everything around them. Following the interaction model, several human and non-human subjects, such as animals, plants, tools, and features of the landscape interact permanently and mutually upon one another. The term 'object' is limited to the dominance model where these things tend to be more or less passive components of the world under the continuous influence of active subjects. In other words, subjects, that is humans, work continuously on the world's objects, change and shape them, and therefore feel called to dominate them.

Both models of world interpretation, the specific Tyvan dominance and the specific Tyvan interaction models, are intersubjective and universalised among Tyvans. Both ways of interpreting the world are well known and shared by all the Tyvans I met during fieldwork. Furthermore, my data suggest that most Tyvans, in using terms like 'tradition' and 'modernity', are aware of the existence of both models and distinguish between them. They use them not only unconsciously but also consciously by deciding for one or the other, or for a suitable mix of both models of interpretation, behaviour, and action. According to their situation and needs, the Tyvans I observed preferred to interpret a situation and to behave or act in it either in accordance with the interaction model or with the dominance model. In doing so, they selected the use of one model of world interpretation in its pure form or quite often a reasonable mix of both models. When Tyvans decided for a special kind of explanation of an event, they were aware of the model they were following, but preferred terms like 'following our tradition' or 'according to Russian and modern influences'.

The definitions of both models of world interpretation include a separation of structure and content. Content means, as described by Schütz and Luckmann, 'intersubjective symbolic meanings that are specific to different cultures and historical eras. They exhibit an enormous "diversity of socio-historical forms"' (2003 [1975]: 657). Whereas the content of models of world interpretations is in a permanent process of modification, development, and influence, the structure of the models, by contrast, appears as global and permanent through time.

Two examples may clarify this. The permanent process of transformation of the interaction model's content becomes apparent when comparing older and more recent ethnographic monographs on Tyvan traditional worldviews. Older sources refer to the acceptance of a multi-layered world consisting of an upper, middle, and under world.[26] This model is well-known in Tyva, but it is relegated to the past and today no Tyvan known to me is of the opinion that the world is really organised as such. Instead, Tyvans today accept the common, natural science-based understanding of the form and composition of the terrestrial globe. In Tyvan everyday reality, this insight is now 'internalized' as 'objective knowledge' (Berger and Luckmann 1966: 129ff), regardless of whether Tyvans speak about their world from the perspective of the dominance model or that of the interaction model.

Secondly, the permanent structural stability of the dominance model can be shown by using the example of the production and use of tools in the Palaeolithic era as well as that of the Neolithic domestication and breeding of domestic animals and plants. I would suggest that the invention, production, and use of simple tools from wood, bone and stone points to an early human tendency to apply the dominance model. So too, does selective domestication and breeding.

The limitation to only two models of world interpretation in the present study does not presuppose that Tyvans are unfamiliar with other

---

[26] Harva (1938: 24f, 56); Potapov (1969: 347); D'yakonova (1976: 275); Alekseev (1987: 65); Budegechi (1994: 12); Vajnshtejn (1996b: 253).

models of world interpretation. On the contrary, Tyvans have as many models of world interpretation at their disposal as other members of globalised Western societies. In Tyva today, apart from the interaction and the dominance models, we also find variants that are oriented toward Tibetan Buddhism (described by Mongush 1992, 2001), Christian variants introduced by American Baptist missionaries, Russian Orthodox, and other European churches, as well as animist models of world interpretation oriented towards European and American esotericism and the New Age movement. These forms have been described by Johansen (2003, 2004), Grünwedel (2008, 2010), and Zorbas (2007), documenting a shift from shamanism to neo-shamanism. Such religious models of world interpretation belong to what Schütz (1945: 551) calls 'realities of religion'. They may mix with other models of world interpretation or complement each other. However, by themselves, and through their interplay with other models of world interpretation, they have thus far not been investigated.

A study of the dominance and the interaction models will suffice to describe plural world interpretations because they exhibit a *global* and *permanent* tendency and taken together are part of and compose the 'world of daily life' (Schütz 1945: 533) or what William James (1890: 290ff.) called 'paramount reality'. Furthermore, they provide a conceptional basis for the majority of other models of world interpretation. Both the dominance and the interaction models are related to other models of world interpretation in the same way that Schütz's 'world of daily life' relates to all other 'finite provinces of meaning' (or what James called 'sub-universes', Schütz 1945: 533). All other models of interpreting the world derive from either or both the dominance and the interaction models, and have to be seen in connection with them.

In the context of Tyvan self-representation, in their narratives, Tyvans usually decide for one of the two extremes. The oppositions mentioned above may then appear in almost pure form, untouched by the opposite pole, that is in a narratively idealised pure form (ideal state). Observing the same Tyvans in interaction with their peers, however, soon made me aware of the wide field of transdifference, the permanent crossing of the border between self-defined 'tradition' and 'modernity' as well as the abidance to and oscillation in the wide space of the continuum between them (factual state, practice). Both models of world interpretation therefore appear as extreme points on a continuum in which the individual depending on his situation or needs continuously occupies new positions. How this permanent change of positions in the transdifference continuum works will be explained and discussed in Part III.

In this section I deal with the problems that emerge when using both models of world interpretation as parallel models, mutually contradictory but at the same time complementary. I show how individual Tyvan research partners deal with the existence of both models of world interpretation in their own personal way. The shift in position on the continuum between the extreme points arises from their attempt to manage situations in their everyday lives by using a suitable mix of both models. The focus will be on describing what rules are followed in shifting between both models. In the following chapters I discuss the reasons and consequences that accompany the model switching, consider the direction of these shifts and their frequency as well as differentiate between spontaneous, strategic, or professional model switching.

The present study does not only deal with the Tyvan practice of plural world interpretations, but also demonstrates – on the basis of my empirical material – the specific Tyvan contents of the interaction model. The interaction model will be described in Part II.

Data on the content of the specific Tyvan interaction model was collected especially during the period of July 2004 to January 2005. Employing qualitative methods, I interviewed people about their views on the natural and artificial environments, plants, wild and domestic animals, as well as (fellow) human beings. Further interviews concerned the meaning of the wilderness and sacred sites, spirits, and the multifaceted roles of these in the lives of human beings. Particular attention was directed at the rules and norms of 'proper behaviour' within a world of permanent interaction between human and non-human subjects. In addition, I present reports of events about exemplary events that local people experienced during encounters with natural subjects, individual spirits, artefacts, and natural subjects possessed by spirits or by people who had been blessed or cursed by spirits. The data from these interviews and narratives is presented in emic terms based as closely as possible on the statements of my research partners. The results reflect the self-representation of my research partners in Tyva and in turn the ideal state postulated by the Tyvans themselves, that is, the 'proper' way to think, behave, and act modelled on the Tyvan interaction model of world interpretation. Finally, Part II is geared to the possibilities of interaction between human and non-human subjects that are well known in Tyva and thus offers a new perspective on existing research with the Tyvan interaction model.

Terms and Definitions

The phrase 'plural world interpretations' that gives this book its title is based on phenomenological and constructivist insights that view human beings as the creators of multiple realities. At the same time, socially constructed realities shape human interpretations of the world as well as their actions and behaviour, which, in turn, are based on these interpretations. Here I define plural world interpretations as human interpretations, as well as human actions and behaviours following these interpretations, that are based upon the flexible use of simultaneous and equivalent models for interpreting the world. These models of world interpretation are coherent systems having both structure and content. They supplement and contradict each other and are part of the knowledge, behaviour, and action repertoire of human beings.

In studying the flexible handling of just two of many possible models of world interpretation by individual Tyvan actors, I use the term 'model' in the sense of a 'social construction' as defined by Berger and Luckmann (1966). Since the world interpretation of an individual Tyvan actor at any given moment comprises a selection from many different archetypes and patterns, I propose to regard these archetypes as models and intersubjective social constructions. As models, they are neither natural realities nor human biological characteristics, but rather products of human creativity. Both models of world interpretation discussed here are socially constructed and members of Tyvan society work constantly on their externalisation (i.e. production [Berger and Luckmann 1966: 52]), objectification (to become an objective reality, ibid. 53-61), and internalisation (i.e. annexation to become a subjective reality, ibid. 129-47).

In the following descriptions of plural world interpretations, I will sometimes simply use the term 'interpretation'. This term is not equivalent to perception because 'interpretation' signifies the behaviour that follows perception. People perceive something with their senses and afterwards interpret it in many ways. For interpreting the perceived we use archetypes and patterns predetermined by our culture, which I call models of world interpretation. Our subsequent behaviour is based on these interpretations.

I use the term 'world' in the constructivist sense of 'life-world' that goes back to the phenomenology of Edmund Husserl (1954 [1936], 1970) and was introduced into sociology by Alfred Schütz (1945: 533; Schütz und Luckmann 2003 [1975]) as 'paramount reality'. Peter L. Berger and Thomas Luckmann developed the idea further as the 'world of daily life' or 'social everyday reality' (Berger and Luckmann 1966: 23-25).

'Social everyday reality' is a 'reality of common sense' (Berger and Luckmann 1966: 20; Berger and Luckmann 2012 [1969]: 23). It is this reality that 'is available to the common sense of the ordinary members of society' (Berger and Luckmann 1966: 19). As one of many realities, it precedes all other realities. 'Among the multiple realities there is one that presents itself as the reality par excellence. This is the reality of everyday life. Its privileged position entitles it to the designation of "paramount reality"' (Berger and Luckmann 1966: 21; 2012 [1969]: 24). Or, as the authors explained, this is the everyday reality that individual persons experience 'in the state of being wide-awake' (ibid.). That is, 'this wide-awake state of existing in and apprehending the reality of everyday life is taken by me to be normal and self-evident, that is, it constitutes my natural attitude' (ibid.). 'The natural attitude is the attitude of common sense consciousness precisely because it refers to a world that is common to many men. Common sense knowledge is the knowledge I share with others in the normal, self-evident routines of everyday life' (Berger and Luckmann 1966: 23; 2012 [1969]: 26). In this sense we need to allocate both models of world interpretation presented here, the dominance and the interaction model, to 'everyday reality'. They are part of and constitute the socially constructed 'world of daily life' or 'everyday reality' (1966: 18-26).

As part of 'everyday reality', one needs to understand the dominance and the interaction model as 'social stocks of knowledge' consisting 'of recipes for the mastery of routine problems' (Berger and Luckmann 1966: 41-43). Being 'socially constructed', we enrich them permanently with new contents when managing problems in a creative way. By repeating and copying them, such routines become common knowledge and factual reality. As such, they pressure us to apply them in managing everyday life situations. We adopt them by several processes of primary and secondary socialisation and transform them into our subjective realities so that we then follow them voluntarily and usually in an unreflective way (ibid. 129-46). This process can be seen as a cycle that steadily feeds into the wider domain of our daily social interactions. The socially constructed 'worlds' we live in are accepted as realities because we become introduced to them when we imitate authorities (e.g. parents and teachers) and peers, and because we share them with others intersubjectively.

Once we accept that both models of world interpretation are products of human construction, then the human ability to flexibly handle a multitude of such models becomes plausible. Because the particular models are distinct from each other, however, they belong each in equal measure to the repertoire of knowledge, behaviour, and action of the Tyvan community and its members. Diversity and variability of the models make it possible to use both to interpret events and situations in a flexible way and to react to and act in them according to the needs of the moment.

This study introduces the flexible use of two models of world interpretation, the dominance and the interaction models, by Tyvan actors. As parts of a specific Tyvan everyday reality, we may define them as common to all Tyvans, and thus as intersubjective.

The specific Tyvan modern worldview draws primarily on the dominance model. This term describes a model of world interpretation based on the idea of the human domination of an environment consisting of rather passive objects of human agency. The attributes of the dominance model can be summarised as follows:

> The separation and juxtaposition of humans and their environment.
> The differentiation between active subjects (human beings) and passive objects of human agency (the natural and artificial environment).
> Purposeful action of humans (subjects) on objects of the non-human environment.
> Interactions that are only possible between self-conscious subjects, that is, between human beings.
> Humans alone having power to consciously shape society and the environment.
> Human power being limited alone by the laws of nature.

The Tyvans call their specific Tyvan form of the interaction model their 'traditional worldview'. It is also known as Tyvan animism or shamanism. But the interaction model is not exclusive either to the South-Siberian Tyvans or to religious worldviews. Examples of secular interaction models are the actor-network theory as summarised by Belliger and Krieger (2006) and the 'interactive paradigm of work' introduced by Spittler (2003). The specific Tyvan interaction model is a model of world interpretation that focuses on interactions in a world encompassing both human and non-human subjects. This model is characterised by features that include:

> The human being appears in it as an integral part of the world.
> Non-human subjects exist and act beside human beings.
> Interactions can take place between human and non-human subjects.
> The world's subjects can be superior, equal, or inferior to each other depending on the situation in which an interaction takes place.

If we are accept the fact that models of world interpretation are the products of human creativity, then the human capability to use them flexibly follows. As contradictory as the models are, they both belong to the repertoire of knowledge, behaviour, and action of Tyvan society and its individual members. The diversity and variability of both models enable Tyvans to interpret situations and events in a flexible way and to react to or act in them based on the individual situation.

The material presented here will show that Tyvan interpretation, behaviour, and action draw on various contradictory and complementary models of world interpretation that are equal and occur simultaneously. Their flexible use results in seemingly contradictory statements about one and the same event and lead to different forms of behaviour in otherwise comparable situations. It is thus necessary to clarify the question of how human beings use the models of world interpretation in their everyday lives. The answer to this question is reminiscent of what Schütz (1945) and Schütz and Luckmann (2003 [1975]) have already argued: (1) Both models are perceived as 'true' and 'correct'; (2) the models of world interpretation are only coherent in themselves. Findings modelled on either one of both models of world interpretation cannot be consistently related to findings modelled on the other; (3) in the sense of 'multiple realities', both models of world interpretations have their own 'specific accent of reality' or 'reality accent' (Schütz 1945: 546ff). Schütz and Luckmann (2003 [1975]) argue that if we bestow the accent of reality upon one model of world interpretations, we accept interpretations modelled on it as true. If the actor shifts the accent of reality to the other model, a new interpretation or truth emerges that can be contrary to the first.

In this sense, the models of world interpretation can be seen as parallel truths of one and the same person. An argumentation modelled on one of them can be perceived as true if we bestow the accent of reality upon it. If one switches from one model to another, that is, if the accent of reality shifts from one model to another, then the previous argument may appear illogical and the new argument, which may be contradictory to the former, may be accepted as true.

Schütz (1945) describes this switching as crossing the line between different 'finite provinces of meaning'. 'The passing from one to the other can only be performed by a "leap", as Kierkegaard calls it, which manifests itself in the subjective experience of a shock' (Schütz 1945: 547). James (1890) and Schütz (1945) point out that the shift between different 'provinces of meaning' is not a contradiction, but rather, a typically human skill. This is also true for the shifting between models of world interpretation. The Tyvan case shows that the plurality of models of world interpretation enriches everyday life. Because Tyvans are able to choose between several alternatives, they can apply them to their personal and general advantage.

Change in Perspective

The change in perspective is a well-known but often underestimated method to gain new insights in and develop a theory about human self-conceptions in their daily life. This project aspires to two changes in perspective. Firstly, it complements analyses of Tyvan animism that in earlier publications mostly focused on the variety of non-human subjects and their meaning for Tyvans. These have been described in numerous works by mostly Tyvan and

Russian authors.[27] Having myself published a monograph about this subject in 2004, it seemed reasonable for the present project to choose a new perspective focusing on the interactions between human and non-human subjects. In this way the present work complements all preceding work on Tyvans.

Secondly, the project looked to shift the focus on the presentation of Tyvan tradition and modern influences to one on the presentation of parallel realities which are equal to each other as models of world interpretation. The present book considers the dominance and the interaction model as distinct models of world interpretation that in their content are subject to a permanent process of transformation, influence, and development while maintaining in their structure a permanent and global stability. Tyvan world interpretations are regarded as the human implementation of a plural and flexible model that consists of the permanent replacement, complementation, and mixing of various models of world interpretation. The continuous repositioning on the continuum between the dominance and interaction models, depending on situation and context, defines the success of an individual actor in managing all kinds of life situations. How successful a Tyvan masters his or her life depends directly on his or her skill in finding an adequate mixture of the models of world interpretation that in turn are constitutive for all further models of world interpretation that are common in Tyva but will not be dealt with in this work.

Summary

This section has looked to introduce the theory and practice of plural world interpretations. The focus of the present book is on two models of world interpretation that are common in Tyva and used flexibly by individuals and groups. On the one hand, there exists a specifically Tyvan dominance model usually perceived by Tyvans as their 'modern' worldview. On the other, there exists a specifically Tyvan interaction model that Tyvans identify as their 'traditional' animistic-shamanistic worldview. Together with a specifically Tyvan Buddhist worldview of Tibetan import, these worldviews are part of Tyvan everyday reality, which is constituted simultaneously with the worldviews. Although mutually contradictory, the worldviews are parallel components of a mental culture that all my research partners in Tyva share and can be used by every Tyvan for interpreting events, and as a guideline for proper action and behaviour. To me, they were often communicated in a narratively idealised pure form. However, they were enacted

---

[27] In addition to those listed in note 17, these include Vajnshtejn (1961, 1963).

only in tendency, that is in mixed or complementary forms according to the situation and context.

Plural world interpretations and their flexible use follow several rules that can be summarised as follows. Both types of world interpretation, the interaction model and the dominance model, can be found side by side among the Tyvans with specific Tyvan content.

In their extreme forms, both models contradict each other in such a fundamental way that an interpretation of a situation based on either one of them seems 'fictitious', 'dissonant', and 'inconsistent' (Schütz 1971b: 397), if compared against the other.

Both models of world interpretation appear in statements made by many Tyvans in a narratively idealised pure form. Many Tyvans admit gladly only one of them.

The actions and behaviour of many Tyvans and their conversations among themselves reveal that both models of world interpretation are applied complementarily or in mixed form. In this dual use, Tyvans oscillate according to their needs from one extreme to another, or change their position on the continuum of transdifference between them.

My conversation partners knew to distinguish between both types of world interpretation and attributed their statements to the emic concepts of 'modernity' and 'tradition'.

None of these models can be attributed exclusively to 'the Tyvans'. Many Tyvans feel at home in both models as well as in the space of transdifference between them.

Both models of world interpretation seem to be stable in their structure. However, they can rapidly change their content as a result of the influence of the media, schools and professional education, science, tourism and travel, as well as esotericism and the New Age movement.

The world interpretation of one person at a given moment in time results from their position in transdifferential space (i.e. the position that a Tyvan adopts in a particular moment, situation, and context and that he is willing to follow at that moment).

For this reason, the world interpretations of the people of Tyva are not only subject to a permanent process of change in their content but also in their structure. Structurally they are not *unambiguous, one-dimensional,* or *static*, but *ambiguous, flexible, situational,* and *plural*.

Religious Life

Plate 36. Tyvans incorporate old Turkish tombs in their ancestor worship (2005).

Plate 37. A stone *ovaa* built for the spirit master of a valley close to the road from Kyzyl to Turan (2005).

Plate 38. The controversial *ovaa* of the Nine Heavens shamanic clinic on the promenade along the Yenisei River in Kyzyl (2005).

Plate 39. A wooden *ovaa* built for the spirit master of a mountain pass on the road to Khandagajty (2005).

Plates 40-41. The *ovaa* of Ak Bashtyg Mountain close to Mugur Aksy in the Möŋgün Taiga (2005).

Plate 42. Stupa and *ovaa* on the road from Kyzyl to Chadaan (2004).

Plate 43. 'The Arat' monument and an *ovaa* near Kyzyl (2004).

Plate 44. A stupa in the vicinity of Kyzyl (2004).

Plate 45. A sacred spring in the vicinity of Kyzyl (2004).

Plate 46. The shaman siblings in Süt Khöl, preparing a sacrificial fire for the spirit master of their homeland (2004).

Plate 47. A shameness lighting a sacrificial fire.

Plate 48. The shaman siblings in Süt Khöl (2004).

Plate 49. A shamaness (Süt Khöl, 2004).

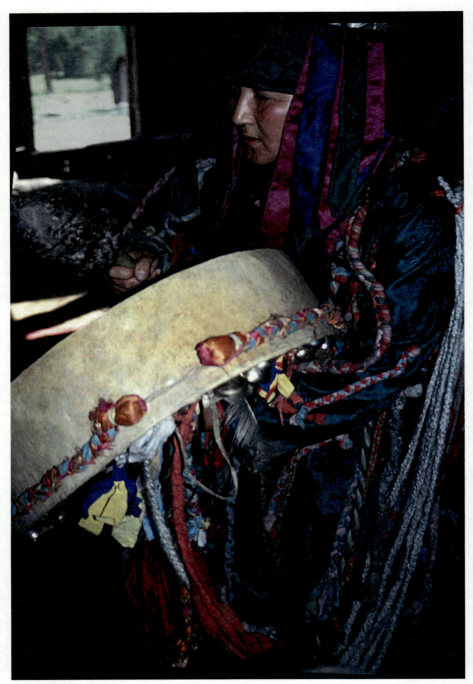

Plate 50. Another shamaness (Süt Khöl, 2004).

Plates 51-53. Shamans of the Nine Heavens shamanic clinic in Kyzyl during the annual consecration of their *ovaa* (2004).

Plate 54. The 'Great Hunter' during *khuvaanak* divination (Ulug Khem, 1995).

Plates 55-56. Shamanic trees close to Mugur Aksy in the Möŋgün Taiga (2005).

Plate 57. Funeral of a horse cranium in a tree close to Mugur Aksy (2005).

Plate 58. A sacred tree (*ydyktyg yjash*), centre (1997).

Plate 59. Monks in front of a Buddhist temple (*kham*) in the vicinity of Kyzyl (1995).

Plates 60-61. A Buddhist temple and a monk in Kyzyl (2005).

Plate 62. A yurt in the Möngün Taiga (2004).

Part II
Ethnography of the Tyvan Interaction Model

Whereas modernity cherishes the illusion that human beings are chosen to rule the world and all objects around them, many social scientists call on us to view the world's non-human entities as 'actors' with whom human beings interact constantly (Latour 1987, 1996, 2005, 2007). They often refer to examples from traditional cultures (e.g. Ingold 1986, 1994, 1996, 2000, 2002); the Tyvan interaction model is also such an example. As argued above, the timeless and universal interaction model is based on the assumption that human beings are in steady interaction with everything around them, regardless of whether this interaction takes place with human beings, animals, plants, material things, or immaterial phenomena. A particular historical or cultural form of such an interaction model does not necessarily have to be based on religious principles alone. Using the example of photocopiers, Gerd Spittler (2003) described how interactions between human beings and machines work. Inviting us to reassess Western modernity, actor-network theory argues that a human being is only one of many actors in networks that include non-human subjects, and shows how complex a network of human and non-human actors can be (Belliger and Krieger 2006). Consequently, the interaction model specific to Tyvan society is only one example among numerous other religious and secular interaction models of world interpretation. It belongs to those models that are based on the conceptual world of animism and shamanism. It has often been described as such.

The following sections therefore aspire to a shift of perspective that, building on previous publications, focuses on the numerous interaction possibilities. A fundamental prerequisite for such a representation is to accept the existence of a collective of human and non-human actors that can interact. In the following, the possible existence of non-human subjects is not questioned. I allow for the possibility that spirits exist beside the human spirit. In so doing I reiterate the emic perspective of my Tyvan research partners. They act on the assumption that some non-human subjects (spirits and gods) deliberately and consciously act, and that some (religious powers and energies) unconsciously act, on events in the earthly world; non-humans set norms und rules for interaction, control their abidance, and punish contraventions. I here take up the perspective of my research partners in order to describe a model of world interpretation that on the one hand is consistent and logical in itself, but on the other hand is largely alien to Western Europeans.

The interaction model is equal to other models of world interpretation in Tyvan culture. It complements the Western assumption that there is no reason or will outside of human reason and will and that therefore human beings are destined to dominate the world. In the following description of the interaction model, I do not see an ideological confrontation with modernity because both models have a place in Tyvan self-understanding. The following section applies a historical-comparative approach in trying to render comprehensible to Western Europeans the specific Tyvan interpretations of events.

Non-Human Interaction Partners and Religious Forms of Interaction

Whereas many a god (Tyv. *burkhan*) – such as the ruler of the upper world (Tengeri or Kubustu Khaan), the ruler of the lower world (Erlik Lovun Khaan), 'father sky' (Tyv. *deer adam*) and 'mother earth' (Tyv. *cher iyem*), sun (Tyv. *khün*), moon (Tyv. *aj*) – has been regularly discussed in the existing literature, these deities no longer play a significant role in the lived interaction model of contemporary Tyva.[28] Although many Tyvans are still aware of the former importance of such deities, their presence and function has been taken over by master and evil spirits as well as by other non-human subjects that for most of my conversation partners seem earthlier, closer, and for this reason more influential. For this reason, data about interactions between human beings and deities such as sky (Tyv. *deer*) and earth (Tyv. *cher*), sun, and moon is harder to come by. Nevertheless, many Tyvans still address several deities, primarily '[my] father sky' and '[my] mother earth', in blessings and invocations as protectors of all human and non-human subjects of the earthly world. These deities regulate, control, punish, and

---

[28] These deities are discussed in Harva (1938); Taube, E. (1974b); D'yakonova (1976, 1977); Alekseev (1987); Kenin-Lopsan (1993, 1994a); Budegechi (1994); Vajnshtejn (1996b). For a summary see Oelschlägel (2004a: 38-53; 2004b).

safeguard them and are in this sense co-responsible for success in everyday work and for fertility, happiness, health, and prosperity.[29]

One of my research partners, a 58-year-old male biology and chemistry teacher living in Mugur Aksy, said the following on 9 October 2004 about the sky:

> The Tyvans pray: 'My blue sky, watch over me!' They pray: 'My black earth, watch over me!' Moreover they also pray: 'My golden sun, my golden moon, watch over me!' If – for example – somebody on horseback stumbles over a root and falls, he prays to the masters:[30] 'Oh, Lord, my blue sky, my black earth, take all bad things from me and watch over me!' Also if a child dies, they pray: 'My blue sky, my black earth, my golden moon, my golden sun, disease and death leave me, take them away from me, watch over me!' The Tyvan people believe that sky, earth, moon, and sun are gods (H1).[31]

Tyvan deities are often enumerated together with a variety of spirit masters of the earthly world.[32]

Another research partner, a 48-year-old female meteorologist who is the daughter of a shamaness and lives in Mugur Aksy, had the following to say about nature, on 13 October 2004:

> At dawn, when the sun rises, I make an offering by sprinkling the first part of my freshly cooked milk tea. By sprinkling my tea I sacrifice and pray to the rivers, the waters, the mineral springs, to my sun, my hills and mountains, my moon, and to my nine deities[33], and say: 'watch over me, my Lord.' My daughter is studying in Tomsk. That is why I speak to my inner self, when I sprinkle my tea: 'May the way of my daughter be good and white, may her education go

---

[29] See also Harva (1938: 248); D'yakonova (1976: 178f, 285); Budegechi (1994: 12f); Kenin-Lopsan (1993: 60f, 63f, 67; 1994a: 66f, 75f, 99f). These are summarised in Oelschlägel (2004a: 39-53).

[30] The Tyvan term *ee* (pl. *eeler*, possessive *eezi*) must be translated literally as 'master'. In Tyvan everyday life the term is used for 'host' or 'landlord'. In a religious sense, however, the term is often used to refer to a 'spirit master' or a 'spirit master of a place'.

[31] The key (H 1, NA 8, etc.) allows for tracing the sources in my other publications. All original texts in Tyvan or Russian as well as their German translations have been published in Oelschlägel (2013b). In this volume, the location of the interview is the informant's place of habitual residence unless otherwise noted.

[32] See also Mänchen-Helfen (1931: 90, 93); Harva (1938: 46); Potapov (1969: 361f, 365f); Taube, E. (1972: 122, 135f; 1974b: 592); D'yakonova (1976: 281f; 1977: 174f, 181, 190, 196f, 199, 202f); Kenin-Lopsan (1993: 44ff, 64, 68; 1994a: 71f, 104ff, 107, 109f, 113ff); Arakchaa (1995: 2); Schenk and Tschinag (1999: 17, 117f);Vajnshtejn (1984: 354; 1996b: 244ff). Summarised by Oelschlägel (2004a: 58-92).

[33] The nine deities are the constellation Ursa Major.

well, may she successfully complete her studies!' For my children, who already work, I pray too: 'May the work of my children be successful, may they not fall ill!' Furthermore I ask during my sacrifices: 'May my people live well!' (NA 8).

Of all non-human subjects, the spirit masters are most strongly involved in the thinking and acting of contemporary Tyvans. They are the most frequently mentioned and most visibly attract religious attention. Especially visible are the many ritual and sacred places (Tyv. *ydyk cher*) dedicated to the service of the spirit masters. Everything that belongs to the Tyvan landscape – the hills, mountains and rocks, taiga and forest, specific trees, the steppes, valleys, mountain passes, rivers, lakes and springs, and all distinctive places in the Tyvan landscape and other parts of nature – are inhabited by spirit masters according to the interaction model. These spirits are the true owners and protectors of everything existing in the Tyvan world. They control their use and punish their abuse or destruction. Special natural subjects, like a sacred tree, mineral spring, or swamp spring (Tyv. *kara sug*), all known to be the domicile of powerful spirit masters, are often used as ritual places. These spirits are the focus of interest of residents and guests, especially during rituals taking place on-site.

A female research partner, a 30-year-old healer living in Mugur Aksy, told the following story about the spirit master of a spring on 5 October 2004:

> We drove upstream to the summer camp in our car. When we arrived in the summer camp, the owner of the yurt received us joyfully. Our hosts, Kashpyk-ool and Dshejma, were just milking cows. We stayed in the camp for several days and nights. After visiting the camp, we drove to Suglug-Khovu, a place in the forest nearby. After arriving there we went to two well-known springs. We waded through the water and one spring was warm, but the other was cold. Then we wanted to find the source, where they came out. At dawn we wanted to return, but had the feeling that somebody was there. We noticed its breath in our back and it held us from behind. When we turned to see who it was, we saw nothing. But we were sure that it was the master of the springs we had visited (HG 37).

The spirit masters of the waters, mountain passes, valleys, hills, and other parts of the landscape who regularly interact with human beings receive from them manmade artificial ritual places in the form of *ovaalar* (s. *ovaa*). They are used as places for mutual communication and interaction. Two types of *ovaa* are common in Tyva. The first type is the *dash ovaa* (stone *ovaa*), consisting of stones that are piled up to form a cone. In these piles of stones the Tyvans stick wooden sticks or branches, which they decorate with colourful sacrificial ribbons.

The other type is the *chadyr ovaa*[34], which is made of long wooden sticks and branches that again are arranged in a cone. In the cone's centre is a long stake, on the upper end of which is a carved figure that reaches into the sky like an arrow, and together with the stake symbolises the axis mundi. The entrance of a *chadyr ovaa* most often faces east.

The type of *ovaa* built by Tyvans depends on whether there are enough stones in the area that can be stacked to make an *ovaa*. If they are in an area where there are not enough stones then a *chadyr ovaa* is built.

With or without *ovaalar*, the ritual places stand out from their surroundings because trees or bushes near them are decorated with colourful sacrificial ribbons (Tyv. *chalama*) as visible gifts to the spirit master of the place they mark. At the ritual place there is often also a larger sacrificial stone, which the Tyvans use for spontaneous or regular smoke sacrifices (Tyv. *sang*). Less common are altars with the same sacrificial function. Whether a passerby only puts a stone on the *ovaa* or ribbons on branches, or whether several persons gather next to the *ovaa* to conduct an elaborate sacrifice for the spirit master of the place and communicate with him, depends on the visitor's situation. In any case, people are obliged to dwell briefly at the *ovaa*, greet its spirit master, and give a sign of faith. Visiting a ritual place is often connected with a short prayer or an invocation including a request for the master's blessing of all future plans.

The granddaughter of a poet, a 43-year-old stockbreeder living in Mugur Aksy, recited on 26 August 2004 the following blessing for Tangdy (the High Taiga, i.e. the taiga in general), as formulated by her grandfather during the annual spring consecration at the ritual place of the taiga's master:

Tangdy eeleringe algangan algyshtar.	Blessing for the masters of Tangdy.
Oran tangdym eeleri!	Masters of my Tangdy!
Ee körüp, örsheengerem!	Watch over us! Protect us!
Dört-le tangdym eeleri!	Masters of my four Tangdy![35]
Ee körüp, örsheengerem!	Watch over us! Protect us!
Bazhy bedik tangdylarym!	Your heads are high, my Tangdy!
Bagaj chyve yngaj turzun!	Evil shall disappear as far away as possible!
Ekti bedik tangdylarym!	Your shoulders are high, my

---

[34] A *chadyr* is a conical Tozhu-Tyva tent built using long stakes and bark.
[35] These are the mountains in the four cardinal directions.

	Tangdy!
Eki chüve beerlezin!	Good shall come here!
Adam-iyem alys churtu,	The homeland of my father and my mother,
Ak-la bashtyg Möngün-Tajgam!	Has a white head, my Möngün Taiga![36]
Buyan-kezhik doktaazyn deesh,	In order for true goodness and well-being to come,
burungaar körüp, tejlep tur men.	I look forward and pray.
Azhy-tölder mandyzyn deesh,	In order for my children to prosper,
algysh-yöreel salyp or men.	I offer a blessing (HG 14).

Apart from spontaneous, small ritual activities when Tyvans pass a ritual place, there may be special reasons for visiting such places, for instance to invite the support of their masters and use their powers. Regularly in spring, in some areas also in autumn, elaborate rituals for the master spirits of the homeland take place. Often precise ideas exist about the spirit masters of the local settlement area.

A 54-year-old male shaman living in Ak Dovurak told the following about the spirit masters of the Möngün Taiga and Ak Bashtyg Mountain on 5 October 2004 during our meeting in Mugur Aksy:

> I first met the female spirit master of the Möngün Taiga when I was 16 years old. She was a little girl riding a little rabbit. The rabbit had a harness, reins, and a saddle made of silver. The girl was pretty, wearing silver and gold clothes. We talked to each other. Moving closer to the *ovaa*, she said: 'I am the master of the Möngün Taiga.' A couple of years later, when I first consecrated the *ovaa* of the Möngün Taiga, I met her again. We asked each other: 'How are you?' Then we went our separate ways. The spirit master of the Möngün Taiga can present itself as an adult or a child. She often meets the master of Ak Bashtyg[37] at the large *ovaa* of the Ak Bashtyg Mountain. I first met the master of the Ak Bashtyg Mountain in June 2004. The master of the Ak Bashtyg Mountain is a Tyvan man dressed in Tyvan clothes, carrying a knife and a lighter. We take care of him by bringing the first part of our meals to his *ovaa*, because this spirit master feeds us (HG 38).

To celebrate the spring consecration (Tyv. *ovaa dagyyr*) of the *ovaa* of a settlement area or that of a clan, people who inhabit the territory of this

---

[36] Silver Taiga – a mountain in south-western Tyva on the border with Russia's Republic of Altai.

[37] White Headed Mountain – a mountain north of Mugur Aksy.

ovaa's spirit master or who descend from the resident clan gather at the end of May or the beginning of June. They see their fate depending on the local spirit master. A few days before the consecration takes place, ritual assistants tidy and perform a cleansing of the surroundings of the *ovaa* (Tyv. *ovaa septeer*). Other participants prepare sacrificial offerings, slaughter sheep, prepare white food (*ak chem*, i.e. foods made from milk) and foods made from flour, cut sacrificial ribbons, and invite at least one shaman or shamaness and sometimes also a Buddhist lama.

On the day of the ritual, all participants gather and go together to the ritual place. Very powerful ritual places, like the *ovaa* of White Headed Mountain, are approached only by men before and during the ritual, while women and children celebrate their own, smaller consecration at a safe distance. The inhabitants of the Mugur Aksy settlement are sure that the power and energy of the *ovaa* and its spirit master are too dangerous for women and children.

There are many reasons for celebrating the spring consecration. People are grateful for the spirit master's clemency and favour in the previous year; and they wish to inquire after the spirit master's wishes and satisfactions, pleasures, or worries about human behaviour. People also address problems in their lives in the hope that the spirit master will help solve them, and request general well-being, fortune and success with stockbreeding, favourable weather, good meadows, fat livestock, and enough food and good health for the people.

Every shaman has his own way to conduct the ritual séance. But all shamans call on the spirit master of the *ovaa*, enter into a dialogue with him or her, make sacrifices with a fire of wood and juniper (Tyv. *artysh*), express the participants' gratitude for favours granted in the previous year and their hopes for the next year, take leave of the spirit master, and finally translate the contents of the communication between the shaman and the spirit master to the other participants. The shamans relay to the participants the spirit master's gratitude for the offerings; forward the spirit master's warnings about bad behaviour; and convey the spirit master's commendations for the rendered services and for the respectful interaction. The shamans inform the participants about the spirit master's demands and instruct them about the master's intentions in the coming year. During the dialogue between the shaman and the spirit master, which is accompanied by a smoke offering, the surrounding participants sprinkle milk, milk tea, and milk alcohol from a bowl with small juniper branches. In this way, laypeople are included in the interaction between shaman and spirit master and participate directly in the ritual.

After the official part of the ritual is over, the spirit master leaves. When the sacrificial fire is extinguished and the quiet prayers are done, the participants relax. They talk about the success of the ritual, discuss the spirit master's messages, and speculate on what the coming year will bring for the inhabitants of the *ovaa*'s territory. Slowly a festive mood emerges. Whether at the same place or elsewhere, the religious obligations are followed by a festival that the Tyvans celebrate with plenty of alcohol and food. These festivities usually include music, singing, dancing, and sportive competitions such as wrestling, horseback riding, and archery.

In addition to the regular annual rituals, the Tyvans conduct numerous spontaneous rituals, for example, when they are faced with problems that they cannot resolve alone. These include diseases, adversities, and serious accidents that the Tyvans want to bring to the attention of powerful spirit masters in order to have them positively influence the situation of the persons involved. Especially popular for celebrating such spontaneous rituals are sacred trees and healing springs. The Tyvans visit the latter at particular times of the year, for example, when in autumn the water matures and develops its maximum force. They try to use its power by direct bodily contact for the recovery of the ill person in order to obtain the favour of the spring's spirit master. Before a Tyvan makes use of the healing spring's water, he tries to contact its spirit master. In especially serious cases, the ill person asks a shaman to undertake the contacting and communication with the spirit master. During the ritual the shaman asks the spring's spirit master what caused the illness. This question is based on the idea that illness arises from bad behaviour, that is, from disrespectful interaction with non-human subjects. Anyone behaving disrespectfully towards fellow human beings or non-human subjects will draw upon himself the wrath of the other and can be punished by falling ill. For this reason, further questions of the shaman to the spring's spirit master ask what behaviour will be needed to recover.

Even if no shaman is involved, the visit to a healing spring is often accompanied by a smoke offering of juniper, meat, and white food. With these gifts, as well as with coloured ribbons and other presents, the Tyvans ask the spirit master of the spring for their help and support.

Another research partner, a 75-year-old retired male stockbreeder from Mugur Aksy told the following about healing springs on 8 October 2004:

> An ill person who goes to a healing spring prays, ties white and blue offering ribbons, and by saying, 'My illness shall heal', requests a cure from the spring's master. The spirit master of the spring will then help the ill person. Sometimes the spring's spirit master presents himself to the ill person, but this happens very rarely. If so,

such a person may never speak about the spirit master he has seen. If he speaks about the master, he will fare badly (Y 20).

To avoid specific problems like childlessness, conflicts in the family, poverty, or similar ills, the consultation of a sacred tree is particularly suitable. In addition to distinctive sites of lone trees there are other attributes of sacred power inherent in a particular tree. There are trees in Tyva whose special quality is expressed in their extraordinary form. These include the shaman tree (Tyv. *kham yjash*) or the shaman larch (Tyv. *kham dyt*) with a partial or completely ball-shaped crown as well as the rich tree (Tyv. *baj yjash*), which is characterised by a multitude of trunks growing from one root, or the forked tree (Tyv. *tel yjash*), which has the trunks of at least three different tree species sprouting from one root. Shaman trees are often frequented by shamans either on their own behalf in order to conduct regular or spontaneous rituals, or to call on the tree and its spirit master for help on behalf of a client, often to help solve a health problem. Tyvans assign the power to have a positive impact on the fertility of human beings, their livestock's prosperity, or the aggrandisement of wealth to the rich trees and their spirit masters. For these reasons, Tyvans consecrate them annually and visit them spontaneously in problematic situations. Forked trees have the greatest influence on fertility, as the thriving of different tree species from one root shows in all-too-evident symbolism. Forked trees facilitate not only fertility, large numbers of children, good health for mother and child during and after pregnancy as well as a gentle delivery, but also the peaceful and happy living together of several persons, like married couples, relatives, or neighbours. All of these can be a reason for visiting and performing a ritual next to such a tree. The sacred trees of the Tyvans are visible in the landscape over a long distance due to numerous coloured ribbons in their branches. The Tyvans regularly and in emergency situations acknowledge the trees and their spirit masters with smoke offerings and libations because they are considered as reliable, less capricious than other spirit masters, and very helpful interaction partners for human beings.

A female 54-year-old interview partner who is a shamaness and teacher in Kyzyl had the following to say about rich trees and their spirit masters. I recorded this interview on 1 November 2004:

> We call a tree a 'rich tree' if from its root grow three, four, five, six, or even seven trunks. Such a tree gives power and energy during a ritual and the rich larch (*baj dyt*)[38] itself acquires power from the cosmos. A rich tree has connections to the cosmos because it has strong roots. Where a rich tree grows strong cosmic energies prevail.

---

[38] 'Larch' is here used as a synonym for 'tree'.

> Therefore this tree has a strong spirit master. Some people invite a shaman to heal them where a rich tree grows. The ritual is conducted in the summer. If somebody has a big problem and he asks a shaman to conduct a ritual next to a rich tree, his wishes will come true. People conduct rituals next to a rich tree, so that their families prosper, their livestock proliferate, and children are born. The rich tree is also a symbol of wealth. You can put coins under the tree to make sure there will be enough money in the family (Y 7a).

The same interview partner also spoke on 1 November 2004 in Kyzyl about forked trees and their spirit masters:

> We call a tree a 'forked tree' if out of its root grow three or more different species of trees; for example, birch, pine, and larch. A forked tree has great power that it pulls from the cosmos. Three points also are the symbol for power. If somebody has a problem with her partner, relatives, or other people, then she conducts a ritual on the place where a forked tree grows. Such a ritual is conducted by a shaman. We call this ritual 'consecration of the forked tree' (Tyv. *tel yjash dagyyr*). After the ritual, the friendship between husband and wife is stabilised. The forked tree is the symbol of friendship because the forked tree is the 'root of every friendship' (Tyv. *najyraldyng dözee*). To make sure that people have unity and closeness, shamans conduct rituals next to forked trees, and ask their spirit masters for strength (Y 6).

The following information was given by the same shamaness and teacher on 10 November 2004, when she spoke to me about shaman trees and their spirit masters:

> We call a shaman tree *kham yjash*. A shaman tree is a larch (*kham dyt*) with an abnormal growth of its branches. The branches of a shaman tree grow like a swirl. Next to such trees we have altars for smoke offerings and in the branches we hang coloured ribbons. They are thin and have a length of about 40 to 70 centimetres: we call them *chalama*. Once a year – in the summer – a shaman performs a ritual for the master of the forest. For the consecration of the shaman tree, the participants bring several kinds of food, for example meat, milk, milk products, or flour products. All this they burn on the altar for smoke offerings and the shaman calls for rain or help to have a good harvest. If such a tree grows next to a spring, then the shaman conducts the prayer for the spring water and the tree in one and the same ritual. We call the place where a shaman tree grows a 'sacred place' (Tyv. *ydyktyg cher*) (Y 13).

Were one to look only upon the visible attributes of religiously venerated, non-human subjects in the Tyvan landscape, they could easily lose sight of the fact that spirit masters are inherent in everything existing. This includes material artefacts produced by human beings, like yurts and other residential and economic constructions, as well as household appliances and tools. Their human owners and users are in permanent daily interaction with the spirit masters of these artefacts. People have to daily acquire and maintain the favour and support of these spirit masters by carrying out smaller and larger demonstrations of respect and veneration. The spirit master of the camp (Tyv. *khonaash eezi*) – sometimes called *baj khonaash* (the rich of the camp) – and the spirit master of the fire in the hearth (Tyv. *ot eezi*) watch over everything belonging to human residential and economic spaces.

One of my interview partners, a 44-year-old woman who works as an anthropologist and folklorist in Kyzyl told me the following about the spirit master of such dwellings. I recorded the interview on 28 July 2004:

> Every yurt, each dwelling has a spirit master. My flat has a spirit master too, and places where yurts or yurt camps stand, the camp grounds, have spirit masters. We call them 'masters of places'. They are the protectors of the yurts or of the places where the yurts stand. It is imperative that we feed the spirit master of the yurt and the spirit master of the camp. If we do not bring them sacrifices, they will become angry. We offer them the first part of our meals. Once a shamaness came to visit me at home. After entering my flat, the shamaness said immediately: 'The male spirit master of your flat is hungry. He is angry. Why don't you feed the spirit master of your flat? If you feed the spirit master, he will support you. As of today you must bring him offerings.' Since then I prepare a plate and bring him sacrifices from our meals. But sometimes I forget to feed him. The spirit master of a yurt or a flat is its real owner. Therefore we have to honour and respect him (NA 11).

All spirit masters demand respectful interactions, even the spirit masters of the seemingly negligible articles of daily use. Their consent and favour are absolutely necessary for the successful use of such artefacts.

At Khamnar Tej (Small Shaman Mountain) on the Ak-Oj River on 27 July 2004, a 46-year-old male interview partner, a stockbreeder from Süt Khöl, said about the guardian or spirit master of the camp (Tyv. *khonaash eezi*) and the evil spirit called *puk* (pl. *puktar*):

> The camp ground (Tyv. *khonaash*) of our family is old. Our ancestors already lived in this place and we have spirit masters. When our ancestors died, they stayed behind on their ancestral domicile and became spirit masters. Sometimes they are in a good

mood, but sometimes they are angry. They can be capricious, sometimes good and sometimes bad. The shaman banishes the evil spirits, but to the kindly spirits we bring offerings. Each old camp ground has its spirit masters. They are the ancestors. A human being who was born in a particular place and grew up there continues to reside there after his death. As a spirit master he protects his homeland. We revere the well-disposed spirit masters of camps. We conduct rituals for them and burn smoke offerings. We do this especially when arriving at the seasonal camp ground. In addition, the housewife makes a libation every morning from the first milk tea of the day. Nevertheless, there are camp grounds where very evil spirits live. If a human being has done very bad things during her lifetime, she becomes a *puk*. Evil spirits also take up residence on our camp grounds. A camp site occupied by a *puk* is called a *puk talgan*. Such a *puk* brings bad luck, the livestock fall ill, and the people die. Therefore we leave such camp grounds and no longer visit them. Or we ask a shaman for help. But a shaman can only banish the *puk* under ground or far away if he is stronger than the spirit. For this reason, the shaman will always first check how strong the *puk* is before pitting his strength against the spirit (NL 13).

A 42-year-old female Russian teacher living in Kyzyl told the following about kitchen utensils and their spirit masters. I recorded the interview on 15 November 2004:

Every utensil, all things have their own spirit masters. If somebody borrows a pan, she needs to put a present inside – for example, sweets, biscuits, or something else – before returning it. Otherwise the spirit master of the utensil will be offended. Moreover, it is important that the dish is cleaned before it is returned. In any case, dishes should always be clean because they have a connection with fire. Otherwise, the spirit master of the fire can become angry which has a bad effect on the wife and the whole family. The present at the bottom of a returned dish we call in Tyvan a 'dish bottom' (*pash düvü*). If we borrow a knife, we call the present 'knife top' (*bizhek bazhy*) (HG 46).

Apart from all visible things of the Tyvan world, the immaterial elements of Tyvan culture need also to be included in any description of the influence and power of spirit masters. To them belong the spirit masters of skills and talents as well as the results of such human talent – art and handicrafts. A good example is the skill of hunting, as elaborated by a 47-year-old female stockbreeder from Toolajlyg Valley. She told me the following on 30 August 2004 in the Toolajlyg cooperative in the Möngün Taiga District:

> My father was a hunter. Once, when hunting, there was no game. As he was returning from the Balyk River, a hunter came flying. This hunter wore a knife of silver and had a [traditional] lighter [for making fire]. The nicely dressed man came up to my father. When my father saw him, the stranger said: 'You will have quary.' What he said to my father happened. This stranger was the master of the place. He led the game to my father (HG 17).

Apart from numerous narratives about interactions directly induced by human beings in the form of smaller or larger rituals and sacrificial acts, there are narratives about face-to-face encounters with spirit masters and other non-human subjects that human beings meet unpremeditatedly. Such narratives remind people again and again of the strong influence of non-human subjects on their lives, both in positive and in negative terms.

The following was told to me by a 49-year-old female interview partner working as a stockbreeder in the Toolajlyg taiga. I recorded the text on 1 September 2004:

> When I was a young girl, the camp of my parents was at a place we call 'wood with ravens'. Once, when I returned from the village to our camp and sat down in our yurt to rest, I heard a whirlwind, and from it sounded the tone of the *doshpulduur* (Tyvan wind instrument). I jumped out of the tent and fell over. I became really ill and was petrified. When we asked our neighbours for advice, they said: 'The spirit master of the place came to you. You were frightened, but he intended to do well. For this reason he appeared.' It took me a while to recover. When I met this being, I was 18 years old (HG 22).

Another interview partner, a 51-year-old retired man living in Mugur Aksy, told me about the place called 'two larches' (Tyv. *iji dyt*) in Toolajlyg on 1 September 2004:

> The following happened in the autumn of 1978, when all the yurts moved to the autumn pasture. In the evening, at sundown, I went from the camp of my younger brother to the village. At that time my younger brother camped at the bank of the river Mugur at the place 'two larches'. I walked towards the place called *döng-shöl*. Suddenly I heard a car behind me. When I turned to look around, it had only one light. I tried to hail it. But when I stopped walking, the car stopped too. When I continued to walk, the car followed. I continued to walk, but suddenly saw that the car's light cast no shadow. I became afraid and jumped down the slope to the place *döng-shöl*. The sound of the car with the single light that I left behind was clearly from a car. But wherever the light shone, the thing cast no

shadow. How I arrived in the village, I do not know anymore. But after me, many people saw this car, as I later found out. Until today I do not know what it was (Y 1).

The Tyvan world of non-human subjects does not only consist of spirit masters. Besides these helpful guardian beings who control and punish, there are numerous spirits intent on disturbing the regulative power of respectful interaction between people and spirit masters. They attack human beings on the one hand to live out their playful yet dangerous nature, and on the other to punish human misbehaviour. The most popularly known evil spirits are *albys, aza, chetker, puk,* and *diireng*.[39] The inhabitants of a certain area know where particular evil spirits live, alone or in larger numbers, and wait to attack careless passersby.

An interview partner, a 75-year-old male retired stockbreeder from Mugur Aksy, the district centre for Möngün Taiga District, said the following about *albys* on 8 October 2004:

In our country there are beings we call *albys*. An *albys* looks like a human being. This spirit confuses the mind of human beings and changes their attitude towards other people. The *albys* shows itself to young men as a beautiful young girl or as a middle-aged woman. This being tries in this way to contact them and to begin a relationship. To girls it presents itself as a man. The *albys* tries to start a relationship with them as well. This spirit speaks like a human being. Furthermore, this being gives advice where one should go to find good luck. At the place called 'on the white lake, where you get the creeps' is a rock where *albys* live. There you can hear them laugh, sing, and cry (AL 4).

A younger 35-year-old interview partner, a male hunter from Toolajlyg told the following about an encounter with an *albys* spirit. I recorded the interview on 4 September 2004:

To a man called Kyzyl-ool, the following happened. He has died of an illness since. I talked to Saida about him. When one day Kyzyl-ool went to work, suddenly a person followed him. From this day on, this person always stayed with him, also when he went home. When he went to work again, this person was with him. Bit by bit this being became inseparable from him. Soon Kyzyl-ool was unable to bear it. He saw the *albys* all the time (AL 1).

Connected to the *albys* is the erotic seduction of human beings by spirits. To begin a long-lasting love relationship, the *albys* appears to a human being as the ideal partner.

---

[39] On evil spirits see Taube, E. (1972: 137; 1981: 54f); D'yakonova (1976: 282f, 283f); Vajnshtejn (1984: 354f); Alekseev (1987: 108f); summarised by Oelschlägel (2004a: 54-58).

Human beings can get into an ardent love affair with an *albys* and acquire numerous personal benefits, like success in hunting or other special talents. The danger consists in a mental aberration of the person involved that he or she does not perceive, but that their fellow human beings do perceive. Therefore the attempt to free somebody from an *albys* often comes from the relatives or neighbours of the person involved. They call on a shaman for help to exorcise the spirit and banish it back to its place of origin. The ability of the *albys* to confuse its victim is so proverbial among the Tyvans that they use the verb *albystaar* for 'aberrate' and 'disorient' as well as 'to sicken' (i.e. like a shaman with an unstable mental condition).

The term *aza* is commonly used among the Tyvans for all kinds of evil spirits that cause various symptoms of disease or damage. From a simple attack to a serious illness that the Tyvans view as the theft of the human soul by this spirit, the *aza* (pl. *azalar*) or *aza-chetker* again and again affects the fate of human beings. *Azalar* are considered incalculable enemies of human well-being.

A 35-year-old male hunter from Toolajlyg told the following about an *aza*. I recorded this interview on 5 September 2004:

> Not long ago the following happened: People say it is very dangerous at the spring of the river Oonachy. Once, when a man arrived there, a being jumped on his back. The man caught it and threw it over his head to the ground. When he inspected it more closely, he could not see anything. The man told me later: 'When I threw this being, I heard it bounce, but the *aza* was invisible.' The name of this man was Eres-ool Bady Ochurovich. He went on and arrived at Batkash. Because he was afraid, he rested there. He told us: 'I threw this guy – to the best of my knowledge – like a real wrestler' (AZ 5).

An older interview partner, a 75-year-old male retired stockbreeder from Mugur Aksy, told me about an *aza-chetker* on 12 October 2004:

> The following happened on the pass called 'mountain saddle with black stones' in the year 1916 or 1917. At that time I was not yet born. When I was a child, I heard about this event from the elders. At night, one of the elders was riding in the higher regions of the taiga and crossed over the pass. As he rode on horseback, suddenly his horse stopped. The horse cocked its ears. Suddenly something invisible started to batter the man. The elder wore Tyvan garb. His clothes were torn and tattered. But he kept a red-gripped whip. After jumping from the horse he began to trace the shadow of his horse with the handle of his whip. It was a moonlit night. Then he started to beat the shadow of his horse that he already had marked with his

whip. He also beat himself and his horse before crossing the pass. People say that moonlit nights are the time when the *azalar* meet each other to play. On such nights one can meet many *azalar*. But they are afraid of whips with red grips. When the old man crossed the pass he had already heard about such events. He did not lose his soul, which is good. Only because he used the red-gripped whip did he survive (AZ 10).

A young interview partner, a 23-year-old male stockbreeder from the Khamnar Tej campsite on the Ak-Oj River in the district of Süt Khöl told me on 29 July 2004 in the spring camp about the *azalar*:

Formerly there lived here a famous lama called Lovun Kheling Gelong. He could see the future and the past of human beings and the people in his neighbourhood knew that he was very powerful. His yurt stood at a place called Adyr-Terek [branched poplar]. One day he rode up to the Ishkin River and visited a camp site. When he arrived a girl was just burning alcohol from fermented milk. Hereupon the girl handed him a cup of milk brandy [Tyv. *araka*]. When the lama left the yurt he asked the girl: 'My child, have you ever seen a living soul?' 'No', the girl answered. The old man said: 'Then come here!' and asked her to step out of the yurt. 'Look through under my arm!' The girl looked under the arm of the old man and saw two *azalar* holding a young girl by her arms and carrying her with them. The girl became afraid and cried: 'Oh, protect me, what a horror!', and broke away from the lama. But the old man started to explain: 'My child, now it is disclosed that – in a month's time – a young girl will die.' Indeed, after one month, a 16-year-old girl died in another yurt camp (AZ 2).

A very young interview partner, an eight-year-old schoolgirl in the third grade in Mugur Aksy, told me this about an *aza* on 7 October 2004:

My teacher told me the following. She herself no longer knows when it happened, but probably it was in 2002 or 2003. When my teacher took the schoolchildren to a holiday camp, one evening they went to a disco to dance. After the disco had finished, they returned to the camp. Suddenly she saw a figure through the window. It was a human being in clothes. The teacher scolded the children because she assumed that one of them had left the house. But when she checked the girls and boys, they were all indoors. After awhile, one of the children saw the figure too. The child had seen a tall *aza*. Because they were afraid, all the children started to sing. Suddenly something blew out the candle, but the children did not see anything. For fear of the *aza* they hid under their covers. While they lay covered, they fell asleep. Suddenly something pulled their covers away. In the morning, when they woke up, the stove was broken and all their blankets lay in a heap. They immediately left by car to return home (AZ 6).

The spirits my informants called *puktar* were described as a kind of transformed soul of a deceased human being that had not yet found its way to the other world, the realm of the dead. As *puktar*, these souls are vengeful and harm living people with whom they had conflicts during their lives. They catch the souls of living people who then fall ill and may die without treatment by a shaman. Tyvans regard the souls of both living and dead persons that wander around at night (and can be observed by seers) as a form of evil spirit. Especially because of their fear of *puktar* and of souls that will be but have not yet been transformed into *puktar*, many Tyvans avoid leaving the house at night between three and five o'clock in the morning, when these spirits are most active.

A 48-year-old female interview partner who works as a meteorologist and is the daughter of a shamaness in Mugur Aksy told the following story about the souls of dying persons, explaining, 'the death of a human being can be foreseen by particular gifted persons.' I recorded the interview on 13 October 2004:

> I have seen souls. I saw them in 2002, in December at about nine o'clock in the evening. When I left the gym these people were still alive. Yet I saw the souls of these people. At first, I heard their voices talking to each other. I then looked around to see who was talking but did not see anyone. Suddenly I saw two people in the darkness who looked down-and-out walking close to a courtyard. One of them was a man, the other a woman. The man was carrying the woman on his back. Curious, I followed them. I was interested in their conversation. I listened to what they were talking about. At first the man said: 'Why are you cowering on my back?' The woman answered: 'I feel my death approaching.' In that moment I recognised her voice. I checked them out. At first I watched the woman. She seesawed with her feet. When I saw their faces I recognised that these were not their faces. Their faces looked like the faces of dead people. I became frightened because I understood that these were their souls. I quickly went home and in doing so spit three times. The next morning I learned that the man had already passed away at five o'clock in the morning. That the woman had died too I found out when her relatives received a telegram. After seeing the souls of both persons, they died (TO 3).

The souls of the deceased, especially of shamans, who – in contrast to the souls of religious laypeople – remain in the earthly world to serve living shamans, can also interfere in the lives of the living. In any case they are a positive or negative power with which every human being has to cope.

A 43-year-old female anthropologist and folklorist from Kyzyl told the following story about her grandfather, who was a shaman. I recorded the interview on 23 July 2004:

> About my grandfather Shagar, a shaman, I heard several stories from my grandmother. My grandmother is a person who is able to see in dreams. My Shagar-shaman grandfather was already dead when my grandmother lost several cows. Many days and nights she looked for her cows but could not find them. Once, when asleep, she dreamt the following: While peeing between the *kharagan* bushes a big bird was sleeping nearby. When she watched the bird, its face was similar to the face of Shagar-shaman, its beak was as big as his nose. Its wings were like those of the eagle [Tyv. *ezir*] and altogether the bird was too big. Suddenly the bird began to talk: 'Have you lost your cows?', it asked. 'Your cows graze over there. Go and fetch them in the morning!' My grandmother recognised the voice and replied: 'What are you for an old man? Why do you terrify me? Leave me alone!' But the next morning, when she woke up, my grandmother looked around. And when she arrived at the mentioned place her cows were indeed grazing there. My grandmother found her cows in the spot that my grandfather had shown her (SCHA 14).

Another type of evil spirit is what the Tyvans call *chetker*. This spirit sucks out the life energy from human beings to nourish itself. To prevent people from dying due to the absence of life energy, a shaman must be called to exorcise this spirit.

The *diireng* (pl. *diirengner*) is considered an importunate jester as well as a reason for the sudden and undeserved prosperity of a person. Any Tyvan who wants to acquire fast wealth may try to find this spirit and win it over. During the contact and the interaction with this spirit, however, there are also negative consequences that cannot be avoided.

A male stockbreeder from Süt Khöl, aged 46, told the following story about *diirengner*. I recorded the story in June 2004. 'A *diireng* presents itself. He can look like a young or an old person. If you meet a *diireng*, you will do well. This spirit will fulfil all your wishes. But you do well to not speak about him. If you want to get rid of the *diireng*, demand from him something he cannot fulfil, for example, to carry water with a bottomless bucket' (DI 1).

A retired 54-year-old teacher, shamaness, and head of the Düngür shamans' clinic in Kyzyl told the following about *diirengner*. I recorded the story on 1 November 2004:

> You can meet a *diireng* at a road junction, in the woods, on the fields, or in the taiga. He looks like the silhouette of a human being or an animal. People who met a *diireng* become rich. The *diireng* brings you all you desire. But on the other hand, the *diireng* is very imposing, he makes jokes, plays, and it is impossible to get rid of him. Anyone wanting to split up with a *diireng* can only do this with phrases like: 'Go there, where I don't know! Bring this, that I don't know!' Only then, when he is unable to carry out your order will he disappear (DI 2).

A 14-year-old schoolgirl in the eighth grade in Mugur Aksy had the following to say about *diirengner*. I recorded the text on 8 October 2004:

> What we call a *diireng* is a young, handsome man who hunts in the taiga. He wears a sable fur hat and rides a white horse. A person who meets a *diireng* can fare well or poorly. First you need to play chess with him. You should intoxicate the *diireng* with milk spirits or vodka; only in this way can you defeat him. If you defeat the *diireng* he will become your slave. He will bring you everything you request. Furthermore, the *diireng* will ask you whether you want to become a shaman, a hunter, or a rich person (DI 3).

Non-human interaction partners of the South-Siberian Tyvans include, further, partner and familiar protecting spirits of shamans, seers, clans, and, as well as persons initiated as oracles or who in any way have been chosen or been given talents by spirits or gods. To the partner spirits belong, on the one hand, the deities mentioned above, like heaven, earth, sun, moon, stars, and stellar constellations. An example of someone who has the sky as a partner spirit is a shamaness who calls herself the 'ancestral shamaness of heavenly descent'; she ascribes her gift to the god of heaven. On the other hand, partner spirits include powerful spirit masters, evil spirits, the souls of deceased shamans, the souls of animals and plants, as well as the powers and energies of the wilderness, the water, and the cosmos that are impersonally represented. All these non-human subjects act in some kind of way on human beings, who for their safety and well-being should interact and communicate with them in a careful manner.

An interview partner of 23 years of age, a male stockbreeder from Süt Khöl, told the following story of his grandmother about her own shaman grandmother. I recorded the story on 1 August 2004:

> My shaman grandmother had two partner spirits. One of them was a bear spirit. When she was in her yurt, she hung him on the

> headboard. The name of the other I forgot, but she hung it up at the foot of her bed. When I was still young I loved to sleep with my grandmother in her bed. At night, when I slept, I heard the bear spirit of my grandmother growling: 'moesh moesh' at the headboard. The partner spirit at the foot of the bed was continuously smacking: 'chap-chap'.
>
> Once, when my grandmother was not in the yurt, I became ill with my liver. I took her cap that she had left in the yurt, put it on my liver, leaned back, and fell asleep. In my dream a very small black old man sat on my stomach. I tried to throw him off. When my grandmother returned to our yurt in the morning, I told her about my dream. She laughed and explained to me: 'Oh, my child, you took the cap-boy and put him on your liver. In your dream you have seen the cap-boy' (SCHA 11).[40]

The same interview partner had told me a few days earlier, on 29 July 2004, about the *aza*:

> In the past an *aza*-bird lived here on the Ishkin River. The bird showed itself in the twilight and at night. Once my grandmother's brother arrived from Övür. He brought red rock salt from there. When he came home he asked my grandmother at night to stake the horses at the river bank close to the ford. It began to dawn. At that time my grandmother was still a child, about six or seven years old. When she approached the river, a giant eagle flew down, landed on the larch tree, letting the rotten upper branches crack. She was surprised and began to look at the strange bird. But the bird began to blurt out curious sounds to warm up its voice, like a singer who wants to start throat singing: 'gmm-khe-khe'. After that the bird started its throat singing. My grandmother's hair stood up, she was scared stiff. When she came to herself and the bird continued to sing, she loosened the horses, and ran home with all her might. At home she told her brother about the bird. He calmed her and explained that the bird forebode the death of a member of the Ondar family. 'The bird is the *aza* of the Ondar family', he said. To this day my grandmother tells me that this bird masters throat-singing better than any human being. The first name of my grandmother is Chassyg, her family name is Ondar, but the father's name I do not remember (AZ 1).

---

[40] The story is not about an ordinary cap, but about the shaman's cap of the child's grandmother. As the narrator explained, the cap-boy in this case is the spirit master of the cap (*bört eezi*).

Both examples concern non-human subjects that have, from the perspective of Western European concepts, 'supernatural' characteristics. Typical non-human interaction partners of the Tyvans are spirits and souls, which are part of a mutually affective network with human beings. But animated beings and things that surround human beings in their earthly world are also classified as non-human interaction partners. Whether living or man-made property, a Tyvan interacts with all parts of the natural and man-made environment, with everything that matters in his everyday life. Many Tyvans perceive themselves in permanent interaction with their domestic and farm animals, with the wild game and the plants of the taiga, with all natural resources they use, and with their tools and other articles of daily use. The cutting of a tree, for example, requires not only the permission of the spirit master of the taiga, who is the real owner of the tree, but it also requires that human beings apologise to the felled tree or the one to be felled.

The daily interactions of the Tyvan stockbreeders with their domestic animals, be they livestock, dogs or horses, take place between subjects that bring their own will into the network of interaction. Often the acting human being remains superior. Nevertheless the Tyvans often discuss in their yurts cases of interactions between human beings and domestic animals or wild game as tense events, in the course of which human beings get to feel the impact of non-human subjects during an interaction. Animals that run away and can be caught by their owner only with great effort or not at all, game that the hunter unsuccessfully follows for hours, ill stock animals, a difficult to handle horse, a uniquely devoted or aggressive dog – they all play the same important role in everyday conversations as broken tools, a defective gun, or even the taiga grass that causes aches in the knees of an old hunter.

An old hunter, aged 74 and living in the district of Ulug Khem told the following about his destiny as a 'famous hunter' in his summer camp in 2005:

> My whole life I have been a hunter. Because of my success in hunting, people in recent years have called me the 'famous hunter'. I hunted and shot as many animals as there is grass in the taiga. Each blade of grass is one shot animal. People said the spirit masters of the taiga love me. But this is not true. Today, in my old age, the taiga spirit masters have become angry with me. Because I killed so many animals, they punish me. Just as I killed so many wild animals as blades of grass grow in the taiga, now every blade of grass causes me pain when I walk. This is the revenge of the spirit masters. Today I am ashamed that I killed so many wild animals (NL 17).

Another example for interactions between human beings and their animals is the following statement, showing the duty of a human being to the horse that devotedly served its owner.

My interview partner, a 49-year-old female bookkeeper in Mugur Aksy said the following about the custom to honour horses after their death. I recorded this text on 11 October 2004. 'We hang the skull of a horse in a tree.[41] So that the horse may live well in the upper world, that is why we Tyvans have this custom. When a good horse dies and goes to the upper world, then it will fare well if we do so' (TO 2).

Respectful Interaction and its Violation

Infringements of the norms of respectful interaction with non-human subjects are part of most Tyvans' everyday lives. From their point of view these are the result of either external influences (especially Russian or Soviet influences), or to a person's character or socialisation. This study will show additionally, that violations of the norms of the interaction model are based not only on the reasons identified by Tyvans, but also in the application of the dominance model. The interaction model regards the violation of norms not only as a sacrilege or sin, but also as an expression of a dangerous human presumption towards authorities whose agency influences the fate of individuals and of Tyvan society as a whole. On these premises it is clear to many Tyvans that the frequent violations of taboos implicate great dangers, as these can result in more or less human harm in the form of punishment on the part of non-human subjects.

In addition to large-scale industrial abuses of 'mother earth', the taiga or the steppes, or of spirit masters watching over all parts of the Tyvan world[42], there are a multitude of smaller deviations from the norms of respectful interaction. The daily small breaches of the interaction model's norms reflect the beliefs of many Tyvans about respectful interaction, its violation, and the resulting consequences.

The interaction model's rules, their violation, and the consequences thereof were a popular subject during conversations with my research partners. They are reflected both in interviews recorded in 2004 and 2005 and in contemporary Tyvan legends or 'true occurrences' that people love to tell at night in their yurts.

A 47-year-old male interview partner who teaches Russian and Tyvan in Mugur Aksy spoke on 10 October 2004 about a shaman tree:

---

[41] On horses see Potapov (1975: 473-87).
[42] For example, nature is overexploited through large-scale mining endeavours for asbestos (e.g. in Ak Dovurak) and gold (e.g. in Tozhu-Tyva), logging, and fur hunting.

For many years we lived together with the Kezhik-ool Marsyns family in a summer camp, close to Suur Taiga. In these years, they regularly consecrated a shaman tree in the summer. When they consecrated the tree, the stock prospered and the residents lived well; their stomachs were full and they were healthy. The shaman tree and its spirit master protected them. Close to the shaman tree was a healing spring and its spirit master. This spring flowed out of a rock only in the summer, on 15 June. On other days it was only a trickle. The spring's water was cold. We regularly hung white and blue ribbons there and conducted smoke offerings. When we arrived in the spring, we first fed the spring and its spirit master before we drank and ate ourselves. We also went to the spring to take a shower and drink its healing water. After some time our relatives no longer blessed the shaman tree. They neglected to consecrate the healing spring. Then began their bad luck. Their stock was stolen by thieves. Their health changed for the worse. Kezhik-ool's wife died. He himself died recently. The reason was that our relatives stopped consecrating the shaman tree and healing spring in the Soviet era (Y 18).

Following the interpretations of the interaction model, a human life path is not only determined by the individual involved. Rather, the fate of a human being is a mix of human will, skills, and actions with the regulating, protecting, and punishing influences of non-human subjects that co-determine the success or failure of human beings. Non-human subjects, especially spirits, demand respectful interaction, which ideally consists of a give-and-take relationship and preserves a balanced network of human and non-human subjects. To this belong annual rituals, like the consecration of sacred places inhabited by spirit masters. Many Tyvans see such rituals as an acknowledgement of the spirit masters' influence on their well-being, as well as a reward for and recognition of past interactions, and a request to secure their favour in the year to come. In the previous example, the human interaction partners abandoned the interaction, which caused an imbalance. They stopped acknowledging the spirit masters as forgers of humans destiny and stopped thanking them for their generosity, whereupon the spirit masters of the shaman tree and the healing spring stopped safeguarding the family and its stock from sickness, death, and other misfortunes. Consequentially, their stock was stolen and the heads of the household fell ill and died.

Whereas Tyvan contemporary legends represent an allegory for a daily routine modelled on the interaction model, many of my conversation partners were very explicit during interviews. The first principle of respectful interaction between human and non-human subjects is the appreciation of the spirit masters' sovereignty over all earthly existence in the Tyvan world, including all kinds of oral tradition and other products of human talent. This interpretation of the position of human beings in Tyvan cosmology is the reason for many Tyvans' conviction that human beings may not use or modify anything according to their own will without requests to the spirit masters and their consent. Either it is simply not possible, or the unauthorised human actor incurs the anger and disfavour of the real owner, the spirit master, who may take revenge. The respectful interaction consists in a contract between human beings and spirits. This contract is based on negotiations undertaken during rituals, in a conversation between a shaman and the spirit masters, whose property Tyvans want to use and whose rules they must follow. The rules agreed upon include the considerate exploitation of natural and man-made resources, the careful application of talents, and regular returns in the form of rituals, libations, and smoke offerings.

The most frequent examples for describing the consequences of ignoring the norms and rules of the spirit masters are human interventions in the wilderness, either concerning plants or animals.

A 44-year-old female anthropologist and folklorist from Kyzyl told the following about spirit masters. I recorded the interview on 2 August 2004:

> The spirit masters of places, waters, and the taiga are all [referred to as] *oran eezi* (spirit master of a place). Every place has its spirit master. Together the *oran eezi* protect visible nature. Furthermore, they are part of nature. They protect and advocate nature. They control and defend nature. They also control human beings and keep them in check. If people behave badly towards nature, the *oran eezi* become angry. We Tyvans explain it in this way: if, for example, a human being cuts down a shaman tree, kills wild game or a bird or any another animate being, he will fare badly or become sick (HG 2).

A 46-year-old male stockbreeder from Süt Khöl told the following about spirit masters. I recorded this interview on 28 July 2004:

> The spirit master of the taiga moves in the high taiga. He is a very young and powerful being. He is likeable and beautiful. Also his horse is very beautiful. Its saddle is covered with silver decorations. The horse repeatedly shakes its head and snorts. The spirit master's shoes and clothes are traditional Tyvan; he wears a Tyvan coat and hat. He rides incessantly through his territory. Moreover, he often helps good people. By contrast, he punishes bad people. We call bad persons those people who do not maintain relations to the taiga and

disturb it, kill lots of wild game, cut down trees, and do not believe in the taiga (HG 9).

Another male interview partner, 51 years old and retired, living in Mugur Aksy, told the following about the spirit masters of the Möngün Taiga Mountains and Ak Bashtyg Mountain. I recorded this interview on 1 September 2004 in Toolajlyg:

> A long time ago my old grandfather Surung talked about the masters of places. Our neighbours called my grandfather Kök Kheling. He was a lama working with *kheling* spirits. He told me the following: the master of the Möngün Taiga is a very young man and rides a black horse. The master of the mountain Ak Bashtyg, by contrast, is a young woman on the back of a white horse. Every year, when we consecrate our *ovaa*, these spirit masters meet each other at the big *ovaa* of the river Mugur. Our grandfather gave us this advice: 'You may not destroy or kill anything, neither the wild game of our earth, nor the trees, or the grass, simply nothing, otherwise the masters of our earth will become angry!' All lakes, all high, high mountains have their spirit masters. You should learn blessings and invocations if you want to hunt the game of the world or collect medicinal herbs. In this way, he advised us, the spirit masters will not become angry (HG 24).

More detailed are my conversation partners' statements about hunters. Hunting seems to be a particularly serious intervention in the domain of the spirit masters because the game is regarded as the stock of the masters of the taiga, who often appear as wild animals. Every time I observed nomads setting out on hunting expeditions of several days or to set traps for fur-bearing animals, I heard them tell about the afflictions and threats that the masters of the taiga send to those who poach in their territory without having made advance offerings or requested the spirit masters' consent to hunt. To make such offerings and requests is the most important rule of respectful interaction between the hunter, the game, and the spirits that provide human beings with game for hunting.[43]

Three sisters (a 34-year-old physician who lives in Moscow; a 30-year-old merchant living in Kyzyl; and a 27-year-old systems administrator living in Mugur Aksy) told the following about spirit masters. I recorded this text on 24 August 2004 in Mugur Aksy: 'Masters of places can turn into wild animals. But such animals all have an anomaly [in their appearance]. If a hunter kills such an animal, this hunter or his family members will fare badly. Our old uncle was a passionate hunter. Hence he lost his sons. People

---

[43] See on this Ottinger (1993: 71); Taube, E. (1977a, 1998).

say that because he hunted too much, he enraged the masters of places' (HG 12).

In addition to food, most nomadic Tyvans collect other materials from the wilderness that are important for their subsistence. For everything Tyvans collect from the wilderness, they have to request and receive permission in advance through respectful interactions with the spirit masters of places.

A 54-year-old female interview partner, a shamaness and teacher in Kyzyl, told the following about the forest and its spirit masters. I recorded this text on 1 November 2004:

> The spirit masters of the forest are called *arga eeleri* in Tyvan. They protect the living world, the plants and the animals. If a human being wants to fell a tree, collect berries or medicinal herbs, or hunt game, then he first conducts a ritual. If he wants to cut wood for building a house, he asks the master of the forest for permission. People light a fire; put food, juniper, butter and oil into the fire; and with the smoke ask the forest master for permission. Only after conducting such a smoke offering, do you get to work. If one does not celebrate a smoke offering, then he will not be happy in his new house (HG 36).

Spirit masters do not only reside in the natural and man-made environment of Tyvan dwellings. Whether in a house or a yurt, virtually every household in Tyvan towns, villages, or yurt camps has a fire pit that is inhabited and controlled by the spirit masters of fire. The male and female masters of fireplaces influence the whole of family life and protect the household's inhabitants against illness, hunger, and especially fire hazards. For this reason the fire spirit master is the first and most frequent interaction partner of all family members who warm themselves at the fire, cook their meals on it, and use it for other economic activities. Practically everything that happens in a family – smaller or greater conflicts between family members; eating, hygiene, and reproduction; fortune and success; prosperity; and the positions of the family members in their social environment – depends on the successful interaction with the spirit master of the fire due to their proximity to human beings. The male or female spirit master of the fire receives the first offerings of the day, libations from the first milk tea, and the first pieces of the meal in the morning. In addition, the fire spirit has to be fed the first part of all foodstuffs that guests bring into the yurt. To procure the favour of their own fire spirit master, the members of the household consecrate the hearth at least once a year under the direction of a shaman. In the framework of this ritual they contact the master of the fire. They try to find out if there are reasons for the fire spirit's friendly mood or anger, invite further protection, and try to clear up misunderstandings in the daily interactions between the fire spirit master and the members of the household in an effort to avert the fire spirit's anger.

The following interview partner (a 29-year-old female stockbreeder from Toolajlyg) said the following on 31 August 2004 in the autumn camp about the spirit master of her fire pit:

> Our fire is sacred and we have a spirit master of our fire. The spirit master of fire can be male or female. Our fire pit has a male spirit master. We honour and respect him by feeding him. Every day we put the first part of each meal into the fire. When I make tea, I always sprinkle the first drops into the fire. Under no circumstance should one throw garbage into the fire. Otherwise, the fire will become angry. If one enrages the fire, a resident of the yurt will become ill. But if we protect the fire, then the fire's master will also protect us (HG 19).

Another interview partner (a 46-year-old male stockbreeder from the taiga in Süt Khöl) told the following about the fire's master spirit. I recorded this text on 27 July 2004:

> A long time ago, there was a rich man (Tyv. *baj*). Close to his yurt he owned a second yurt in which a simple herdsman was living with his family. Once the spirit master of the rich man's fire and the fire spirit of the poor herdsman had a conversation. The rich man's fire spirit spoke: 'My landlord is very bad. He does not feed me. I am always hungry.' The poor man's fire spirit replied: 'My landlord, as poor as he is, always gives me the first part of his family's meal, before eating himself.' The rich man's fire spirit then stated: 'My landlord is rich, but he does not give me my share. I will punish him!' And so it happened that soon after this conversation, the rich man's yurt burned down. If you do not offer the fire spirit his share of your meal, do not honour and respect him, and do not thank him for his protection and gifts, then he will punish you (NL 14).

Fortune and Misfortune in Response to Human Behaviour

Although human action takes place in the self-interest of humans, it often affects non-human parts of the environment. Every human action can induce reactions from the world of non-human subjects, to which human beings have in turn to react. On the one hand, human behaviour is a reaction to the actions of non-human subjects, because human beings – according to the beliefs of many Tyvans – can only realise what spirits and other non-human subjects made realisable for them. On the other hand, non-human subjects also react to human behaviour in their earthly territories. In both cases, Tyvans often ascribe human success or failure retrospectively to the respectful or disrespectful communication and interaction of human beings and non-human subjects. Many narratives report on failed interactions and their negative consequences for people, unmistakably disclosing the controlling, ordering, safeguarding, and punishing influences of non-human subjects.

An interview partner (a 60-year-old male stockbreeder from Toolajlyg) told me about the spirit masters of the taiga on 1 September 2004:

> When I went hunting once, I met an old hunter. From him I heard the following story. This man – who like me went hunting – told me in great distress: 'When I hunted once, I killed a wild animal. When I levelled my gun and shot, it was already getting dark. Because it was late, I could not skin my game. I only disembowelled the animal. Then I left. When I returned in the morning to take the game, it was strange because the head of the animal was gone. After that I fared badly. You are a hunter too, that is why I warn you. "Other" wild game lives here too. I have seen it. Don't shoot game you do not know. This animal runs wild in this forest until today. It may be the master of the place.' The next day I went into the forest. I was interested in this wild animal. I wanted to see it. It was a white-spotted musk deer (Tyv. *toorgu*). This kind of animal does not actually live here. It stayed close to me, but at first I could not see it. It was probably the spirit master of the taiga (HG 36).

An interview partner (a 46-year-old male stockbreeder in Süt Khöl) spoke on 2 August 2004 about spirit masters:

> This event happened on a mountainside of the Great Kyzyl Taiga in the years between 1970 and 1980. Once a hunter hunted in this area. He was unsuccessful for several days and nights. But one morning he came to a small piece of grassland close to a summer camp; a giant maral deer with eighteen points was grazing there. The hunter aimed and shot the deer with his gun. It tried to run, took a few steps, and then collapsed. When the animal sank to the ground, the hunter heard a female voice calling: 'Oh, how could you do this?'! At that moment the hunter became scared.
>
> After skinning the animal together with his friends, they returned home. When he arrived in his camp he fell ill. The physician could not do anything for him. He had been paralysed. Finally they invited a shaman and showed him the hunter. He said: 'You killed the rare game of the taiga master (Tyv. *oran eezi*, lit. master of the place)! You are a man who heard her voice.' The hunter died soon afterwards. For this reason hunter do not kill rare or large wild animals (HG 5).

Another interview partner (a 60-year-old male stockbreeder in Toolajlyg) told me on 2 September 2004 about the spirit master of the taiga:

> If somebody meets the master of a place, he should never talk about it. The following has happened: A hunter, who snuck up to an animal to shoot it, saw how another person was sneaking up from the other side. When he shot, the other hunter shot as well. After both had skinned the animal, he started for home going downwards but the other shouted after him: 'Do not talk to anybody for three days!' When he arrived in his yurt camp, he remained silent for one day. But the second day they distilled fermented milk (Tyv. *khoitpak*), drank it, and talked. After they had amused themselves, the hunter remembered and thought: 'Why did I speak?' The following three years he was unable to shoot a single animal. As much as he tried, he could not succeed. Being distressed about it, he remembered the event and related it to other people. The other hunter had probably been the taiga spirit master who had put the hunter to a test (HG 27).

Breaches of social norms or of adequate interactions among humans also seem to be controlled by the spirit masters. To break a taboo in the social domain can provoke reprimands by non-human subjects. These cases are also the subject of numerous narratives.

An older interview partner, a 75-year-old male retired stockbreeder, living in Mugur Aksy, told me on 16 October 2004 about what happens to those who behave badly:

> A woman went down to the village. Suddenly a whirlwind blocked her way. On closer inspection she saw an old man. The woman had stolen money in a yurt camp during the night and was going home. She tried to stop a car but did not succeed. So she went back to her village on foot. After this she fell gravely ill. A shaman treated her, but her condition became worse. That was when the shaman said: 'On the banks of the river Mugur you have stolen money!' and 'You have done bad things!' (AN 1).

Spirit masters do not only mete out punishment. They can also search out their own victims. Spirit masters of large bodies of water are regarded as especially capricious and hot-tempered. They are often the subject of narratives about the theft of human lives because they strike suddenly and unexpectedly, for example, if they do not like the conduct of people taking a bath.

A young schoolgirl (14 years of age, living in Kyzyl) said the following on 24 September 2004 about the spirit masters of water: 'Every year people drown in the Yenisei River. We say the river master has taken them. This spirit master fetches people who are drunk or people whose character he does not like' (HG 29). She continued: 'A fisherman related the following event about Lake Chagataj to me: "Once, when I was fishing, people were bathing in the water. Suddenly clouds arose. At the same time a swirl formed itself in the centre of the lake. The swimming people were drawn under water by the swirl. The master of the water hates human beings who pollute the water by bathing, and fetches them." [This is what] the fisherman told me' (HG 30).

The spirit masters, if they are in a good mood, like to test people who visit their territory in order to decide on the basis of their guests' behaviour if they will grant them what they came for. If the human beings succeed in delighting the spirit masters, they can be overwhelmed with gifts and talents. Tyvans often tell stories about true events in which poor people became rich and rich people became poor because they obtained or failed to obtain a spirit master's favour.

A female bookkeeper in Mugur Aksy who was 50 years old told me the following on 3 October 2004 about the spirit master of a lake: 'One evening a couple of fishermen sat at Lake Khindiktig. They ate and drank tea. In the late evening, a woman joined them. She sat down with the fishermen, and chatted and ate with them. When casting their nets the next morning, they caught many fish. Only then did the fishermen realise that the spirit master of the lake had paid them a visit' (HG 31).

A male stockbreeder from Süt Khöl (49 years old) spoke on 28 July 2004 in Kuu-syra about a master of the taiga:

> Once there lived a son of the Kyrgyz from Ulug Khem District who descended from the clan Ondar. When he arrived at our place, he started a family with a rich man's daughter and lived with her. He was that kind of guy. But the wife he had married did not give birth to children. He asked a lama 'Why don't I beget children?' After he had asked, the lama checked and answered: 'Because you do not fit your wife. A famous healer lives with his daughter in the yurt camp on the other side of the river. If you live together with her, you will live well and have children', he said. Thereupon the Kyrgyz man married the girl from that yurt camp and began to live with her. A year later she gave birth to a son. Azhyk-Karak was pleased with his son and waded through the river to ask his wife's brother for a sheep. But he did not give him one. Returning to his yurt camp, he slaughtered the calf of his sole grey cow to strengthen his wife. He then went to the spring of the Ishkin to hunt in the Great Kyzyl Taiga. After hunting for a while, he met a man of the same age. This man asked him: 'What distresses you?' The Kyrgyz told him about his predicament: 'I am a man with a single son. Therefore I have

come here to ask the taiga's master for help.' 'Well, if that is so', he answered: 'then return here after having hunted squirrels for several days and nights.' He left and hunted squirrels, killed a few, and was happy about this. Then the man said to him: 'Do not talk about our meeting. Your wishes will come true.' So the Kyrgyz man returned to his camp, where there was lots of livestock. These animals did not have an owner, and so they became his livestock. After months and years had passed, he encountered a big 'rich tree' at the spring of the Cheede River and made it his own tree. In this way it happened. The Kyrgyz never told anyone how he had become one of the richest people (HG 8).

To take some of the potential danger from the daily and difficult interactions between human beings and spirit masters, many Tyvans tell each other cautionary tales about unsuccessful interactions and their negative consequences. By orally propagating cases of human breaches of the interaction model's norms, the 'proper' guidelines of human interactions with non-human subjects in the Tyvan world are kept present. And the knowledge of such events and their possible consequences enables the experts of such narratives to interpret life situations modelled according to the interaction model and to adapt their behaviour to the norms and rules of this model.

A 58-year-old male teacher of biology and chemistry in Mugur Aksy told me on 9 October 2004 about nature and pollution:

> Anyone destroying or polluting nature at the sacred places, on the *ovaalar*, in the vicinity of springs, of fire, or of sacred trees runs the risk of angering the spirit masters. After that, human beings who behave badly will fare badly. For example, if somebody during a journey stops at an *ovaa* and pollutes the place, then his car – when he drives on – may break down on the insecure and steep roads of the taiga, or he can fall ill after his arrival. He may even die. If we Tyvans do not follow the rules of our spirit masters, then war can even break out. Anyone not following the rules of the spirit masters will fare badly. Good things will happen to him no more. The spirit masters of the sacred places punish people if they are permanently angry. The result is that such people cannot live well, that they either fall ill or die. To prevent this from happening, we must keep nature and the sacred places clean. Anything that has become polluted should be cleaned again. After cleaning a sacred place, one should conduct a fire sacrifice (i.e. Tyv. *sang*, smoke offering), attach a ceremonial scarf (Tyv. *khadak*) or coloured ribbons to bushes or trees nearby, and then pray the following words: 'My world and my

mountains, protect me. I did nothing bad. May you give me good things. May you take away bad things. Protect me!' (NA 7).

A 48-year-old meteorologist, the daughter of a shamaness from Mugur Aksy told the following on 13 October 2004 about nature:

> Our district is not an ordinary country. In our district there are the Silver Taiga Mountains and the White Headed Mountain. The Silver Taiga Mountains and the White Headed Mountain are pure and sacred places. Moreover, they are very powerful. The spirit masters of the Silver Taiga Mountains and the White Headed Mountain see, hear, and know all that happens. The people of our district pray to the Silver Taiga Mountains and the White Headed Mountain, they pray to both. Some people become rich here. But if they leave the country and go away, they will fare badly. Because the spirit masters of our country are angry with them. The spirit masters receive guests from other districts as well. When these people have become rich here and thank the spirit masters of our country, then they fare well when they later live in another place. But anybody who does not thank them when they leave will fare badly because the spirit masters have given them everything (NA 9).

Pleasing the spirit masters and obtaining their favour and gifts is not easy. The most common way of asking the spirit masters for help are small rituals at sacred and powerful places where the spirit masters are able to fulfil the desires of people seeking support.

A 75-year-old male retired stockbreeder living in Mugur Aksy spoke on 8 October 2004 about shaman trees:

> Shaman trees are very rare in the world. We consecrate them, attach white and blue ribbons to their branches, pray to them, and make fire sacrifices for them. Furthermore we sacrifice milk tea and fermented milk by sprinkling it. My grandfather was a hunter. When he went out hunting, he first put white and blue ribbons on the branches of a shaman larch, prayed to the tree, and only after finishing his prayers went hunting to kill game. The spirit master of the shaman larch sent the game his way. If one prays to the shaman larch, then this tree's spirit master will help them during the hunt (Y 19).

Talent and Gifts as Obligations in the Interaction Model

When writing about 'talents' or 'talented persons' among Tyvans, many historical and contemporary authors refer primarily to shamanism and shamans. It is generally and correctly known that the shamans' abilities to travel to non-earthly worlds, approach non-human subjects, communicate with them, and positively affect relations between humans and non-human subjects are gifts of their partner spirits. Shamans are selected for their functions in Tyvan society either by their partner spirits or inherit their talents from one of their ancestors, which is equivalent to their being chosen by their partner spirits. In both cases, the awareness of being gifted with shamanic talent results from a very painful history of illness caused by the partner spirits of the future shaman to force them to follow their calling.[44]

A 40-year-old policewoman from Kyzyl told the following about shaman illness:

> The wife of my older brother [was] called Olga. She [had] just turned 46 [when] she experienced the following in the village of Teeli. In 1999, this woman celebrated her wedding with my older brother Volodja. After the celebration they left at about four o'clock in the morning.[45] When walking down the street, my sister-in-law suddenly seized my brother's hand and sat down on the ground. He asked her: 'What is wrong?' She answered: 'Look, there are dead persons walking about! The dogs are barking at them! Let us sit here for a while.' And she held my brother. My brother told me later that he did not see or hear anything. A short while after this episode my sister-in-law died. My brother told me about the incident. He also died after a short while (SCHA 4).

The conversation following this narrative makes it possible to better understand this 'true event' or contemporary legend. The narrator commented on the events after her sister-in-law had died. On the forty-ninth day after Olga's death, her relatives invited a shamaness, as usual. The shamaness contacted the dead woman and explained that Olga had been seriously afflicted by a shaman illness. Because she had not followed the call of the spirits when they appeared on her wedding night, she had to die. It was thus clear to my Tyvan conversation partners why the person mentioned was able to see and hear the wandering souls of the dead.

Due to the public attention to Siberian shamanism, the core features of Siberian shamanism have garnered wide public attention, also in the West (Vitebsky 2001a, 2001b; Zorbas 2007; Znamenski 2007; Grünwedel 2008, 2010, 2012; Voss 2008, 2011). These descriptions present it in an isolated form[46], which to my mind is only partially justified. In my observations,

---

[44] This typical interpretation of shaman gifts is described in detail in a Kazakh text, written down and published by Divaev (1896: 38-45) that has been translated into German and analysed by Taube, J. (2008: 81-140).

[45] The time between three and five o'clock in the morning is considered especially dangerous since various types of spirits, especially *aza* and *puk*, linger on the streets at night.

[46] Mänchen-Helfen (1931: 116-19); Vajnshtejn (1961: 176-94; 1996b: 252-85; 2005: 197-213); Diószegi (1962, 1978); Alekseev (1987: 245-72); Peters (1993); Hoppál (1994); Kenin-

extraordinary talents among the Tyvans cannot be reduced to this kind of calling. One interview partner (a 43-year-old female anthropologist and folklorist from Kyzyl) provided on 21 July 2004 a spontaneous and thus fragmentary list of possible Tyvan talents: 'We consider blacksmiths, shamans, overtone and throat singers, wrestlers, storytellers, hunters, and elders "gifted". People regard them as *sacred* persons. They are chosen people. They impart wisdom and the fate of our ancestors to ordinary human beings. These chosen people have a special relationship to nature as well as to the spirit masters of places and bodies of water' (BE 1).

Tyvans attribute to gifted people a special relationship with non-human subjects. In the example cited above, my interview partner alludes to the ancestors, nature, and the spirit masters of places and bodies of water. These are only three of many more non-human subjects to which the Tyvans ascribe suzerainty over material and immaterial elements of the Tyvan world. To the latter belong all kinds of talents as well as those cultural traits that are realised by gifted Tyvans and that we can summarise as 'art', such as music, dance, singing, poetry, narration, painting, smithing, leather and fur stitching, wood processing, soapstone carving and other arts and crafts, but also sports (wrestling, riding, and archery), religious and medicinal skills (shamanism, divination, and healing), economic skills (successful stock-breeding, successful hunting), and other exceptional skills including those of scholars. As in Western perspectives, a wide palette of possible talents exists in Tyva, and these talents are not only to be enjoyed, admired, or envied. In the Tyvan interaction model, talents and gifts as well as their implementation and attentive use have as much to do with animism as does the praxis of shamans. Human abilities are not considered to be inborn and do not arise solely as a result of genetic predestination. They are the gifts of spirits who are responsible for such talents among human beings. The spirit masters of talents determine who among Tyvans will receive a special talent to be put into practice. A human being who wants to acquire a special talent can try to induce its spirit master to transmit it to them. But – following the interaction model – he or she should give evidence of a sense of responsibility and may not anger the spirit masters through incorrect behaviour or egoistic ambitions. Both are the case in the following example in which a man tried to request a talent but enraged its spirit master.

A 31-year-old male stockbreeder from Süt Khöl told the following narrative on 26 July 2004 at Kara Chyra in Süt Khöl District about the spirit masters of throat singing:

Lopsan (1994a); Johansen (1998, 2001); Vitebsky (2001a, 2001b); Reid (2002); Deusen (2004); D'yakonova (2005).

In the Kyzyl Taiga there is a place where one can meet the spirit masters of Tyvan singing (*khöömej*) and especially of throat singing (*kargyraa*). They award the gift to learn and perform the art of throat singing. Once a man went there and performed a ritual in order to win the spirit masters over and learn the art of throat singing. But he was drunk and conducted the ritual wrongly. In so doing he enraged the spirit masters. He fell ill and died 60 days later (NL 5).

The awarding of a special talent by the spirit masters is – according to the Tyvan interaction model – equivalent to the duty to use it. The contract between gifted Tyvans and the spirit masters of their talents stipulates that anyone who is able to do something must practise it! Thus people have the duty, upon threat of human suffering, to use responsibly the talents given to them by the spirit masters. Moreover, gifted individuals must not be sparing in the realisation and the quality of realisation of their abilities. If people ask a gifted person to give an example of their abilities or to employ their skills for the community, then the gifted person is obliged to do so. If the gifted person fails to apply their talents for a time, then they can fall ill. If they refuse to serve their talent and its spirit masters, then they must face the consequences and possibly an early death.

An interview partner (a 43-year-old female anthropologist and folklorist living in Kyzyl) explained the following about shamans on 20 July 2004:

In Khandagajty there lived a shamaness. She was a famous shamaness and was feared by the people. She had borne many children. Her youngest son, for example, became director of a school. But she did not want to pass on her shaman's gift. Her son, the school director, had three daughters. Finally all three daughters came down with the shaman's illness. I saw it myself. The eldest daughter had bad luck. The middle daughter went to university, finished medical school, and worked as a paediatrician. She also became ill. The youngest daughter came down with the shaman's sickness when she was seven. People say that it was the fault of their grandmother because she did not pass her skills and knowledge as a shamaness to her children (SCH 3).

The duties of gifted people also include the obligation not to use their gift carelessly, not to play with their own skills, and not to abuse their abilities. This is shown by the deadly dangers that come from frivolous divination.

In June 2005 I lived for two months in the household of Tanja in Kyzyl. She had children, among them 15-year-old Olga who engaged in different kinds of divination and was considered gifted. One morning we heard that a close male relative had passed away the night before. This was a big shock for my host family. He was only 28 years old. Numerous narratives about the course of his death circulated in the family. The entire family met and buried the young man with all honours and at a high financial cost. After the funeral, I noticed changes in my acquaintances' behaviour. Tanja's daughter Olga could not be calmed down; she cried often about the death of her second cousin. Tanja tried to encourage her daughter, but Olga told us that in the previous year, she and her cousin had tried a new oracle. She had only read briefly about the oracle, which is why she had mastered it insufficiently. During the oracle they had called its spirit and asked him about their life expectancy. However, they did the oracle only for fun. When Olga had asked the spirit about her cousin's life expectancy, he answered: 28 years if he does not become more careful. Both had laughed and ascribed the result to their inability to handle the oracle. But now she knew that the oracle had been right. She saw the cause of his early death in their careless use of the oracle and their careless contact with the spirit who had spoken to them through the oracle. She lamented that she herself was responsible for the death of her cousin.

In Olga's interpretation, the spirit addressed during the oracle was angered by its disrespectful handling, had warned both of them, and had finally punished her cousin with a tragic death. Thus a new interpretation entered the family's explanation of the young man's premature death. The misfortune – according to the interaction model – was at least co-determined by non-human subjects that Olga and her cousin had addressed in their oracle.

The handling of a person's talents can be affected by fear. Usually the gifted individuals ponder diligently the right time to realise their talent. Especially religiously talented persons do not want to risk misusing their talents. Erika Taube observed the fear of misapplying a talent and of ensuing punishments by its spirit masters in the following example of a shamaness: 'When I recorded her singing and as she called her protective spirit, she showed such extreme physical reactions (the reddening of her face, breaking out in a sweat, trembling) that I broke off the recording for fear of her health. On her part she later said to me that she panicked with the idea that the spirit would come and punish her for calling him without reason' (Taube, E. 2004: 7).

Numerous stories about hunters reveal warnings about the misapplication of talents and the ensuing punishments that are meted out by the spirit masters associated with them. Narratives about the rules of hunting, the reasons for success in hunting, and the connections between hunters and the spirit masters of the taiga who watch over the wild animals and at the same time provide the hunters with prey make up the biggest part of the texts

I was able to collect. Often they allude to severe punishments if a hunter kills game in excess of his needs or only for pleasure.

A female interview partner (44 years old, an anthropologist and folklorist from Kyzyl) talked about hunters on 3 August 2004:

> Famous, gifted hunters do not kill much game. They only shoot what they can eat. If they – for example – shoot a big animal, they do not kill another one. They shoot no more than one or two animals. They do not kill big, rare, or beautiful animals because such animals can be the master of the place (*oran eezi*) or are his property. Tyvan hunters adhere strictly to the rule that they only kill as many animals as they need to feed themselves or their family. They do so because the spirit masters of the taiga severely punish those people who kill many animals or who kill only for their amusement (HG 1).

A male interview partner (31 years old, a stockbreeder living in Süt Khöl) told on 28 July 2004 about spirit masters and hunters:

> Before hunters go hunting to kill game they make sacrifices for the masters of the taiga. When they rest prior to the hunt, they offer the first part of all the food that they brought with them. They make a fire, cook tea, and sprinkle its first drops. Only then do they drink themselves. In addition, they offer the first part of the bread, the meat, and other food. If hunters spend the night in the taiga, they tell each other stories to please the spirit masters. Because spirit masters love to be entertained, they reward those hunters who tell them interesting stories with good game (HG 47).

A further rule of the interaction model is not to profit unfairly from one's own talents. Religious laypeople today often demand this from professional shamans and use the principle to distinguish contemporary shamans from the 'real' shamans of the past.

A 43-year-old female anthropologist and folklorist from Kyzyl said on 26 September 2004 the following about shamans:

> Today, shamans market themselves. They present themselves to the ordinary populace, advertise themselves and announce: 'I am a shaman, I am able to presage with 41 stones, heal human beings, ritually clean the house, and conduct the ritual of the forty-ninth day after the death of a person'.[47] Earlier, this situation did not exist. Shamans did not promote themselves; they hid their talent and did not reveal themselves to the people. The people knew which shaman was real. They went to a shaman themselves. And, if necessary, they

---

[47] On the forty-ninth day after the death of a person, the bereaved contact the deceased for the last under the guidance of a shaman. In this context they conduct several rituals, commemorate the deceased, and speak their last words with him.

spoke with him about their needs or their problems. They asked the shaman for help. A real shaman agrees to help, but you need to ask him and sometimes persuade him. Only after pleading with him for a long time would the shaman accept your invitation (SCHA 1).

Several research partners pointed out that contemporary shamans are primarily interested in making money. They would not flinch from inventing rituals to earn money, such as rituals for blessing cars, making fortunes or being successful, or earning more money.

The equation in Tyva therefore is not that one's talent is a gift or a favour that elevates one above others in the community, but rather that talent is an obligation to be used carefully and in the service of the spirits and one's fellow human beings. For this reason, in the time before shamans had the opportunity to earn money as professional shamans, many Tyvans regarded this talent as a heavy burden that people tried to avoid rather than accept (e.g. Mänchen-Helfen 1931: 116-19). The following eye-witness account by the Austrian sinologist and historian Otto Mänchen-Helfen, who was the first non-Russian to travel to and write about Tyva, shows this very clearly: 'The shaman is not a priest nor a member of a caste. He enjoys no privileges. He is a cattle breeder just like his neighbours and relatives' (ibid. 116). And,

> Anybody who has listened to a shaman during his vivid dialogue with his partner spirits, how he exclaims amazement, laughs about what his spirits – audible only to him – say to him, nods or winces, will no longer doubt the fair-mindedness of these poor people. Because they are to be deplored. Parents are horrified when they find a sign on their child that shows it to be a future shaman. The practice of shamanism is physically hard work. The young woman from Khöndergej working as a shamaness every evening, the heavy coat on her fragile shoulders, the heavy drum in her hands, from nightfall until midnight, but often enough until two or three in the morning. Spiritually, the production of visions, the creation of another world is an enormous achievement. After the last beat on the drum she sinks down, pale-faced, drenched in sweat, exhausted, almost unconscious. And her pay? Nothing, or a slim ribbon for the grip of her drum (ibid. 118).

An example beyond the much-cited sphere of shamanism is provided by the spirit masters of fairy tales (Tyv. *tool eeleri*). Erika Taube published the fairy tale, 'Why a Storyteller Should Not Allow Himself to Be Begged too Long' (1977b); it was an orally transmitted Tyvan text from the Mongolian Altai that describes and substantiates the rules of storytelling among the Tyvans (Dyva) living there. Her comments on this fairy tale, as well as other articles about the connections between 'religious customs' and 'folk poetry'

(Taube, E. 1990, 1991, 1992, 2000, 2004, 2008) indicate that Tyvans see the talent of a storyteller as the cause and the consequence of interactions between humans and non-human subjects. Talents are transferred by interactions between human beings and spirit masters of talents and seem only rarely to be actively sought after by the people involved. Moreover, they have nothing to do with a free decision of people about their actions or the use of their talents.

On the one hand, Erika Taube (1997b, 2004) sees the skill of storytelling as a gift that storytellers get directly from the spirit masters of narratives (i.e. 'the masters of knowledge', Tyv. *erdem nomnung eeleri*) in order to pass on the treasure of Tyvan spiritual culture and instruct the people.

For this reason the spirit masters of fairy tales and knowledge watch over the storyteller and the process of storytelling to make sure that the talented person uses his or her skills to the fullest and does not employ talent carelessly, using it insufficiently or wrongly. Erika Taube, who collected numerous examples of all genres of oral tradition among the Altai-Tyvans of Mongolia and China (Taube, E. 2008), understood the artist's obligation that results from talent as the cause of several imperatives and prohibitions related to storytelling, singing, or making music. These include the rule to not begin a narration or intone a song unless the artist is sure that he can perform and finish the text or the melody correctly. In addition, the talented person should not misapply the treasure of Tyvan arts or use it in inappropriate situations, for example by whistling during work. Every contravention would be an affront to the spirit masters for whom the sacrifice is intended and who safeguard the talents and give them to the people. These are the non-human subjects that permanently interact with human beings.

Here is an excerpt of the Altai-Tyvan story 'Why a Storyteller Should Not Allow Himself to Be Begged too Long':

> A young man, after learning the art of storytelling to perfection and acquiring a great deal of knowledge was about to be married to the daughter of a Khan. At the wedding reception the guests asked him to tell a few fairy tales; everybody wanted to become acquainted with the young man's elocution. But however much they begged him, the son-in-law did not give in, not even when the Khan himself asked him. [On the evening of the festive day the bridegroom sent a boy to his yurt to get his knife]. The boy went to the new yurt, but just as he wanted to enter, he saw three men inside. They were lying on top of the fireplace, each using the feet of the other as a pillow and talking to each other. The boy stopped in front of the door,

listened and heard what they were speaking about. 'This young man is actually a bad person! He has acquired rich knowledge, but conceals it from everyone. Therefore he has no right to live. We will kill him tomorrow, when he moves home with his yurt, takes his wife with him, to be followed by his stock and all his property.' [The three men agreed on how to kill the denier of his talent]. They were the masters of knowledge (Taube, E. 1977b: 22-23).

That there is a connection between spirit masters who award talents and people who receive and implement talents is a widely distributed view in Tyva. Another interpretation suggesting an interaction between the storyteller and the protagonists of his fairy tales and heroic epics seems no longer to play a role in contemporary Tyva. As far as I could observe, this interpretation is no longer known. But it was common in the past (Taube, E. 1998: 48f; 2004: 6ff) and is an interesting possible interpretation of performing arts according to the interaction model.

The Dolgan, a Mongolised Siberian group, studied by Popov in the 1930s still acted on the assumption that if they told heroic tales, the figures of the tales would enter the lives of human beings, would even become visible in a shadowy way, and interfere directly in the community for the common good. Popov pointed out that we may assume that their appearance resulted from mentioning their names. But if the storyteller does not know the name of the hero or that of his horse, or not accurately, then the figure cannot appear or can do so only imperfectly in favour of the imperilled human beings, so that their assistance cannot have the intended effect. The lack of knowledge of the correct names thus impedes the appearance of a positive figure – for example, of the hero or his horse, so indispensable in Central Asian hero tales – and thereby also the figure's effective interference. The inaccurate knowledge of names could cause the relevant figure not to appear in full possession of his powers and possibilities and therefore lose the battle with dangerous powers. Both possibilities should be avoided, and not even be risked, because a figure's misappearance or lost battle could weaken or even destroy the community concerned. This explains the preoccupation with the correct rules of storytelling (Taube 1977b: 33-34; 2004: 6-7).

If this interpretation of storytelling in the context of the interaction model is correct, the interruption of a narrative will have the same consequences as its inaccurate or flawed narration. On the one hand, the protagonists in the story will not be able to complete their actions for the good of human kind; on the other, they may be offended and become resentful. The interruption of a narrative is equivalent to the forsaking of the non-human subjects awakened by the storyteller. According to the rules, the storyteller is committed to relating the subjects' heroic deeds. This understanding of storytelling has been better documented in a Khakassian example: in 'The Storyteller Agol' (Kaziev 1983: 100-03), the interruption of the narrative results in the heroes of the fairy tale taking revenge, the loss of the storyteller's talent, and his premature death.[48]

One is not only obliged to use one's own talents for the public good. To care for the gift is also an imperative of the permanent interaction between a talented person and those non-human subjects that award a talent. To such interactions belong the journeys of many contemporary shamans to their home and clan areas, to those places where they can contact the partner spirits who once awarded them their talents and powers. These annual voyages mainly serve to refresh these talents by means of regular communication with the spirit masters of the shamans' homeland.

A 54-year-old shamaness and teacher from Kyzyl told the following about shamans on 10 November 2004:

> Shamans travel to the taiga for a year or longer, especially to absorb power. They sew and animate their shaman-garment in the taiga. The shaman awaits the beginning of the month and sews his garment. When he has finished sewing, he awaits the thirteenth day of the lunar calendar. On this day he takes the shaman-garment and his attributes, and with both travels about seven or eight kilometres into the taiga. There he hangs his shaman-garment and his drum in a tree. The shaman then leaves and waits for the seventeenth day of the lunar calendar. After four days he returns to pick up his garment. For this he must conduct the following ritual. At the tree he prepares a smoke offering. He builds a fire by piling wood. On the wood he puts juniper, concentrated butter, crushed Tyvan flour, millet, and tea, and lights it all. Into the fire he sprinkles milk and fermented milk. When the fire is burning, he kneels and asks the spirit master of the taiga for shaman-power. Then he purifies himself three times with the smoke of the burning juniper. Only then does he take the shaman-garment from the tree. He puts on the shaman-garment, takes his drum, and sings invocations. In this way, he thanks the spirit master of the taiga. Only if the master of the taiga provides the shaman with power will the shaman be successful after returning to the people (HG 43).

The care for talents is not only undertaken by people who want to attain maximum skill. The strict control of talents and the above-mentioned rules that is exercised by spirit masters is founded on a reciprocal dependency. On

---

[48] See Funk (2005: 10): 'shamans and storytellers, just as healers and sorcerers, were simultaneously in charge of the same social functions'.

the one hand, human beings practise the talents awarded to them in the human world for their own benefit and that of the community. Talents help people to enrich their lives and ensure their prosperity. On the other hand, the existence of the spirit masters of the talents depends directly on the vitality of the gifts they give and their proper realisation. The logic of the Tyvan interaction model substantiates the duty of human beings to foster their talents in ways such that they safeguard the existence of the spirit masters through the preservation and practice of the talents that they have given. The loss of an ability in the world of human beings and the neglect to practise a talent leads to the decrease and ultimate disappearance of its spirit master. Therefore, in the interaction model, both human beings and their non-human interaction partners are existentially interested in the diligent cultivation of talents and the knowledge of practising them.

The abilities of human beings are the result of successful interactions with non-human subjects that have power over human talents. However, the talented person does not always associate only positive, peaceful, stress-free, fascinating, or foreseeable interactions of give and take with his non-human benefactors. Menacing and monstrous interactions that people prefer to avoid also play an important role in the bestowal and maintenance of a talent. Tyvans mention this side of their talents, for example, in connection with successful hunters who stay in the taiga wilderness for a long time.

A 65-year-old female stockbreeder from Toolajlyg told on 5 September 2004 about an *albys*:

> My father often went to a hunting tent and spent the night there. During the night an *albys* often stayed there with him. However, when he woke up in the morning, he could not see this spirit. When the spirit arrived in the snow, he could hear the snow crunching, but the spirit itself was invisible. He also heard that it carried a stick and how it breathed. My father was convinced that he only hunted very successfully because he stayed overnight with this creature. He told me that if this being did not come to the tent, he did not have a successful hunt (AL 2).

Oral tradition does not only serve to entertain people; it is also an offering that non-human subjects much appreciate and that – similar to singing and instrumental music – can be seen as a service to the spirits. Another reason for performing Tyvan arts, therefore, is to please non-human subjects by narrating, singing and making music.

A 46-year-old stockbreeder from Süt Khöl on the Ak-Oj River told the following on 27 July 2004 about hunters and the spirit masters of the taiga:

> A few years ago, two young men went hunting in the Kyzyl Taiga. One of them was a musician. For a long time, they hunted without

any success. There was hardly any game. One evening one of the hunters asked the other to play for him on his *igil* (a Tyvan stringed instrument). The musician played his *igil* while the other hunter sat and listened to the sound of the *igil*. However, the latter was a seer (Tyv. *karang köör*).[49] Suddenly he saw several beings approach their tent. They pushed each other at the entrance and into the tent. Each wanted to be as close as possible to the musician. They listened to the music attentively. These beings were the masters of the local area (Tyv. *cher eeleri*). Only the seer was able to see them. The musician played on unaware for the whole evening. The next day the seer was afraid to tell his friend about the spirit masters who had been listening to him playing the *igil* because it is impossible to talk about these beings without angering them. On that day they finally were successful in their hunt. They hunted lots of game. If somebody is able to make music, then he pleases the spirit masters of the place, and in return they give game to the hunter. Therefore, the next day, the seer asked his friend to play his *igil* again. They hunted for several days and shot lots of game. In the evening the same procedure was repeated. The seer asked the musician to play his *igil* and evening after evening more and more taiga masters came to listen.

One evening many spirits assembled again. Inside the hunters' tent was a very strange being; his eyes were blind and he limped. He made his way to the hunters in a strange gait. The seer began to laugh. The one playing the *igil* became angry, interrupted his playing and asked: 'Why do you sit here and laugh at me?' The seer was afraid to tell him the truth and replied: 'I am laughing about something else.' However, the beings became angry too. They said: 'He is blind', and decided: 'The musician interrupted his playing! This guy, now we will give him his last bull.' The next morning, the hunters went to their traps. A very big maral deer was lying there. They gave this maral deer to the hunter, who had played his *igil* so wonderfully (HG 10).

Many Tyvans consciously use the insight that spirits enjoy talents like storytelling, singing, and making music to curry favour with non-human subjects. In doing so they apply the talents of the spirit masters not only for carrying out their duties to these spirits but also to effect more favours, like success in hunting or for handling other problems.

---

[49] A seer has fewer abilities than a shaman, but is able to foresee the future and the past of human beings as well as the spirits in their surroundings.

A 44-year-old female anthropologist and folklorist from Kyzyl told me on 5 September 2004 about spirit masters:

> The following is known to all Tyvans. After hunters have gone to the taiga, lit a fire in the evening, and boiled tea, it is imperative that a talented person tell an interesting story or perform overtone singing or throat singing. People say our taiga master is a young girl and she enjoys this. Thus we ask the taiga master for success. Sometimes the taiga master is a very beautiful girl. This young girl listens to the hunter's stories, enjoys them, and then gives the hunters success. It is very difficult for our hunters to please the taiga master. That is why – after boiling tea – they sprinkle nine drops of it as an offering. With it they pray (HG 3).

Annual sports competitions and performances of different Tyvan arts are closely connected with the entertainment offered to influential non-human subjects, like the gods 'father sky' and 'mother earth', but also to clan spirits or spirit masters of places. They are usually included in regular seasonal rituals, for example in the spring or autumn sanctifications of *ovaalar*, the annual Naadym festival and New Year's celebration, or on occasions like weddings. Sports competitions in all Tyvan regions, at least during the Naadym festival, always include the three traditional Tyvan disciplines: wrestling, riding, and archery. They are often supplemented with music, dance, theatre, poetry, beauty and talent competitions, as well as craft exhibitions that today also serve the purpose of trading hand-made products. These festivities are accompanied by specific rituals intended to establish interactions with non-human subjects and influence them in a positive way. A ceremony does not only serve human beings as a welcome diversion and amusement, but also has clearly transcendent features. It gives all participating people the opportunity to meaningfully use the spirits' talents for continuing good relations and positive interactions between human and non-human subjects for the purpose of mutual pleasure and benefit.

Misfortune, Illness, and Death as Punishment by Evil Spirits

To explain diseases, contemporary Tyvans consult modern medicine. However, for Tyvans this in no way limits the possibility of interpreting failed interactions with non-human subjects as the real causes of illness or misfortune. In the interaction model, biological causes for illness or the rational reasons for misfortune are symptoms of regulating, controlling, protecting, and punishing actions of non-human subjects, especially of spirits.

A 58-year-old male teacher of biology and chemistry in Mugur Aksy had the following to say about nature and environmental pollution on 9 October 2004:
> People who behaved badly are punished by the masters of the world and of the mountains by being sent evil spirits, like *aza, chetker, buk* [i.e. *puk*] *albys,* or *shulbus* [another evil spirit]. The spirit masters ponder whether the person's misbehaviour was serious or not. If one has committed a serious offence, either killing a human being or mistreating a wild animal, then they send the spirit *buk*. The children of the person become disabled. If one, for example, scaled a living fish and then threw it back into the water, their offspring will get a disability similar to the injury of the fish. They will be born with a flaky skin. We call such people 'human beings made by *buk*'. In addition to their own generation, the second and the third generation will have this dandruff as well (NA 7).

Among Tyvans we often find an alternative explanation for illness and misfortune alluding to the dangerous playfulness of some spirits. They seem to wait for the moment when they can fool passers-by or the careless, to play with them and pit their strength against them.

An interview partner (a 51-year-old male pensioner from Mugur Aksy) told me about spirit masters on 1 September 2004 in Toolajlyg:
> Our horsemen fear crossing the hill called 'mountain saddle with black stones' in the Möngün Taiga district at night. Because people say that the horses suddenly stop there, as if paralysed, unable to proceed. Once, when my brother-in-law came to visit us from the village, it was already twilight. At that time, our yurt camp was behind the pass of the hill 'with black stones' in the place we call 'dark wood'. When my brother-in-law arrived, his whole face was scratched. But my brother-in-law is a shaman. He warned us: 'In the pass "with black stones" suddenly my horse stopped. Do not cross this place at night! When the horse stopped, it stepped back and forth, as if it were shackled.' He further explained: 'If your horse stops there, you have to jump from its back and with your red-gripped whip [pretend to] free the shackles.' When my brother-in-law freed the shackles with his whip, the spirit master of the pass was totally invisible to his eyes. The spirit clawed him, he told us (HG 23).

In the spring camp on Khamnar Tej in Süt Khöl, close to the Ak-Oj River, a 23-year-old male stockbreeder re-told the following story from his grandmother about her father's encounter with an *aza*. I recorded this story on 1 October 2004:

> My [great-grand]father told [his daughter, i.e. my grandmother] the following. At that time we were living on an open hill, without trees. One night my wife was in bed together with our child. But I lay on the floor in the back of the yurt (Tyv. *dör*). As I was lying there and looked around, somebody opened the felt-close of the door. Then a beam of light shone in. It transmuted into an ugly, long and grey woman dressed in a Tyvan summer coat. She looked around the yurt for some time. I quickly threw my coat over me, lay still and watched from under its edge. I pretended to sleep. She moved quietly, looked at me and looked to the bed. 'So that the poor mother and her baby are not frightened, she should come to me', I thought and lay very quiet. Suddenly the woman came quietly to me. She straddled and sat down on me. 'Why do you sit down on me, *eshpi*?'[50] I shouted quietly and spat. With all my power I hit her in the ribs with my hand and she fell down with much noise. A shiny light shone in and then she jumped away, out of the yurt. Outside the cows began to low and the dogs barked. The old man, our neighbour, shot his gun in the air. I also went out of the yurt and saw that she fled and that her hip burned blue. Thus I hit an *aza*. If I would have had a knife, I would have knifed her to defeat the monster (AZ 3).

Attempts of several spirits to steal human souls count as much more dangerous. Especially notorious is the *albys*, a spirit that appears as a young and beautiful woman or a handsome young man to its victims, seducing them into a love relationship that soon turns into madness.[51] The spirit blinds the mind of its victims and in this way commits them to itself. *Albys* spirits are often seen as shaman partner spirits that confuse and torment their victims for such a long time that they are forced to serve them as shamans or die as a consequence of their refusal.

An interview partner (75 years old, and a pensioner and stockbreeder in Mugur Aksy) spoke on 8 October 2004 about *albys*:

> A long time ago a young woman met an *albys* at the Mugur spring. She lost her heart to this spirit. At that moment the shaman Chydym, who was able to catch *albys* spirits, arrived. The confused young woman, possessed by the *albys*, wandered all around the place. Her relatives invited the Chydym shaman to drive out the *albys*. The shaman started to hit the young woman with his red-gripped whip

---

[50] Pejorative term for 'woman'.

[51] Analysing texts from more than 100 years ago (Miropiev 1888; Divaev 1896; Kastan'e 1912, 1913), Jakob Taube (2008: 9-60) describes the *albys* as a seductress and wife among the Kazakhs. All the consequences that such a relationship may have for the people concerned are the same among the Tyvans.

shouting: 'Say the name of your *albys*!' But the woman possessed by the *albys* did not want to give its name away. She felt good with the *albys*. The woman who had been whipped tried to trick the shaman about the *albys*'s name. She gave him false names. Only after he had hit her very hard did she give away the correct name. But at the moment she called the right name of the *albys*, the spirit came out fighting. Therefore the woman began to cry. But the shaman sent the *albys* back to its own world (AL 5).

A 54-year-old shaman from Ak Dovurak told the following about the *albys* on 5 October 2004 in Mugur Aksy:

> The being we call *albys* or *shulbus* has no nose. Its feet are invisible and you cannot hear its voice. This being is deaf and it flies. The being we call *albys* has a grey yurt, a human figure, eyes and mouth. If it meets a human being, the spirit takes the human's head, holds it under its armpit, and befogs the mind. The person goes crazy and so they go on together from then on (AL 3).

Tyvans have developed a multitude of protective measures to defend them from the dangerous influence of evil spirits. These are based on their extensive knowledge about the behaviour, preferences, and fears of such evil spirits. Such measures include for instance, the colour red; the red branches of prickly *kharagan* and *söösken* shrubs that grow in the steppe; and the purifying smoke of juniper collected in the mountains.

A 43-year-old, female anthropologist and folklorist, living in Kyzyl, told on 30 October 2004 about the means of protection against evil spirits:

> The dreadful evil beings we call *aza-buk, aza-chetker,* and *albys-shulbus* fear the colour red, fire, and the red and prickly *kharagan* shrubs.[52] To protect us from evil spirits, we also make our whips from a branch of the red *söösken* shrub. We hang a whip made from the wood of *söösken* over the cradle or the beds of small children. Above the entrance to a yurt or house we hang prickly red *kharagan*. This protects us from the *aza*. To burn juniper also protects us from *aza*. At the same time, the smoke cleans our houses and attracts spirits with good intentions (ÜG 2).

Playful evil spirits have a preference for the souls of little Tyvans – the children. All kinds of spirits are attracted by the candour of children. Their charm seduces the spirits to steal their souls. The belief of dangers especially for children is widespread, which is why Tyvans try to protect them in several ways. A proven method is to camouflage them or make them invisible. If the attendance of small children during rituals cannot be avoided,

---

[52] This informant combined types of spirit in her telling. Where such variants appeared in interviews, I have maintained them.

for example during the blessing of the hearth or rituals for the spirit masters of the yurt or the camp, which concern all members of the household, the parents blacken their children's faces with grime and soot so that the spirits to be called do not see them. A dot of black grime on the forehead is enough to make the child unrecognisable for spirits, or at least unsightly and therefore uninteresting. Another widely known method to permanently protect children from attacks by spirits is to give them unattractive names. This form of protection is used especially among families that have already lost one or more children.

The same interview partner spoke on 17 August 2004 in Kyzyl about the protection of children against *aza*:

> The Tyvans do not give their children truthful and beautiful names. Even if they are tender with them, they do not speak to them with beautiful words. They speak differently to them [than they mean to]. If, for example, they love a small child, then they do not talk sweet words to the child but ugly ones. They do this because the *aza*-spirits hear the words and could take the child away. The child would die. In the past, we protected young children from the *aza*. We gave them different names. For example, 'bad boy', 'ugly boy', 'bullshit boy', 'black girl', 'glutton', or 'muddler'. My younger brother's name is 'bad-boy'. His identity card says 'Eduard', but at home we only call him 'bad-boy'. We do not give beautiful names to children who are young. We only call them by their nicknames (AZ 4).

The Pursuit of Stability in the Interaction Model

Many Tyvans are convinced that the Tyvan world can only function optimally if the interactions between human and non-human subjects are stable and proceed in a balanced way. Both sides are thus equally interested in well-balanced interactions between both groups of actors, who mutually presuppose and depend on one another. In the interaction model, the spirit masters ensure their self-perception as masters over everything existing and their own existence with the help of human action. On their side, humans ensure their existence by having the spirit masters provide for everything they need.

The former includes the protection of all that is owned by spirit masters. When a spirit's property is damaged, for instance when it is used wrongly or destructively, the power of that spirits decreases. And with its ultimate destruction, the spirit master dies. If a talent awarded by spirit masters to human beings is not used, people do not only forget their knowledge about the talent and its realisation. With the extinction of a human art or craft, its spirit master disappears as well. Humans thus have the responsibility to preserve the spirit masters' property and in turn the spirit masters' very existence.

The latter includes the dependency of humans on everything the spirit masters provide. If spirit masters refuse human beings their support, human survival is threatened. From a simple tool to health, everything that matters to human beings comes from the spirit masters. Thus, spirit masters are responsible for the well-being of humans.

The pursuit of harmony, balance, and stability in the framework of the Tyvan interaction model leads to an enormous number of interactions between humans and non-human subjects. These include daily interactions like the respectful handling of everything Tyvans need for living their everyday lives, short ritual interactions, and extensive spontaneous or periodical rituals. Many rituals, especially shamanistic séances, also imply divinatory elements in the form of an oral exchange. Also common are exchanges with spirits and other non-human subjects with the help of material media like stones or the shoulder blade bones of animals (Oelschlägel 2004a: 97-121; 2005a; 2006).

Today, the most important rituals are the ritual accompaniment of the deceased. The surviving members of the family of a deceased person are duty-bound to perform these rituals. They are the necessary human part of a successful interaction between the bereaved family members and the deceased person. As already mentioned, the soul leaves the earthly world for the other world on the forty-ninth day after a person has died. It will later be reborn, but prior to that new state, the soul is in permanent interaction with still-living relatives and acquaintances, wandering through the places of its once worldly existence. Many contemporary legends are stories of 'true events' of encounters between a deceased person and the people he had contact with during his life. Such true events clearly show how particularly sensitive people notice the souls of dead persons. Souls present themselves for several reasons. On the one hand, they still need the care and attention of those from whom they had to depart. The soul of a recently deceased person still feels awkward in its new form and therefore needs the support of the living to provide, for example, food and light. On the other hand, many deceased, especially people who died suddenly, only slowly come to terms with the fact that they are no longer among the living. Again and again, the deceased present themselves to their relatives and acquaintances in the hope that the living will suggest by their reactions that they are not dead, but still living their earthly existence. People able to observe the souls of the deceased therefore attempt to appease them and explain their condition to them.

The contact between the living and the dead is always dangerous. Two of the greatest risks are the desire of a deceased to take a beloved person along on their journey to the other world, or to take revenge on those whom they feel injured them in life. To help the deceased during their transition to the new condition, support them in overcoming the hazards on their journey to the other world and reduce the dangers from the deceased to the still living, Tyvans handle the separation of a dead person from his family with a great deal of attention and mutual consideration. For them it is not enough to wash and dress the corpse, lay it out for saying goodbye, and then bury it. Much attention is paid to protect the soul, which only slowly accustoms itself to its new disembodied state. The soul must be provided with food, drink, and a light on an altar by its relatives so that it does not become hungry and thirsty and can find its way to the other world through the darkness. In addition, many Tyvans feel impelled to protect themselves against the hazards that come from the soul of the deceased.

For both reasons, since perestroika it has again become common to conduct rituals on the seventh and the forty-ninth day after a person's death. Relatives invite a shaman because the most important – and, for the people involved, most interesting – part of both rituals is a long conversation with the soul of the deceased. Both rituals serve to secure or reinstate stability and harmony in the relations between the deceased and the survivors in the framework of a last contact between the soon to be forever separated. An example of such a conversation is the case of informant TO 1 below, which reveals the interests of all participants in the ritual, including the separation of people who loved one another, mutual material and immaterial support, divinatory insights into the current situation of all participants, the future of both the deceased person and their living relative and the hazards threatening them.

During the ritual, the relatives sacrifice food, beverages, and other presents to the deceased person, which they burn in a fire with juniper. The non-human share in the interaction presented here reveals itself especially in the content of the conversation during the ritual. The conversation between a shaman and the soul of a deceased woman is summarised by the shaman himself and explained to the bereaved after the leave-taking of the soul at the end of the forty-ninth day ritual.

A 57-year-old shaman from Kyzyl conducted a ritual 49 days after the death of a female bookkeeper, aged 59, that included the following conversation with the soul of the deceased. The ritual took place in the deceased's native village of Mugur Aksy on 3 October 2004. Attending were the three daughters of the deceased (a physician from Moscow, aged 34, a merchant from Kyzyl, aged 30, and a systems administrator in the district administration of Mugur Aksy, aged 27).

Shaman: A. is a loveable person.

A. [as repeated by the Shaman]: I will leave no bad things behind, no black things.[53] My whole life I have only raised my children, did well to other people and committed no sins, so tell this to my daughters and relatives. It could not be foreseen that such a terminal illness would strike me. The children have done everything possible for me.[54] Now there is nothing we can do to change things. Everything my children have done for me was right, but this disease was stronger and now I am in this [other] world. It is strange, my younger brother [addressing the shaman] and our older sister died of the same illness, and now I passed away in the same manner. Please take a look at my children, check them to see if they have the same illness!

Whence did you come, my son?

Shaman: When I replied: 'Your children invited me from where the sun is rising',[55] she spoke on.

A.: How well our people fed me, how good this was, this is very fortunate. I brooded about whether the people would come, but in the end everybody came.'

Shaman: When people offered her cigarettes and put them into the fire, she was very happy. She said:

A.: Here, in this [other] world, I met the father of these [my] children, here we found each other [again].[56] In less than three years, in two years and seven or eight months, I will return to this yellow world.[57] A mother, as I was, I will become again. I will be born with a white soul, like the milk of my mother, so I will be born again.

Shaman: She said, 'Tell it to my children in this way!'

---

[53] A. loved her grandchildren very much. That is why her daughters were afraid that she did not want to be separated from them and take one of them with her to the other world. For this reason the first question the shaman addressed to the deceased was whether she intended to take a relative to the other world. A. repeatedly indicates that she did not want to do bad things to her relatives. This includes taking revenge for injustices committed against her and any intentions to kill relatives by seizing their souls and taking them with her to the other world.

[54] A. means all the efforts of her daughters to provide medical care and obtain medicine from a Tibetan lama, for which one of her daughters travelled to Tibet.

[55] The shaman lives in Kyzyl, to the east of Mugur Aksy.

[56] Her husband died in 1997.

[57] In the celebration the shaman reported that A. would be reborn as the daughter of one of her own daughters.

A.: When I am born again, give me the names of two persons, so that they are bound with a hyphen in the middle, for example, Gold-Flower or Moon-Heart. The names of three persons would also be good. It has become clear that my name was very short – this was bad. I do not want to leave sorrow to anybody. After my children come younger children. Tell my relatives to be good to the fathers of their children, do not fight. There is another peculiar thing. I heard it said here: 'One of the men could die.' I do not want this myself, I wish only the best. Offer white milk and blessings. I found a white way[58], my son.

Shaman: When we gave her the book, she was very happy. She said: 'Oh, my children have forgotten nothing and will not [forget].' She liked eating grapes, she loves such fruit. She drank juice and tea, but hardly ate any meat.

A.: Oh, my illness I did not watch out.[59] [...] Look, this is what we call the life of a human being. There are people who get such a serious illness. I would have liked to see how the sons of my children marry. But I did not manage that.

Shaman: She said [this]. And: 'This offends and afflicts me. It seems that our elder sister also died from this illness.'

The deceased's daughters interject: This is true. The sister of our mother died the same way. People thought she had an illness of the liver. But she had the same symptoms.[60]

Shaman: Your mother will be reborn from the water and the stars. When I work with my drum, we will beseech the stars for it.

A.: When I fell ill, I only felt a slight pulsating pain, but I paid no attention. Then I got acute and finally violent pains. If I would have had a son, he would have drunk [the illness] with the breast milk. But my daughters probably did not have enough strength for this illness.[61]

This poor foreign girl, when I was ill, she came to the hospital. It made me feel better in my soul.

I never drank any vodka. During festivals and weddings I only sipped it. But my husband drank regularly. Pour the husband something from the white fermented milk![62] [63], He [my husband] has

---

[58] A good, happy way.

[59] A. ignored her illness for a long time. That is why the cancer remained undetected for a long time.

[60] The elder sister was never diagnosed with cancer, but had the same symptoms.

[61] A few years before she died, A. fell ill with breast cancer.

[62] *Araka* (distilled fermented milk) belongs to the white foods.

already been reborn into the yellow world. Here only a part of him remains.⁶⁴

Shaman: When she left, it was strange, she headed east. When she left, she said: 'I will now travel into the cosmos.' Does she fly from the east into the cosmos?

Daughters of the deceased: To the east lies the valley of Toolajlyg. There lies the Oorzhak-*ovaa* of our mother's clan.⁶⁵

Shaman: Then she was right to fly the way she did. Oh, she is a very good person, for sure nothing bad will come after her. She was very concerned about the men [of the family], that something could happen to them. She said: 'In our family there are sons-in-law, younger brothers and also elder men. They should be very careful. That is why you have to protect these good men!' (TO 1).

The conversation between the shaman and the deceased woman begins with a positive evaluation of her life. The shaman informs her relatives that A. does not intend to inflict pain upon the bereaved. He calls her a 'loveable person' and praises her religious attitude. The deceased had decided to visit the clan *ovaa* as her last goal before travelling to the other world, to say goodbye to her ancestors and to the spirit master of her clan area. This showed him that her relatives had nothing to fear from such a soul that was following the rules of interaction with both human and non-human subjects in such a respectful way.

A second part of the conversation consisted of words of reconciliation and gratitude from the deceased to the bereaved. The shaman listed in detail everything that made the deceased happy. She was glad for the help she received during her severe illness, especially from her daughters, who – according to the deceased's statement – did everything they could to ease her suffering and lengthen her life. She put her daughters at ease that they could not have done more. Her situation had been hopeless. With these words she took from her daughters any feelings of guilt and encouraged them to live free of any agonising doubts. At the same time, she expressed regret about having to leave her family so early and tried to appease them by willingly accepting her fate. She was grateful for the rituals on the seventh and forty-ninth day of her death, as well as for the offerings. She praised both rituals and pointed out to her relatives which offerings she had especially appreciated. In this way, the conversation created an appeasing atmosphere

---

[63] When the shaman poured vodka into the fire, all relatives present wondered aloud: 'She asks for vodka?' Thus the shaman explained to them why she demanded vodka.

[64] The participants explained to me that she meant the shadow of her husband.

[65] See H 19 and Y 3

of conciliation, enabling both sides to take leave of each other and let go in love, mutual gratitude, and binding confidence.

The third important topic of the conversation concerned the deceased's rebirth as well as warnings to her family about the future lives of her relatives that A. wanted to contribute on the basis of insights newly acquired with her death. First, she explained to her daughters that she was not the first victim of this disease, as her sister had died from cancer as well, albeit undiagnosed at the time. Second, in an omitted section of the text, A. warned her daughters that the family should pay attention to the symptoms of cancer, which she again described, and should have regular check-ups in order to combat cancer in time. She also warned the bereaved that one of their male relatives could die next and urged her daughters to care for the fathers of their children.

In addition, she told her daughters about their father who died in 1997. Already reborn, 'only a part' of him remained in the other world. She told them that she found him again, which provoked joy among the participants of the ritual. She also announced her own rebirth and reported on when, how, and with what characteristics she would return to the earthly world. The discussion of these three issues was at the core of the meeting between the soul of the deceased, the shaman, and the bereaved. The ritual of the forty-ninth day ended for all participants in a satisfying way. The care of the bereaved, their respectful observance of their duties during the interaction with the soul (the invitation of a shaman, rituals and conversations with the soul as well as offerings of food, drink and light), and the handling of the dead body (transfer to the homeland, dressing, laying out, and funeral) had been received positively. In return, the deceased had given insights into the future, warned them of possible dangers and relieved them of feelings of guilt. Thus the interactions between all sides achieved their purpose of creating stability and harmony.

If danger has entered the life of a human or if a phase in life was characterised by more than average misfortune, like deaths, illnesses, poverty, infertility, economic or individual failures, many Tyvans will act on the assumption that the cause of these misfortunes lies in failed interactions between human and non-human subjects. The list of human failures in the interaction model ranges from neglect of interactions with non-human subjects to accidental or deliberate contraventions of the norms and rules of the interaction model. Following the rules of the interaction model, the consequences of such failures often require a clarification of the precise reasons behind them. The person involved first has to find out what has caused his bad luck. Then, often with the help of a shaman, a Tyvan undertakes a reconciliation ritual to arbitrate the conflict. During the ritual the person involved promises to modify his long-term behaviour. This modification of behaviour – usually a shift to respectful interactions in the future – should avoid a recurrence of any misfortune.

Both human beings and spirits are anxious to restore stability and harmony in the interaction model. The following example will demonstrate how this process takes place. A Tyvan colleague elucidated how the analysis of a string of bad luck led to the finding of a connection to failed interactions. This is followed by the invitation of a shaman, who limits the damage and brings about a reconciliation between both parties. It ends, finally, in a long-term modification of behaviour by the human interaction partner.

My 44-year-old female friend who works as a social scientist in Kyzyl told me about her life in long conversations. She mentioned that after a series of private misfortunes, she had invited a shamaness to her flat in 2002. The shamaness sanctified my friend's flat by ritually cleansing it to reconcile her with the flat's spirit master, and in this way rectify the reasons for her bad luck. The shamaness said the male spirit master was hungry, and suggested that my friend feed him regularly (see NA 11 above).

Both the shamaness and my acquaintance attributed her misfortune to the angry spirit master of the flat. During the ritual they tried to appease him, and they succeeded. However, the shamaness explained that peace would only be short-lived if respectful interaction was not cultivated in the future. After the ritual, my friend's life changed for the better. She herself explained to me that she could only make offerings for a short time. But her daughter had continued to do so later.

When I met her again in 2005, she complained about depressions and that her friends had abandoned her. She spoke again and again about her misfortune and seemed desperate. Finally she said she had found the true cause of her misfortune. The spirit master of her flat whom she had culpably neglected was at fault, she thought herself. Her daughter, who fed him regularly, was doing well – she said – but with her, he was angry again. She decided to change her behaviour. We conducted a ritual cleansing of the flat, and from then on she fed its spirit master regularly.

I later asked her if the ritual had worked. She said that she felt much more relaxed and cheerful and was happy again to meet with friends and acquaintances.

The cause of bad luck is not always seen as related to failed interactions. Whether or not Tyvans explain the cause of bad luck with the interaction model, making contact with relevant non-human interaction partners may help to rectify a situation. The people concerned determine the framework of such contacts themselves. Such interactions range from a short visit to a sacred place, where people conduct several ritual acts, like invocations, blessings, and offerings (see Y 10 below), to complex and costly rituals that are prepared and organised with the help of professional shamans (see Y 5 below).

A female research partner, aged 54, who works as a shamaness and teacher in Kyzyl, told the following about a sacred place on 1 November 2004:

> This sacred place is located in Kungurtug. There is a rock there. On the rock you can see the natural image of a woman with a young child, like a silhouette engraved into the rock, but at the foot of the rock are seven natural cavities in the form of cups. This place is also a sacred place. Anyone unable to give birth to a child, sews a doll and hangs it there. The female spirit master of the place then decides whether or not the woman will become a mother. Many women give birth to a child after doing so. The woman with the little child on the rock is the female spirit master of the place (Y 10).

The same woman told the following about springs and their spirit masters:

> Once a woman came up to me and asked for help: 'Look, they want to amputate my leg.' The surgeon, however, had gone to Moscow for a conference. 'My leg hurts every day', the woman told me. I considered whether I should ask for power from a shaman tree or a rich tree for her. Then it came to me that I could ask the spirit master of a spring for power. We drove to the spring, and I conducted a 'consecration of a spring' ritual. I proceeded in the following way: I built a fire by piling up wood. On top of the wood I placed juniper, butter oil, milk tea, cream, dried curd, cheese, grain, and crushed Tyvan flour. I asked the woman to sit down near the fire and the spring. During the ritual I sang blessings and invocations, asking the spirit master for help for her to recover. After a year I met the woman again on the street. I saw that she was very happy. Since then, five or six years have gone and she still feels good. She gave me her address. Look, this is the way in which the master of a spring heals (Y 5).

The actuality of the pursuit of stability in a world of interactions between human and non-human subjects does not only appear in the multiplicity of true events or contemporary legends. The need for successful interactions and with them the pursuit of stability and harmony in the interaction model also become apparent in the multiplicity of invocations. Tyvans make invocations and blessings mainly in ritual contexts in order to make contact with non-human subjects and express in a dignified way their gratitude or make requests. The examples of this genre – as with 'true events' – are not only long-established oral traditions. I often observed that Tyvans invented new invocations and blessings during rituals and festivities. The ability to compose such texts is a widespread talent among Tyvans, awarded by the spirit masters to singular persons who therefore have to practise it. The widespread distribution of new invocations and blessings in contemporary literature, especially in poetry, is remarkable. Volumes of poetry often include such invocations and blessings. They can be found in the yurts or houses of many South-Siberian Tyvans. The following example is a transcription from the diary of a woman who copied down texts dictated to her by her father (HG 15). An invocation (Y 17) I excerpted from a publication of one of my research partners follows.

The following invocation (*algysh*) was recorded by a female interview partner, aged 43, who was a housewife in Mugur Aksy. I transcribed the text from her diary on 26 August 2004:

Möngün Taiga algysh	**Invocation to the Möngün Taiga**
Ulug Möngün-Khajyrakan!	Great silver Lord![66]
Udur körüp, 'oog' dener!	If you watch it directly, say 'Oh!'
Biche Möngün-Khajyrakan!	Small silver Lord!
Birgeer körnüp, 'aa' denger!	If you behold it, say 'Ah!'
Avam bolgan Mögen-Büren!	Mögen Büren[67], that became my mother!
Aldyy, Üstüü Sajyrlarym!	My lower and upper hills,
Ugbam bolgan Shegetejler!	Shegete[68], that became my sister!
Ulug, biche Despengnerim!	My smaller and bigger forest glades!
Algysh-samym,	When I sing and dance the Tsam [a Buddhist dance],
Ajan kiirger!	It becomes harmonic music.
Kösku-khöreem,	When the whole upper part of my body makes music,
Khöön kiirger!	It becomes a harmonic melody (HG 15).

---

[66] The high, snow-covered mountains.
[67] Area to the south-west of the Möngün Taiga near the Altai Mountains.
[68] Shegete is a landscape close to Mögen Büren.

A 47-year-old teacher of Russian and Tyvan in Mugur Aksy recited blessings for the fire on 10 October 2004. He had published these in his volume of poetry entitled *Bodaldar* (Thoughts):

    Fire – our father, our mother

    Near the stove we never put waste;
    To the territory of my fire-lord bad powers can never attain.
    The spring of my life, my great fire, may constantly burn!

    My thirteen-headed fire-mother, you create peace in my homeland!
    Us, your sons, your daughters, you will steadily keep warm:
    Each time we go over seven passes, when we wade through seven rivers,
    Each time we remember you; Oh, our fire-mother!
    Master of the three stones of our hearth, you are the antlers of three wild animals,
    Thirty-headed, having come down from the upper world; Oh, our fire-father!

    With your red coat, made from fur, you cover us warmly,
    With your shining flames you warm us,
    Our dear, loving father, safeguard us,
    Take us with you, warm our way, our father.
    Our thirteen-headed fire-mother, our thirty-headed fire-father,
    Your sons, your daughters we are, your warm words we will hear,
    You are the spirit masters of our homeland and we live happily!

    Flames, the warm words of our fire-father, our fire-mother
    Are true, strong and wise.
    They are our and our children's hearth-stones!
    (Kazyrykpaj 2000: 18f; my translation)

The concerns about a successful interaction between human and non-human subjects and the efforts made to ensure a harmonic and stable relationship between both becomes especially clear in the norms of proper behaviour discussed in many true events. As discussed above, stories of such events often broach the issue of the relationship between the breaking of rules and the consequences. The punishment of human beings who break the norms of the interaction model by the spirits shows their ambition to secure the reliability of human conduct based on these norms.

An interview partner from Erzin, aged 22, who at the time was living in Mugur Aksy and working as a teacher, told the following about a healing spring near his home village Shuurmaka:

> Women are not allowed to go to the spring for healing heartburn. If a woman would go there, the healing spring would dry up. Once, when we went to the healing spring to drink from its water, it did not flow. This was because a Russian woman had gone to the spring. We therefore conducted a smoke offering. We conducted the smoke offering for the male spirit master of the healing spring. We split wood and lit a fire. Into this [fire] we sprinkled milk and on it we placed biscuits, chocolate, meat, bacon, and juniper (HG 13).

Other examples of spontaneous or periodical rituals point to the need for stability for those who want to ensure the goodwill of non-human subjects by correctly following the norms of the interaction model. In order to ensure security in the difficult field of such interactions, many Tyvans again and again contact those non-humans subjects that seem to be involved in their lives and fates.

A 47-year-old stockbreeder in the Toolajlyg cooperative, talked on 31 August 2004 in about 'black water' (i.e. a muddy spring):

> In 2000 we consecrated a 'black water' close to the *baza* of the Toolajlyg cooperative. The ritual was led by a shamaness who was living in our valley. Five other shamans attended. Swedish shamans also came. All these shamans were working with their drums. [They] conducted a smoke sacrifice and fed the spirit master of the black water. They found out that the spirit master of the black water is a young girl on a white horse. The shamans tied ribbon offerings. We also tie ribbons when setting out on a long trip. Then our journey will be successful (HG 18).

Another female interview partner, aged 54 and working as a shamaness and teacher in Kyzyl, told me on 1 November 2004 about springs and their spirit masters:

> Fire has a spirit master (Tyv. *ot eezi*). That is why we have to bless each fire. We call this ritual *ot dagyyr*. The blessing of the fire is conducted in spring and autumn, prior to our move from the winter camp to the summer camp or back. Tyvans conduct this ritual and ask the spirit master of their fire to safeguard them from having a fire on the new camp site, to keep them well, prevent burglaries and disease, so that all family members remain healthy, and so on. Tyvans bless the fire in the following way: They slaughter a sheep and prepare food. Before conducting the ritual, people knead the figure of a goat from dough prepared from flour and crushed Tyvan

flour.[69] They put the goat on a piece of carton and around it several other foods and a bit from the meat of the slaughtered sheep. Then they put the carton into the hearth (Tyv. *suugu*). In addition the shaman says invocations and blessings (HG 35).

A third interview partner, a 75-year-old retired stockbreeder living in Mugur Aksy, told me on 8 October 2004 the following about the spirit masters of the Silver Taiga and White Headed Mountain:

> The spirit masters of the White Headed Mountain and the Silver Taiga are closely connected. They regularly meet each other. The master of the White Headed Mountain is a handsome young man riding a white horse. The master of the Silver Taiga, by contrast, is a beautiful woman also riding a horse. Close to the Silver Taiga is a part of the taiga we call 'small table'. The female master of the Silver Taiga meets the master of the White Headed Mountain on the Small Table Taiga. When they meet, they protect and safeguard the wild animals of our world. They are the spirit masters of this world. Our people pray to the spirit master of the Silver Taiga. They sacrifice white milk with a libation spoon and spread food around. The Silver Taiga has an *ovaa*. Close to the White Headed Mountain there is also an *ovaa*. Both *ovaalar* exist to the present day. People to this day go to these *ovaalar* to pray and bring smoke offerings. If people pray to the spirit masters of the Silver Taiga and the White Headed Mountain and believe in them, then these will safeguard the people because they have made offerings (HG 44).

Balanced interactions, as described earlier, can also be endangered by non-human subjects like evil spirits, which Tyvans characterise as playful or vicious in contact with humans. If such spirits interfere into the fate of humans, then the danger to the persons involved can be just as severe as in the case where they are themselves at fault. In such cases, shamans have to spring into action in order to try, with the help of their partner spirits, to push back, banish, or annihilate the evil spirits.

Wilderness and Pure Ground

Pure ground (Tyv. *aryg cher*) is for many Tyvans simultaneously sacred ground (Tyv. *ydyktyg cher*). Even more importantly, it is also powerful ground (Tyv. *küshtüg cher*). We can use these three terms not only for sacred places where *ovaalar*, sacred trees, or healing springs are situated, but also for areas called wilderness, that is areas that are preserved in their natural

---

[69] Tyvan flour is hand-milled with a stone mill. The resulting flour is closer to crushed grain than it is to finely ground flour.

condition, untouched by human intervention, and rarely or never frequented by humans. These include trackless areas in the taiga that only hunters frequent or areas that not even hunters visit, like certain mountains and mountain peaks.

A male interview partner, aged 58, working as a teacher of biology and chemistry in Mugur Aksy, told about the sacred ground:

> If a place has extraordinary energy, then it also has a powerful spirit master. A mountain, a rock, or a pure and wild place, for example, has a strong spirit master. We call those places sacred (Tyv. *ydyktyg*) that have much energy, where human beings do not go, and that for this reason are pure places. The axes of the big mountains become sacred places with their strong electromagnetic radiations. In such places there are many spirit masters. We build *ovaalar* for such areas that have much energy and power. There we practise our religion, sanctify the *ovaa*, bring smoke offerings and celebrate festivals, like the Naadym festival. We also tend livestock at such sacred places. If we consecrate animals at sacred places, we hold a special ceremony. Consecrated animals absorb much energy at sacred places. That is why they have a positive influence on the stock. The livestock does not die and the herd prospers. Where there is much energy, the spirit masters also have much energy. The power of a spirit master depends on the place where the spirit is living. Where there are powerful spirit masters, the people pray because the spirit masters give energy to human beings and heal (Y 12).

Whether an area has a strong and useful or dangerous power for humans depends on its distance from human settlements. The spiritual powers of these places increase with their distance from settlements and the ways of people. The more impassable the territory, the more powerful the spirits.

Areas that are frequented by humans lose power or have their positive energies changed to negative. In the latter case, it becomes worthless for religious activities. According to the interaction model, a spirit master can only have as much power as the place where it resides. If a Tyvan needs a strong spirit master to petition or for a ritual, especially seasonal rituals or for healing an ill person, then he must seek a place with much energy.

A shamaness and teacher from Kyzyl, aged 54, said the following on 1 November 2004 about sacred places:

> A sacred place is a place that helps people. Already our ancestors prayed to such places. They knew that sacred places help them to solve a problem or recover from a disease. From a place called *ydyktyg cher* comes great power. The spirit masters of such places are very strong. The term *ydyktyg cher* includes all these features.

> Sacred places can be passes, rocks, rivers, mountains, springs or a healing spring (*arzhaan*), but also a shaman tree, a rich tree, or a forked tree. You can go to a sacred place and do a smoke offering. Then the spirit master of the sacred place will help you (Y 9).

The potency of rituals does not only depend on the power of a particular place, but also on its physical features. The latter also dictate for what reasons people contact the master of a particular place. The physical features of a place or an area are a symbol of the abilities and possibilities that the Tyvans assign to its spirit master. The features that symbolically determine the function of a place and its spirit master include the shape of bodies of water, different kinds of springs, or the ways in which sacred trees grow.

The same shamaness and teacher told the following about springs and their spirit masters. 'If a person falls ill, then the shaman asks for power from the spirit master of a body of water. A spring flows below the ground and comes out of the earth. At the place where the spring flows out it is connected with the sky and the cosmos. From there it begets its great power. That is why the spirit master of a spring is very powerful' (Y 4).

In the same way that the spirit masters of the camp, the yurt, or the fire are responsible for the well-being of the family, so are the spirit masters of a clan's homeland responsible for the well-being of all clan members.

Another interview partner, 44 years old and working as a social scientist in Kyzyl, told me on 3 August 2004:

> Every clan has its own sacred place. For example, the Mongush, Dongak, Küshüget, and Oorshak clans have specific sacred places. The clan members sanctify these places and regularly conduct offering rituals there. The Dongak of the Övür region regard the Teeli area as sacred. The ancestors of the Dongak clan lived there. Today this is part of Mongolia. That is why the Dongak cannot get to their sacred place. But if Dongaks drive near Teeli, it is essential that they sacrifice food by scattering it (NA 3).

The spirit masters of the powerful wilderness ensure a healthy balance in the natural environment. They compensate the exhaustion of settled areas with their own religious powers that are bound with the purity and untouched state of the wilderness. For this reason, Tyvans are anxious to protect certain areas from human use, partially even from human access. This includes a taboo on climbing certain mountains. Today's boom in alpine tourism, especially in western Tyva, has become a problem in this context, as it has in Russia's other Siberian republics (e.g. Halemba 2002, 2006).

A 54-year-old shaman from Ak Dovurak told in summer 2005 the following about nature and 'pure ground':

What we call nature (Russ. *priroda*) are mainly the wild animals, the forests, and the boggish springs. 'Pure ground' is all that is not town or village. The pure ground is more powerful than towns and villages. There are also spirit masters in towns, but the spirit masters of the pure ground are more powerful than those of the town. The former help human beings, they help them if people feed them (NA 6).

Many Tyvans want to take part in the religious powers of the wilderness. There are many possibilities to do so. First, for particular areas the Tyvans build *ovaalar* as ritual places where they can contact the spirit masters of these places and ask for their help to solve human problems. Second, humans can appropriate the power of the wilderness by hunting wild animals, collecting herbs, onions, or wild berries, and by eating them. A third possibility is the collection of stones for divination, which to be effective must be collected from 41 bodies of water or other sacred places far away from human settlements.

A 44-year-old interview partner, working as a social scientist in Kyzyl told on 21 July 2004 about divination:

> Tyvans love to foresee the future with [the oracle of] 41 small stones (Tyv. *khuvaanak*). In foreseeing with 41 stones, a result can be obtained with good thoughts and words. We perceive the stones to be powerful, alive, and full of wise thoughts. The powers of nature and the spirit masters of waters and places gave this power to our oracle stones. The purest stones, that never err, are collected from pure rivers in deserted areas that human beings never enter. We believe forests, rivers, waters, and lakes that are never entered by human beings are religiously pure and clean. We see these places as the most powerful places (OK 2).

Due to the religious power that is inherent in pure ground, humans who wander in the taiga are regarded as more powerful and healthy. They are permanently exposed to a higher but apparently compatible dose of power and energy in the wilderness. Townspeople and people living in villages lack these powers. In this way, Tyvans explain why townspeople become ill more often, look less healthy, seem more stressed, and are faced with many problems that nomads seem not to have. Lower fertility and child poverty in the cities are explained by the unbalanced energy level of townspeople, who participate less often in the powers of the wilderness. Health, fortune, and wealth are linked to a balance of religious powers. Many townspeople, therefore, make a point of trying to acquire the powers of the wilderness from time to time. They regularly obtain animals for slaughter from their relatives in the taiga. They buy milk products from their relatives, buy or collect wild berries, herbs and onions, and prepare jam and mixed herbs. Many townspeople try to visit their relatives in the villages of the taiga at least once a year. Many families regularly send their children to relatives in the yurts during school holidays to share in the everyday life of pastoral nomads and take part in the work of Tyvan stockbreeders. Apart from the economic interests connected with it, all these methods are instruments for acquiring the power of the wilderness and to stimulate health and quality of life.

Summary

The previous sections were dedicated to examples of different kinds of interaction in the collective network of human and non-human actors. The examples have been taken from Tyvan folk religion, reports of events and experiences (including contemporary legends), interviews, records of ritual texts, and contemporary folklore texts. To describe the multifaceted interactions between human and non-human subjects, I presented the emic perspective of my conversation partners. For more detailed examples, see Oelschlägel (2004a), which describes the Tyvan folk religion on the basis of my own research as well as published works of Tyvan and Russian ethnographers.

Tyvans attach great importance to the spirit masters, who are regarded as the principal interaction partners of human beings. The presence of these spirits in Tyvan thinking and interpretation is immediately clear to any outside visitor. All places with religious importance, where powerful spirit masters live, are decorated with fluttering coloured ribbons that catch the eye from a great distance. This tradition is based on the assumption that everything on earth is dominated by spirit masters, who are the real owners and protectors of everything that exists and who watch over how humans treat (Gmn. *behandeln*) the world. Not only the landscape, but also people's property such as the hearth fire, tools for daily use, livestock, yurts, and whole camping grounds fall under the spirit master's protection. Human health, wealth, and fortune are subject to their power. Tyvans also view all talents and skills as directly dependent on spirit masters. For this reason we can interpret all human actions as interactions between human and non-human subjects.

A central notion of the interaction model for many Tyvans is therefore the recognition of the spirit master's suzerainty over everything existing and the orientation of human actions towards their standards for its proper use. Connected to this principle are the regular and strict adherence to respectful interactions and the redress of mistakes and misapprehension. The latter concerns, for example, situations in which interactions have become unbalanced and people incurred the spirit master's wrath. Interactions are the obedience or violation of norms and rules set by spirit masters as well as the smaller and larger rituals of reconciliation, appeal, or gratitude that are carried out regularly.

Already because of the ambiguity of plural world interpretations, violations of the norms and rules of the interaction model are part of many Tyvans' daily life. They are in a permanent conflict, having to meet the standards of at least two mutually contradictory normative models of proper conduct. Beside the compliance of their religious duty to interact with spirits in a respectful way, Tyvans work in their environment in a purely pragmatic way. In doing so, most Tyvans usually ignore the spirit master's rights to co-determination. Everyday actions often occur only with pragmatic aims in mind. Driven by the desire for quick economic success, the environment becomes an instrument of human needs. Only after a misfortune occurs do many Tyvans pause in their day-to-day routine and remember that the interaction model has set norms. This model stipulates that all human interventions into nature need a spirit master's consent. Human beings can create and achieve nothing without first acquiring a spirit master's agreement and benevolence.

To follow specific rules of correct behaviour assures Tyvans of not alienating the spirit masters. Rituals of request and gratitude serve to achieve agreement with spirit masters about everything that people want to acquire or use for their own purposes. Contemporary legends especially provide examples of situations in which human misfortune and their breaches of the interaction model's norms are associated retrospectively. The regulating influence of the spirit masters returns to mind especially in cases of human suffering, and the need arises to correct an unbalanced interaction. Tyvans carry out these corrections in several steps. First, the events have to be interpreted according to the interaction model. If the persons involved suspect that failed interactions with non-human subjects are the cause of their misfortune, then they often invite religious specialists, like shamans or divination masters, to review and explain the situation. Then follows a ritual of reconciliation and the solemn promise to modify behaviour in the long run; this means a conscious decision to follow the rules and norms set by the spirit masters.

As punishment for incorrect behaviour, often evil spirits attack humans with illness and other evil. Only shamans and their partner spirits are capable of freeing human beings from these dastardly spirits.

With the help of their special skills, shamans are especially suitable for clearing up the causes of harm, defeating evil spirits, and reconciling other non-human subjects involved, like wrathful spirit masters. To this end a shaman gives advice and communicates the rules of proper behaviour that may prevent further damage.

From the examples given in the preceding sections, the following characteristic attributes can be derived:

Tyvans do not perceive themselves as the only intelligent beings or as masters of their universe. They are connected to non-human subjects in a network and constantly interact with them, both consciously and unconsciously. Human well-being depends on the success of these interactions. For this reason, Tyvans attach great importance to compliance with the rules and norms of the interaction model and a consciously respectful interaction with non-human subjects.

Considering the frequency of references to and interactions with the spirit masters, these can be considered the most important non-human interaction partners for human beings. As the real owners of all that exists, spirit masters watch over the world, provide norms and rules for human interaction with non-humans, ensure humans' abidance, and punish non-compliance.

All human activities can be seen as interactions between human beings and spirit masters. Positive aspects of these interactions include the acknowledgement of the spirit master's mastery over all existing parts of the world, the observance of standards, norms and rules prescribed by the spirit masters, rituals of gratitude, requests and reconciliations, different aspects of spiritual culture, and the utilisation of aptitudes and talents bestowed upon a person by the spirit masters. Every non-compliance with the norms and rules of the interaction model and the result thereof must be understood as a negative element in interaction between human beings and spirit masters.

With help of their narrative tradition, Tyvans keep alive the interaction model through their interpretations, behaviours, and actions. One of the most important narrative genres are 'true events'. Typical subjects of such contemporary legends are human failings in the respectful interaction between human and non-human subjects as demanded by the spirits and the resulting punishments, such as crises, illness, or death. Legends that inform about wondrous rewards by spirits to those who distinguish themselves in their handling of rules and norms as per the interaction model are also popular.

Human beings often only become aware of breaches of norms after a crisis occurs in their lives. To avert the consequences of such transgressions, Tyvans have to take several steps: (1) interpret the crisis retrospectively according to the interaction model; (2) invite a shaman to review the situation, find out which spirits were involved in what way, and give advice on how the problem may be solved; (3) conduct rituals of reconciliation (possibly under the direction of a shaman); and (4) promise to behave in a more respectful way with the non-human subjects.

Tyvans consider human talents as connected to the activities of the spirit masters as well. Talents are not inborn attributes and are not considered a form of distinction. Special talents – for the Tyvans – are obligations. In fact, the spirit master of specific talents select and oblige individuals bestowed with such talents to serve these talents by using them in the world of human beings. A person chosen by the spirit masters of a specific talent has to represent it in the human world, is obliged to practise and apply it with the best of his or her ability and not to hold it back, misuse it, or gain unfair advantages because of it. To do otherwise incurs punishment.

The interaction model ensures harmony, balance, and stability in the field of reciprocal dependencies between human and non-human subjects. If a Tyvan compromises this balance, he or she runs the risk of being punished by the spirits. The spirit masters will call forth a crisis. But spirits can also compromise the stability of respectful interactions. For example, attacks by evil spirits, who Tyvans regard as playful or vicious, are a constant source of danger for human beings.

The people see themselves as being permanently dependent on the goodwill of various spirits. But the existence and the well-being of the spirits is seen as depending on human behaviour and action as well. On the one hand, people depend on that which the spirit masters provide. On the other, if people apply incorrectly that which the spirits have given them or destroy it, this may have negative consequences for the spirit masters, and not only for the people. If people destroy the property of a spirit master, they destroy the spirit master as well. The incorrect handling of a spirit master's property may rob the master of its power; neglecting to use a bestowed talent or forgetting bestowed knowledge about its proper practice may cause the spirit master of the talent to disappear.

Shamans endowed with powers by the spirit masters find their function within the interaction model. They are intermediaries between human and non-human subjects. With the help of their partner spirits, they clarify situations that endanger interaction. When interactions become unbalanced, they help to return them to a state of stability and harmony. In so doing, shamans are obliged to reconcile people with spirit masters and to fight against several kinds of evil spirit. They conduct rituals of reconciliation, appeal, and gratitude. Furthermore, they act as advisers and remind people of the correct path in the respectful interaction with non-human subjects.

Thus all aspects of all human and non-human subjects in the Tyvan world are interconnected and interdependent.

Local Economy

Plate 63. Stocks of sheep and goats are a source of wealth for all pastoral nomads (Süt Khöl, 2004).

Plate 64. 'Two Larches' near Mugur Aksy (2004).

Plates 65-66. The five species of Tyvan stock animals include sheep, goats, yaks, camels, and horses.

Plate 67. Girl milking goats (Süt Khöl, 2004).

Plate 68. In the summer, women and girls milk the yaks in the morning and in the evening (Toolajlyg, 2005).

Plate 69. Yaks grazing above a yurt (Toolajlyg, 2005).

Plate 70. Yaks carry the yurts and the equipment of the pastoral nomads through the taiga in the most western parts of the Republic of Tyva (Toolajlyg, 2005).

Plates 71-74. Tyvans especially keep horses as mounts (71, 73: Bij Khem, 1997; 72: Toolajlyg, 2005; 74: Kyzyl, 1995).

Plate 75. Bactrian camels are found in northern, central, and southern Tyva (Kyzyl, 2005).

Plate 76. A herd of camels in Ėrzin (2005).

Plate 77. A herd of camels in Ulug Khem (2004).

Plate 78. Cows often complement the five species of stock animals in Tyva (Baj Tajga, 2005).

Plate 79. Comparatively rare is for Tyvan herders to keep pigs (Kyzyl, 1995).

Plates 80-81. In the north-east of the Republic, nomadic Tozhu-Tyvans keep reindeer (2004).

Plate 82. One of the most important events in the annual economic cycle is the castration celebration. The boys catch the animals while a veterinarian castrates the young animals born that spring (Ulug Khem, 2004).

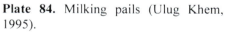

Plate 83. Tyvan women spend most of their time processing milk into several milk products (Kyzyl, 1995).

Plate 84. Milking pails (Ulug Khem, 1995).

Plates 85-86. Tyvan housewives boil the fresh milk, filter it with a scarf, and skim it using a centrifuge (1995).

Plate 87. The women ferment the skimmed milk to produce *khojtpak* (Ulug Khem, 1995).

Plate 88. Cheese is produced from whey and fresh milk (Ulug Khem, 1995).

Plate 89. Goats like to nibble from the drying curds (Bij Khem, 1997).

Plates 90-92. To produce flour, Tyvan women separate the grain from the chaff, roast it, and grind it with the help of a stone mill (Baj Tajga, 1997).

Plate 93. Some old hunters still produce their ammunition themselves. They fill the rounds with home-cast lead shot and gun powder (Ulug Khem, 1995).

Plate 94. To lure deer and maral in the autumn, hunters imitate their rutting calls. The instrument shown here consists of several rolled and drawn film negatives. Originally such instruments consisted of a band made from birchbark (Ulug Khem, 1995).

Plates 95-96. Hunting includes storytelling and making music to entertain the spirits of the taiga in the evening. The first part of the hunter's tea and food are offered as sacrifices (Ulug Khem, 1995).

Plate 97. A hunter's knife (Ulug Khem, 2004).

Plates 98-99. The 'Great Hunter' on horseback, and his son at the entrance of a bear's cave with the bear's winter feed (Ulug Khem, 1995).

Plate 100. A stream serves as a nomad's refrigerator (Ulug Khem, 1995).

Plate 101. A slaughtered sheep inside a yurt (Möŋgün Taiga, 2004).

Plate 102. The Ulug Khem (Yenisei River) is both thoroughfare and provider of fish (Ulug Khem, 2004).

Plate 103. The 'Great Hunter' with two of his trophies (Ulug Khem, 1995).

Plate 104. Russians love hunting just as much as Tyvans (Bij Khem, 1997).

Part III
Tyvan Plural World Interpretations

> The Kombinat Tuvaasbest in Ak Dovurak is said to be one of the largest open pit asbestos mines in the world. Half the mine is no longer operating and of the 3,000 people who used to work there only 600 now have a job. We asked the ones we met about the risks of asbestos poisoning. They smiled and said they had heard it was dangerous but quickly added that they felt fine and, besides, at least they had a job.[70]

Asbestos and shrinking employment opportunities are a daily reality in the life of Tyvans living in the town of Ak Dovurak (White Powder). Most of Ak Dovurak's inhabitants have been or are now afflicted with asbestos poisoning. One of them, a 54-year-old shaman, explained to me why traditional Tyvan boots have upturned points. The design of these boots, he said, ensures mother earth does not get hurt when one walks. If she were to become angry, she might punish people (see Oelschlägel 2004a, 2004b). The Tyvans of Ak Dovurak seem no less familiar with the interaction model than Tyvans living in other parts of the Republic of Tyva. However, like the above-cited shaman, they have reconciled themselves to living next to an open mine and mining dump. The Tyvan inhabitants of Ak Dovurak are no less religious than those encountered in the previous part, but they also live in permanent contradiction to the model of respectful interaction between human and non-human subjects that is characteristic for the many Tyvans I interviewed. Many Tyvans – even if they believe in spirits (animism) – do not always observe the rules prescribed by the Tyvan interaction model. I observed men who crossed rivers with jeeps, but bowed their heads at sacred springs. I have seen makeshift roads in the steppes that in places are 80 metres or more wide traversed by drivers who made libations with milk tea or vodka for their cars in order to safeguard them and their passengers from

---

[70] Cited on http://www.fetchaphrase.com/russia/tuva/asbestos/asbestos01.html (last accessed 22 September 2014).

danger. Also typical are women who offer the first part of the morning milk tea to the spirit masters of the camp and of the landscape around it, but simply throw the garbage behind the yurt in the evening. What all of them have in common is a flexible handling of both contradictory models of world interpretation presented in this book.

The present book's main goal is to present two mutually contradictory models of world interpretation that are flexibly applied in everyday life: the dominance model and the interaction model. In Part II, the interaction model was described as an alternative to a dominance model in Tyvan society that was strongly influenced by its Sovietisation. At first glance, the two models seem to exclude, ignore, or even oppose one another. However, both exist parallel in many Tyvans' thinking and action and both are believed to be equally true or correct. They are applied alternately, either in inclination or in their extreme forms. In everyday practice they can be replaced, complemented, or mixed as a specific argument requires: While their replacement correlates with the switching from one form of world interpretation to the other, the complementing and the mixing of both models of world interpretation show the transdifferent space between the two extreme forms. The complementing and mixing of both types of world interpretation correlate in a visual sense with a situational and contextual repositioning on the continuum of transdifference between both extreme forms. In so doing, one person at certain moments tends more to the one extreme and in another context more to the other extreme. Here I will therefore analyse how individuals make use of both models in various situations in order to interpret an event or experience, to act in a specific situation, or to communicate about the experience.

Tyvans' reflections on events, their reactions to them, and their actions and behaviours are inconsistent. We need to consider these contradictions to be able to give a realistic description of Tyvan world interpretations. These contradictions in particular present clear insights into the (current) situation of folk religion and linked to it the variety of models of world interpretation. They are worth being examined and should not to be ignored or excluded. They show us how people can explain and shape their everyday life in multifaceted ways. In addition, an analysis of these events and their management by individual people shows us the advantages, disadvantages and limitations of each model.

In the second stage of my fieldwork (May to October 2005), I thus focused on the following questions: What attributes characterise the two models of world interpretation, the dominance and the interaction model? Which model of world interpretation do Tyvans prefer in which situation? How does the switching between different models of world interpretation come about? Under what conditions do Tyvans switch between different models of world interpretation? In which direction does switching take place more often and can therefore be considered as typical? What are the reasons and consequences for such switching between different models of world interpretation? And, what are the consequences of the implementation of each model of world interpretation?

These new questions require a change in perspective. I will shift in the following section from the emic perspective, and pursue events among the Tyvans from the etic point of view.

Two Models of World Interpretation and their Parallel Existence

The self-representations of many Tyvans suggest that they follow only one model of world interpretation. It is a matter of following either modernity *or* tradition. In Part I, 'The Theory of Plural World Interpretations', I called a type of world interpretation, to which a Tyvan exclusively adheres, the narratively idealised pure form. This form is connected to the representation of the preferred model as an ideal that a Tyvan feels obliged to follow in order to interpret human existence in the world, and to align his or her actions and behaviours. Such idealised pure forms are narratively purified from the contents of other models and often are opposed to other models of world interpretation as if they are the only true model.

In adhering to a particular narratively idealised pure form, Tyvans create an ideal state. Many Tyvans interpret events or circumstances according to such a pure form especially during interviews. By contrast, observations of contradictions between the ideal state and Tyvan reality reveal the factual state of plural world interpretations. As a social anthropologist, my presence provoked the performance of a narratively idealised adherence to the interaction model (to Tyvan tradition). That is why this model seems to be the ideal state preferred by many Tyvans. It is thus the founding model of generally accepted codified norms (oral or written norms) as well as social norms (social expectations about the behaviour of individuals) that, however, do not necessarily correspond with empirically observable behaviour in Tyvan practice. When I called a Tyvan person's attention to the fact that she did not always abide by the norms and rules of the model she had said she followed, she either reacted with a circuitous explanation leading back to this ideal or debunked the antagonism as 'false' behaviour, informing me of the spirits' punishments for people who act contrary to the spirits' intentions.

Since perestroika, the return to so-called traditional values has led to a change of preferences relating to interpretations of the world. Whereas during socialism, the politically accepted ideal state was exclusively geared to the Soviet dominance model, since the 1990s the interaction model has come again to the fore. This observation led to the insight that for many Tyvans today, the interaction model is again seen as the ideal state of Tyvan culture. This interpretation is underlined by the fact that many of my research partners adhered immediately and clearly to the interaction model. My interest as a social anthropologist in this subject and my questions about it led to statements by many Tyvans that correspond to their ideals. My research partners told me only about those elements of their thinking and action that they wanted to be retained in my work. They drew for themselves an amiable self-portrait.

However, my observations led to the insight that Tyvan world interpretations are multifaceted. Especially because the so-called modern worldview takes up an important position in Tyvan world interpretation, the latter is stamped by contradictions that express themselves mainly in Tyvan action and thus in spontaneous reactions and successive explanations. Especially data that refer to observations rather than to interviews show the factual state (or practice) of dealing with world interpretations, which differs remarkably from the ideal statements of many Tyvans. The interpretation of the world as a field of interaction between human and non-human subjects is possibly older, but it is more likely that there was never a world interpretation based exclusively on this kind of thinking.

In any case, today the interaction model only exists alongside the dominance model. Life in Tyva cannot be imagined without the dominance model. Therefore we have to consider it in an account that aims to be as complete as possible.

The factual state, that is, observable practice, consists of permanent switching between the interaction and dominance models as well as a mixing of both models. The human dominance over nature, for example, is often ignored in the anthropological quest for the typical or 'original' Tyvan way of thinking (i.e. tradition). But a dominance model of world interpretation must be accepted also as part of Tyvan culture, and its presence can probably not be attributed solely to Soviet or Western influences. I want to open my analysis with the following example, which exemplifies the parallel existence of and the possibility of mixing both models. The Tyvans of the Möngün Taiga District complained again and again about the theft of stock animals. They laid responsibility for the theft on the nomads of the Baj Taiga District. But in Baj Taiga, in turn, the nomads told me that bandits from Möngün Taiga regularly invaded their region by crossing the mountain pass, and abducted whole herds of animals.

That people steal livestock is an unpleasant fact in Tyva. It opposes another fact of Tyvan culture, namely that the spirit masters have authority over all human property. Theft is seen as a breach of the interaction model's norms. As such, it is punishable by the spirit masters. Nevertheless, most Tyvans do not wait for the spirit masters to take revenge. If thieves drive livestock away, the cattle owners feel that their property rights have been violated – in accordance to the dominance model – and gather their neighbours and friends to pursue the perpetrators.

The apparent contradiction in this example can be resolved by assuming that both world interpretations are simultaneously applied. It thus becomes apparent that many Tyvans think in two directions about their property.

On the one hand, all human property, including all articles of daily use that people make themselves, belongs to specific spirit masters. In its possessive form *eezi*, the term used for spirit master literally means 'master of something' or 'its master'. From the perspective of the interaction model, humans are only second-rank owners. In the hierarchy of all the parts of the world, humans rank lower than the spirit masters. Humans follow the spirit masters in second position. Finally, in the third position, all animals, plants, and other parts of the human environment can be found. The latter can be understood as an accumulation of subjects with which humans interact. The world is a complicated network of interaction partners that act on each other.

On the other hand, humans have property at their disposal that they can use for their own purposes and defend against attacks or encroachment. Humans do this because they consider their possessions to be their property which they have procured and on which they depend. In urban settings, Tyvans fear burglaries and thefts to such an extent that they secure their apartments with steel doors. By contrast, the doors of yurts are always open. Tyvan nomads have nothing to fear apart from the theft of their livestock. Human property in the dominance model is characterised by human supremacy over everything that they possess. From this perspective, property is seen as something that is available to human beings at their command. Property is made, kept, augmented, secured, tended, and used by humans. In this way, humans dominate their property as more or less passive objects of human agency.

But Tyvans are not always certain which interpretation model should be followed regarding their property, as in the following case observed in 2004.

One evening, a family of stockbreeders found out that rustlers had driven a part of their stock away. As the situation became clear and the commotion had settled, the owners asked a master of divination to conduct an oracle with 41 stones. The people involved explained to me that they wanted to find out if they would be able to catch up with the thieves and get their cattle back. If the oracle answered in the negative, they said, then they would not chase the rustlers.

The oracle did respond negatively, but after a discussion, the men nevertheless decided to search for the cattle. However, the result of the oracle had influenced their mood. The men had lost faith. After a few hours they returned to the camp and justified their abandoning the chase with the result of the oracle.

The pursuers had justified their search with the result of the oracle, but also used it as a loophole out of a predicament. This observation can be augmented by data from other similar cases I recorded in 2004 and 2005. Cattle theft is usually undertaken by groups of armed and bellicose young men who are often not professional rustlers. Nevertheless, they plan every 'campaign' in detail and are prepared to use force. It is therefore possible that the chasers feared a violent conflict and abandoned the chase because they were not well prepared and were only a small group. Thus they decided to call the police and put their faith in the wrath of the spirit masters. From this perspective, the reference to the negative result of the oracle was a pretence allowing the chasers to save face and conceal their fear of further violence.

This example shows how my research partners used both models complementarily, seemingly without being aware of it. First, the Tyvans involved became aware the theft. Following the dominance model, they interpreted the situation as the action of thieves on their property. Then they divined the spirit masters of their environment about their chances for a successful chase. This indicates a clear interaction between stockbreeders and spirit masters because Tyvans generally believe that spirit masters can appraise the situation better than they themselves (Oelschlägel 2004a: 100f, 117ff.). The people involved were clearly of two minds as to whether they should claim their rights as property owners, chase the thieves, and recapture the cattle (dominance model), or follow the spirit masters, who advised against a chase (interaction model). The chase, in turn, could very well result in a dangerous fight with possibly heavily armed thieves. The stockbreeders then decided to chase the thieves (dominance model), but soon desisted. The chasers' quick discouragement seems to have been influenced by both the negative result of the oracle (interaction model) and the objective dangers to which they were exposing themselves. Their response to their predicament turned out to be a complementary application of both interpretation models.

Both interpretation models exist in parallel and they are applied complementarily in appraising a situation and reacting to it without regard to any etic contradictions. How this mixing of both models or shifting from the one model to the other in daily practice takes place will be detailed in the following sections.

The Conflict between These Models in their Extreme Forms

Tyvans articulate the conflict between both models of world interpretation particularly in relation to the Soviet period. This era was characterised among other things by the persecution of actively practising shamans who legitimated their professional activities with the interaction model. How Tyvans themselves remember, reflect on, and talk about this era can be seen in the following true occurrence I recorded in Kyzyl on 23 July 2004. The story, 'The Shaman and the Snake', was told by a female folklore scholar, aged 43 and living in Kyzyl, about her grandfather, who was a shaman:

> I had a grandfather. People called the old man, who was a great shaman, Shagar-Shaman. He was one of the greatest shamans of Övür District. He died when he was 70 years old. The communists abused the old man again and again with the words 'you shaman'. My grandfather himself kept it a secret that he practised shamanism. Once, the chief of police put him in prison. The old man then said to him: 'Release me, my son, I cannot sit in prison!' But the chief paid no attention to him and he remained in jail. The old man became angry and said: 'I am going to show you. I will send my terrible snake.' The chief of police only laughed.
>
> At night, when the chief of police was sleeping, he put his hand under his pillow. He suddenly felt something moving. He stood up and looked at what it was. It was a snake. The chief of police was so scared that he immediately went to the police station to free Shagar-Shaman. In Khandagajty, where this happened, snakes are very rare. Actually, people say they do not exist there. That is why the situation was clear [to the chief of police], when he found the snake under his pillow. People talked a long time about Shagar-Shaman's snake. I heard this story from my mother (SCHA 9).

This is but one account of the persecution that shamans experienced in the period between Tyva's incorporation into the Soviet Union in 1944 and the latter's dissolution. During this time, even the ownership of shamanistic utensils could lead to severe punishments. Shamans therefore either abstained from conducting séances at all or – if this was impossible for health reasons[71] – worked without shamanic dress, drums, or other devotional items. They kept their activities secret. In Russian, the term

---

[71] Shamans are obliged by their partner spirits to conduct rituals. If they refrain from doing so, they risk punishment by the spirits, such as disease or death.

'shaman' (*shaman*) was used as an expletive by the communists. Nevertheless, the story also shows that Tyvan opinions about shamans were not consistent: we can find much sympathy for them in memories of the Soviet period.

The allegorical and humorous story is not only about a conflict between the chief of police and a shaman, but also about the conflict between two models of world interpretation in the era of the Socialist Republic of Tyva. During this period, the communist version of the dominance model was in conflict with the Tyvan animistic-shamanistic version of the interaction model. The Soviet ban on shamanism refers first of all to the dominance model. Using the example of the shaman's imprisonment, the story confronts the Soviet dominance model with the traditional Tyvan interaction model. The chief's laughter about the shaman's threat shows that he does not believe in the shaman's power and therefore not in the interaction model. But the shaman's threat comes true. The shaman provides evidence of his power and of his relation to non-human subjects. He convinces the policeman of the interaction model's truth. The shaman maintains his world interpretation while the policeman has to change his. By believing in the shaman's power he accepts the interaction model. That is why he frees the shaman. The switch between both models occurs because of the policeman's fear at finding the snake under his pillow, an incident that convinces him of the shaman's extraordinary abilities, and therefore of the interaction model's truth.

When this story is re-told, the listener is invited to come to the same conclusion as the chief of police: the interaction model must be true if the shaman can conjure the placement of a snake under the police chief's pillow. These reports of events and contemporary legends function to convince the hearer of the interaction model's importance for humanity. Narrating examples maintain faith in the interaction model and intensify people's discussions about their rights and duties in the interaction model.

The example refers to the time before perestroika. The Soviets propagated a pure dominance model. Staunch communists advanced a model of world interpretation that tolerated no 'supernatural' phenomena, that is anything that could not be explained rationally. Thus, the shaman's activities and his role as mediator between the world of the spirits and that of human beings was to become obsolete. If spirits did not exist to co-determine the fate of humans, then communication and interaction with them was no longer necessary. In the communist form of the dominance model, the Soviets not only denied the Tyvan shamans their power, but also accused them of being liars and frauds. Staunch communists accused shamans of simulating the existence of intelligent non-human beings to their clients and of creating a universe of faked interdependencies between the world of spirits and that of humans in their dramatic performances. They accused shamans of capitalising on people's gullibility to accumulate power, enrich themselves, and in so doing, hinder the eagerly awaited progress towards a righteous world. Religion was an illusion for the unjustified accumulation of power and wealth of individuals, or, as Karl Marx had described it, 'opium' for the people. Religion was a conscious deception that served to conserve and legitimate existing power relations.

While in the communist dominance model, the human rises above all supernatural phenomena, the interaction model rests on the possibility of the existence of things that are beyond human control. To this day, efficacy, intelligence, consciousness, rationality, and willpower are ascribed to non-human subjects. Humans experience again and again unforeseeable events in the network of interactions. To be happy, successful, healthy, and productive, humans – following the interaction model – are forced to consciously make contact with the non-human subjects of the earthly world, to win them over, or to at least be considerate of them. Humans need repeatedly to negotiate the conditions of their life with non-humans. In more difficult cases, shamans are called upon to communicate with the spirits and find safe forms of interaction and translate their findings for religious laypeople.

The two forms of world interpretation presented here are fundamentally contradictory. Still, the initially unbelieving policeman from this story found his way (back) from the extreme of the communist dominance model to the animistic-shamanistic interaction model. The switch was triggered by the appearance of a snake, announced by the shaman. Because of the 'unexplainable snake' under the policeman's pillow, the shaman and his form of world interpretation again became credible, which is why the chief of police felt impelled to correct his interpretation of the world.

The existence of two models of interpretation offers Tyvans the possibility to understand and explain and react to an event in two ways. Both models are so contradictory that their mixing can cause irritations on the level of rationality. Sometimes they appear as two sides of a coin that we cannot see at the same time. It is difficult to imagine approaching simultaneously one and the same phenomenon from the perspective of both forms of world interpretation. If we view the world from the perspective of one of them then – it seems – we automatically blend out the other. That is why the dominance and the interaction model in some cases appear as absolute and pure. I could observe both models in their pure form mainly during conversations about the 'traditional Tyvan worldview'. In such conversations, Tyvans tried to explain the interaction model unaltered and free from influences of the dominance model. Sometimes a Tyvan initially explained an event from the perspective of one model, afterwards adding how it could also be seen from the viewpoint of the other model.

Internal conflicts are also often connected to the choice of one interpretation, for example if the commitment to one model is seen as ideological. In the following example, a man initially told his wife about an experience he had had in accordance with the interaction model, but later he revised his initial interpretations, which he associated with superstition, and offered an interpretation that followed the dominance mode. He only allowed his wife to tell me about his encounter in the mode of the interaction model after I agreed not to mention his name. Seeing himself as an 'enlightened atheist', he did not want to be associated with the interaction model.

The following story was told on 4 October 2004 by a female interview partner, aged 27, working as a systems administrator in Mugur Aksy:

> Two or three years ago my husband travelled from Mugur Aksy to Kyzyl. With a friend he drove through Adar Tösh. However, an *aza* lives there. An old man on the side of the road tried to stop them. It was dark, and my husband was tired and irritable. That is why he did not stop. His companion was sleeping on the back seat. After a little while, about one kilometre down the road, the old man who had wanted to stop the car was suddenly sitting beside my husband. He looked just like the man on the road. My husband drove on. When he looked a second time, the old man had disappeared. Upon arriving in Shagonar, he woke up his companion and told him about the old man. Then they ritually cleansed the car with juniper. But the car broke down. They did not have to go far, but because of the damage to their car they needed a long time to arrive at their destination (AZ 6).

In her telling of the event, the storyteller associated the breakdown of the car with the old man, whom she identified as an *aza*. In contrast, by the time I was told of the event, the woman's husband believed that it could have been a simple breakdown. He now assumed that he had seen the hitchhiker sitting beside him in the car because he had been tired and irritable. These interpretations of the event contrast both models of world interpretations. Whereas the explanation of the driver's wife was founded on the interaction model, her husband explained the event by drawing on the dominance model.

The driver's wife saw in the event an interaction between the driver, his companion, an *aza*, and the car. The *aza* tried to stop the travellers, but the driver drove on. Suddenly, the *aza* sat beside the driver in the passenger seat and finally the car broke down, which she interpreted as damage caused by the *aza*. The travellers ritually cleaned the car with juniper to eliminate the negative influence of the evil spirit. Since this blessing came too late to prevent the damage, they were delayed on their journey. Human and non-human subjects both influence the event. And as it turned out that the *aza*, as an intelligent and active subject, had more influence on the situation than the people involved.

The storyteller's husband knew how to interpret the situation based on the interaction model, but refused to believe in the existence of intelligent non-human interaction partners. Hence he preferred to base his interpretation on the dominance model and limited his analysis of the event to the empirical breakdown. Interpreting the old man in the car as a hallucination caused by his own tiredness and irritation, he reasoned that the misfortune of a broken car can happen to anyone and had nothing to do with the actions of spirits.

The example shows how – in the terms of many Tyvans – the dominance and the interaction models appear in very clearly polarised forms, that is, in a narratively idealised pure form. How Tyvans talk among themselves, their behaviour, and their actions are indicative of the wide domain of 'transdifference' (Breinig and Lösch 2002). In passing the borders between different models of world interpretation and by changing positions in the continuum between the interaction and dominance models, my Tyvan research partners sometimes tended to the first model, at other times to the second. Whereas replacement and alternation are in accordance with an oscillation from one extreme to the other, complementing and mixing shows the transdifferent space between the extremes and the constant situational positioning of many Tyvans along the transdifference continuum.

The seeming incompatibility of both interpretation models becomes apparent mainly from the Tyvan emic perspective. Today, Tyvans often propagate the 'traditional worldview' (i.e. interaction model) as an ideal state and refute actions following the dominance model as being 'false'. Perhaps for this reason, scholars incorrectly identify the dominance model with Russian or modern influences while connecting the interaction model with authentic Tyvan action and behaviour. As argued in Part I, both models exist in their specifically Tyvan modes and are older than the Soviet Union's annexation of Tannu Tuva in 1944.

The allocation of labels like 'right' and 'wrong' also explains why many Tyvans consequently opted for one kind of world explanation and stood by that choice during all my conversations with them. Many Tyvans wanted to explain 'correct' behaviour to me. If I pointed out to them that the religious norms reported by them were not commonly adhered to, they repeatedly mentioned the reprimands that those who break the rules can expect.

The following story about spirit masters was told to me by a 54-year-old shaman living in Ak Dovurak. I recorded the text on 5 October 2004 in Mugur Aksy:

> Shaman: If you meet a spirit master, you should not be afraid. You should remain calm and be quiet in its proximity. If you do not want to anger the spirit master, then you should not drink alcohol, throw away any garbage, or destroy anything. The spirit master will then do no harm to humans.
> A.C.Oe.: What happens when you do not comply with this advice?
> Shaman: If a spirit master becomes angry because a person behaves badly, he can take that person's life in short order (HG 40).

The following example is the answer of a research partner who explained to me what happens with those who break the spirit masters' rules. According to some shamans, the consumption of alcohol constitutes a breach of these rules. Alcoholism is widely spread in Tyva.

A 58-year-old research partner, working as a teacher of chemistry and biology in Mugur Aksy, told me about alcohol and bad spirits on 9 October 2004: '*Albys* and *shulbus* can be found in the company of people who drink much alcohol. Finally, the *diireng* also take hold of them. A person who staggers or attacks others has an *aza*, a *chetker*, or a *diireng* (with him). Such people are very dangerous to others. They are capable of killing or striking another person. For this reason it is good to keep your distance from people who are drunk' (ÜG 3).

Drunkenness is here allegorised as a pact with evil spirits. All beings mentioned are spirits which higher beings or shamans can send to humans as punishment or who attack people by their own free will. They are the carriers of illness and other evils.

I argue that the consequent adherence to one perspective is related to many Tyvans' desire not to lose their credibility. To them it is impossible to argue, in serious conversation, that they are in permanent interaction with spirits and live their lives in accordance with the will of non-human subjects, while at the same time they propagate their own freedom of choice.

The Spontaneous Switch and its Most Common Trajectory

Numerous observations during my fieldwork showed consistently that a spontaneous reaction (action or statement) to an event usually followed the dominance model while later reflection on the same event and the accompanying behaviour often tended towards the interaction model. One form of world interpretation can be completely substituted or complemented by the other form or mixed with it. The following example, taken from the funeral previously described in Part II, illustrates this well.

In summer 2004, my fieldpartners and I transported the coffin of a deceased woman in a convoy of relatives and acquaintances from Kyzyl to her native village. The journey took about ten hours, mainly through the night. We started in the late afternoon and stopped repeatedly to drink vodka and conduct brief rituals at several *ovaalar* along the road. In the night, the vehicle with the coffin went off the road and began to slip down the slope toward a stream. Because the slope was steep, the men had a lot of trouble pulling the car onto the road again.

The deceased's daughters and I were in the first car behind the hearse. When we stopped and asked about the disruption, the people explained to us that the driver of the hearse had fallen asleep due to fatigue and alcohol. That was why he went off the road.

The next day, in the house of the deceased, her daughters and other guests looked back on the incident. For no apparent reason, the line of argumentation had changed, centring on the time that the hearse had gone off the road – at about half past three o'clock in the morning. The time between three and five o'clock is the most active period for spirits. That is why it is dangerous to leave the house at that time, something Tyvans usually avoid. Suddenly, it became clear to the daughters and the other guests that the deceased herself had intervened in the event and voiced her dissatisfaction. For awhile, they reflected on the situation and finally came to the conclusion that the deceased wanted to remind them that her sacrificial table should be supplied with enough food and a candle, so that she would not go hungry and so that she would have a light during her difficult trip to the other world. Her relatives had thus far withheld both from her. They had planned to prepare the sacrificial table only after their arrival in her home village several days after her death.

Thus, the accident that had initially been explained as caused by the driver and the condition of the road had acquired after some consideration a new interpretation derived from the ideal state of the interaction model. An event that first was seen as an accident that could be explained rationally was suddenly perceived as determined by the deceased and explained as her doing. The interpretation shifted from being based on the actions of the driver, who was no longer in control of the situation due to drunkenness and fatigue, to an interaction between the deceased and her relatives. When the coffin was transported to the home village of the deceased by her relatives, her soul stepped in during the 'time of the spirits' to remind them of her right to offerings, as demanded by Tyvan tradition. The bereaved got the message and provided her soul with an appropriately lavish sacrificial table. A spontaneous explanation from the perspective of the dominance model was followed by subsequent reflection from the perspective of the interaction model. The bereaved discussed the deceased's impact on the event, interpreted it, and responded to it with concrete action. Because there was no need for changing the interpretation, from an outsider's perspective we can assume that in this case a spontaneous switch took place from one model to another, namely from the dominance to the interaction model.

The pattern of interpretation with which Tyvans perceive negative events afterwards as punishment meted out by a spirit or a warning against inappropriate behaviour can be found in many contemporary legends and reports of events. One example will illustrate this. Three sisters had the following to say about spirit masters in the Möngün Taiga.

The eldest sister was a physician, aged 34 and living in Moscow; the middle one was a merchant, aged 30 and living in Kyzyl; the youngest was a 27-year-old systems administrator living in Mugur Aksy. I recorded this text on 24 August 2004 in Mugur Aksy: 'Masters of places can transform themselves into wild animals. Such animals have some kind of particularity. When a hunter kills such an animal, he or his relatives will fare badly. Our old uncle was a passionate hunter. That is why he lost his sons. People say that he angered the master of the taiga because he hunted so much' (HG 12).

Such narratives entail reflections and interpretations of events or occurrences. They address incidents in the lives of relatives or acquaintances and interpret them subsequently according to the interaction model. These interpretations occur in connection with a switch from the dominance model to the interaction model. In such cases, the chance that a switch from the dominance to the interaction model occurs increases in correspondence with the intensity with which a Tyvan experienced an event (e.g. how shocking the experience was) and with the distance in the past with which the event took place. Many Tyvans begin to think about the spirits' actions when it is too late (i.e. when the damage has already been done). Only then will they undertake – with the help of a shaman or a lama – conscious interactions with the spirits concerned to appease them, mend the damage, and turn fate around.

The subsequent interpretation of an event as a punishment for preceding misbehaviour can be found quite often, both in rural and in urban contexts. The following example again shows the most common direction of the switch between the models of interpretation. At first a spontaneous reaction according to the dominance model takes place to be followed by a subsequent explanation in terms of the interaction model. Even shamans are susceptible to this kind of switching between models. Just like laypeople, they often spontaneously apply the dominance model, even if we could assume that shamans – because of their professional association with the interaction model – are the ideal representatives of the interaction model. Since even shamans cannot abstain from the dominance model, I would argue that in fact an interaction model completely independent from a dominance model never existed.

In July 2004 I was fortunate to be invited, together with two other foreigners, to accompany a well-known shamaness of Tyva, her younger sister and her two younger brothers (all of whom also work as shamans) on a journey to their homeland. The reason for their trip was religious. Tyvan shamans regularly travel to their homeland to renew their contacts with the spirits residing there, and to recharge their powers in the wilderness – in this case, in the taiga. The wilderness far away from human settlement is considered full of energy. That is why it is important for Tyvan shamans to partake in nature's energy and renew their powers at least once a year. In addition, most shamans feel indebted to the spirits of their homeland by whom they were usually called to become a shaman and find it important to maintain professional interactions with them. Finally, the spirits want to be attended, otherwise they might withdraw the power and skills from the shamans who do not care for them.

For the journey, the four shamans borrowed two jeeps from friends. During our trip one of the jeeps broke down. All persons involved, including the four shaman siblings, interpreted the breakdown as due to the age of the vehicle. Some parts of the engine were worn out. The rough tracks we used through the muddy taiga, across rivers, and in the woods were a strain on the vehicles. The persons involved reacted to the situation by trying to repair the car. It was a spontaneous and rational reaction to a problem and an attempt to solve it in accordance with the model of human dominance. All persons involved saw how they were driving, the condition of the jeep, and the rough tracks as the cause of the problem, and sought the solution in the repair of the vehicle.

During the repairs, the oldest of the four shaman siblings suggested in addition to conduct a ritual for those spirits that might have an influence on the condition of the vehicle, and thus ensure a further problem-free journey. However, because the men were busy repairing the car, because it was getting late, and because it was still a long way to our accommodation, the siblings abandoned this plan and instead hurried to get the repairs done. Unfortunately, they failed to succeed. With the coming twilight, one of the men went on foot to the next camp of yurts and returned with one of the villagers and another jeep. The men solved our problem by towing the broken car to the camp. There they needed several days to find the spare parts and temporarily repair the car so that we could use it to return to Kyzyl.

I accompanied the shamans for ten days before the other two foreigners and I returned to Kyzyl on our own. Two months later I met the oldest sister of the shaman siblings again, and asked her how they had fared with the broken jeep. She told me the following: 'After our trip to the taiga both jeeps were badly damaged and their owners demanded large sums of money.' I then offered to contribute some money, but she did not accept it, saying: 'What would the spirits say, if I would allow you to pay my bills?'

The shamaness associated the broken cars and their owners' demands with the fact that they had taken us foreigners along on their journey and that they had revealed to us their secrets. The spirits had revealed the secrets of shaman practice to them for the sole reason that they cooperate with the spirits, not to divulge the secrets to others. We were not shamans and had no intention of becoming so. Therefore our interviews amounted to a breach of trust towards the spirits of the shaman siblings. During our conversation the shamaness showed remorse about this mistake. She told me that she had thus been punished by her spirits, among others, in the form of the financial reparations.

The shamaness explained further that she had neither succeeded in contacting the spirits as intensively as had been necessary, nor had she accumulated enough power in the wilderness. The spirits had abandoned her for a long time because we foreigners had disturbed them and because she – as a guardian of the knowledge about spirits – had been too frank with us. She said she would never again undertake such a professional journey in the company of nosy foreigners, not even if they were scholars.

When I asked her how she was going to pay for the damages, she explained that she had not repeated her mistake. She had not spoken to any foreigner about her business as a shaman since our trip and she had conducted several reconciliation rituals. Her partner spirits had shown themselves willing to help her again, so that she could earn the money she needed in the shamanic clinic Adyg Eeren (Bear Spirit). Her business went well, she had many clients and at the time, she was the most demanded and expensive shamaness in the clinic. She ascribed her recent success to the fact that she had realised her mistakes and that the spirits had regained confidence in her.

The initial situation and the purpose of the journey of the four shaman siblings had been conditioned by the interaction model and were based on their contract with their homeland spirits. The planned contact with the spirits and the recharging of spiritual powers served – in the framework of the interaction model – their function and work as shamans.

However, after one of the cars had broken down, the interaction model became initially irrelevant. The men tried to solve the problem in a rational way by trying to repair the broken car. The suggestion of the oldest shaman sister to conduct a small ritual suitable to the interaction model was overruled. At this stage the interpretation of the situation as well as their actions were conditioned by the dominance model.

Later, in a stage of reflection, the eldest of the shaman siblings had modified her interpretation of the events. Her report, two months after the event, attested to the value of the interaction model that now influenced her interpretation as well as her further actions and behaviour.

She identified her own mistakes as the cause of the damaged jeeps and the subsequent financial demands of their owners, deriving her argument from the rules of respectful interaction. Her openness towards foreigners, she now believed, had constituted a breach of her duties within the interaction model and had induced her partner spirits to punish her. The new interpretation of the event led to changes in her actions and behaviour. The shaman siblings atoned their mistakes with the help of reconciliation rituals and the promise to change their behaviour. They decided no longer to share their shamanistic knowledge with uninitiated foreigners.

Even some time after our journey, the eldest of the shaman siblings was experiencing problems, which she only solved by being sensitive to the interaction model. She interpreted the events and her professional and financial situation based on the interaction model. In our conversation she explained that her situation had changed only after her attempts to appease her partner spirits. Only then were the spirits willing to help her again and to compensate her for her financial losses. In the months following our journey she was again successful in treating her clients and was much in demand in her clinic.

The example of the shaman siblings is characteristic for switching from the one to the other model of world interpretation. The sequence of actual situation → dominance model → reflection → interaction model is most common but not the rule. As the example of the theft of livestock illustrates, the shift between these models can also take place repeatedly and in both directions. The interpretation of an event based on the interaction model does not necessarily remain stable, but can shift to the dominance model.

At the same time, the reason for the journey of the four shaman siblings, their search for repeated interactions with their partner spirits and the energies of the wilderness of their homeland, as well as the fact that they – independent of this goal – took three foreigners along with them shows that both kinds of world interpretation can be combined, complemented, and mixed. That a combination of both models of world interpretation is possible, despite their contradictions, will be shown in the following section.

The Spontaneous Switch to the Interaction Model and its Consequences

In the preceding sections I demonstrated that the dominance and the interaction models, despite mutual contradictions, can exist simultaneously and be valued equally. They can therefore be applied as parallel truths by one and the same person. Their parallel existence in a person's repertoire of interpretation, behaviour, and action appears to be characterised by a permanent change of position on the continuum between the extreme forms of both models of world interpretation. Many Tyvans change their minds about events and therefore their behaviour and action, according to the situation, place, time, or conversation partner.

It is possible to quite often observe a change in interpretation in the case of negative events or situations that appear difficult to solve. In such cases, the dominance model is a first point of orientation for a spontaneous reaction. Initially the person involved tries to solve the situation in a self-determined, pragmatic and – following their knowledge of the circumstances – goal-oriented way. But the dominance model often reaches its limits in an irreversible catastrophe (e.g. the death of a person, the loss of livestock due to epidemics or thieves, accidents, and other strokes of fate), or when people lack the instruments to improve a situation (e.g. disease, childlessness, poverty, epidemics, or ecological disasters). Less spectacular events can also reveal the limitations of the dominance model, such as the breakdown of cars, conflicts in the family or neighbourhood, general unhappiness, burglaries, or chronically sick children. If a Tyvan feels that he cannot master a difficult situation on his own, then he pauses and enters a stage of reflection on the situation. This stage of reflection is often the moment in which Tyvans consider interpretations in accordance with the interaction model and check their ability to address a problem through it. If the interaction model provides a fitting interpretation and a way to address a problem, then the person concerned may switch to the interaction model and base further actions on this interpretation.

In this way an event is reinterpreted and the person involved will try new ways to react to and deal with a situation. The interaction model provides first of all the possibility to look at a problem from a different perspective. People begin to think about whether they might have angered spirits in their behaviour. Harm or damage is often caused by the will of non-humans subjects, calling attention to situations where people have broken the rules of the interaction model. If an angry spirit is the reason behind a negative situation, people will find ways to appease the spirits. From this insight follow subsequent actions. At first, the person concerned needs to contact the angry spirit. To do so he often needs to employ a shaman. The shaman listens to the person's problem and together they decide how to contact the spirit. The shaman determines where and when the ritual will be conducted, what sacrificial offerings must be prepared, and which form the ritual shall take. At the fixed day, when all preparations are concluded, the shaman makes contact with the spirits in a séance. The shaman will try to find out which spirits are responsible for the incident and why they brought it about. The shaman makes the sacrificial offerings and negotiates with the spirits about what they expect from the people concerned. Furthermore, the shaman tries to reconcile the spirit with soothing words. After the shaman has gained sufficient knowledge of the situation and the spirits have fed and taken their leave, the shaman will inform the client about the results of the ritual. An important demand of an angered spirit is often a long-term modification of behaviour. The spirits do not only demand regular rituals and offerings but also respectful interactions with them. This demand to adhere more strongly to the norms of the interaction model in everyday behaviour quite often has long-term effects on behaviour.

In the above example, the vehicles that the shamans had borrowed were seriously and irreversibly damaged. Attempts to repair them failed. They needed the attention of professionals. The vehicles' owners demanded that the shamans pay for the costs. But the shamans in turn did not have financial resources to pay for the damages. The potential of the dominance model to solve the situation seemed exhausted.

But the application of the interaction model provided a way out of the predicament. The new interpretation of the events not only offered an explanation for the cause of the misfortune (i.e. the curiosity of foreigners, the shamans' openness towards us, the breach of confidence towards their partner spirits connected therewith and their consequent anger). These interpretations also showed ways for counteracting the bad luck. By using the interaction model, the shamans again became capable of action. They conducted rituals of reconciliation, repented the breach of confidence with their partner spirits and promised to change their behaviour (i.e. to no longer make such journeys in the company of foreigners).

The behaviour modification was not directed towards the vehicles but to non-human subjects to which shamans are indebted. The shamans found a way to counteract their bad luck and to avoid similar events in their future. Subsequent events proved to the shamans that they had been right. After their reconciliation rituals and through their consistent behaviour modification, they once again had good relationships to their partner spirits. These partner spirits helped the shamaness earn enough money to finance the damage.

Thus the interaction model turned out to be more useful for handling the crisis than the dominance model.

If someone is unable to solve his problems himself, then his efforts to master the situation by acting directly according to the dominance model fail. After switching to the interaction model, he tries to indirectly influence the situation. Acting interactively is the attempt to enlist non-human subjects to improve a situation. In such a case, people remain dependent on the will, the favours, and the decisions of those non-human subjects with whom they interact.

People who have several models of world interpretation at their disposal can only benefit from them. The possibility to flexibly use several models gives them numerous alternatives to manage their lives with all its events and strokes of fate, not only more easily but also in emotionally healthier ways.

Since it is above all negative events where the dominance model fails that provoke a switch to the interaction model, it is possible to assume that the interaction model is applied less often when the problems can be solved by the people themselves. Most activities in the stockbreeders' everyday lives are uncomplicated and barely concern interpretations modelled on the interaction model. Herding, milking, slaughtering, and treating minor illnesses among the livestock are rarely associated with non-human subjects such as spirits or energies. Such tasks are performed on basis of experience. My observations indicate that with the progress of scientific knowledge and the possibilities to effectively solve problems (for example by using veterinary medicine), Tyvans less frequently use the interaction model.

Situational and Contextual Complementation and Substitution

The focal point of Tyvan everyday life is stockbreeding, which provides the basis for the livelihood of the rural population. In the following, I will show how the dominance and interaction models can complement one another and be mixed in meaningful ways using the example of stockbreeding. I begin with the narrative of a 46-year-old stockbreeder from Süt Khöl, who explained several strategies of successful stockbreeding from the point of view of the interaction model. I recorded the interview about the spirit masters of the livestock on 27 July 2004 in his summer camp on Khamnar Tej near the Ak-Oj River:

> Apart from the spirit master of the camp (Tyv. *khonaash eezi*), the place where the corrals and sheds for the livestock are built also has

a spirit master (Tyv. *kazhaan eezi*). We call the spirit master of the corral and the livestock (Tyv. *mal suzu*). This spirit protects our livestock. We regularly bring him offerings, pray to him, and conduct rituals. In this way we insure ourselves of his help and support.

In order to keep the flock fertile and to continue to enjoy the powers of the livestock's spirit masters, some rules must be observed. For example, if we give individual animals away or sell them, we wipe the animal's nose and muzzle on the corral, pull a few hairs from the fur and the tail and deposit them in the corral. Furthermore we pay attention never to give animals away when it is dark. If a buyer comes to the yurt of a stockbreeder in the twilight, we invite him to spend the night in our yurt and do not sell the animal before dawn. This will help prevent the power of the livestock's spirit masters or the spirit master himself from leaving the family with the animal that is given away or sold. Without the spirit master's protection the flocks can suffer, wolves can kill animals, and epidemics can break out.

Once every year, at New Year's (Tyv. *chagaa*) [corresponds with the Chinese New Year], we conduct a ritual called 'the closing of the gate of the corral' (Tyv. *kodan khaalgazy khaar*) to ensure that the *mal suzu* does not leave and remains friendly to the family. To this end we invite a shaman or a lama, speak invocations, and conduct a smoke offering (NL 12).

This explanation is a narratively idealised pure form of the interaction model. But in regard to animal husbandry, they have become rare among the Tyvans. Instead, animal husbandry in Tyva today appears to the observer to be strongly marked by the dominance model. Stockbreeders are very self-confident in their dealings with their livestock. To do their work, they use their experience and inherited knowledge about strategies for protecting the livestock from diseases and epidemics, predators and other threats, for stimulating the growth of the flock, and for extracting or processing the products of animal husbandry. To a large extent, animal husbandry is a self-determined, pragmatic, and goal-oriented economic activity that serves human well-being. The people look to ensure that their livestock prospers. They focus their abilities on animal husbandry and consciously and intelligently use the possibilities that the environment offers. Animal husbandry not only takes place for the benefit of people, but also according to their will.

However, despite the fact that people apparently dominate animal husbandry, the animals seem to have the ability to counteract human intentions. I will call this instinct or 'self-will' (cf. Spittler 1998, 2003). Following Spittler, the work of a herdsman can be seen as 'interactive work' (i.e. as interaction between subjects). But how do Tyvan pastoral nomads themselves interpret their animal husbandry between the dominance and the interaction model? I argue that they practise a combination of both models of world interpretation.

According to the dominance model, animal husbandry can be described as the work of humans on their livestock. Tyvans distinguish between successful and less successful stockbreeders and in so doing often refer to their resources and abilities.

But many Tyvans also see their animals as individuals. Each animal has its own characteristic properties distinguishing it from other animals. Stockbreeders have lively conversations about these properties. They give their animals names, often based on outward attributes (e.g. 'the yak with a blaze', 'the brindled horse', or 'the limping sheep'). The naming of animals enables the communication of their owners about incidents and intentions with specific animals. Furthermore, children often know all the animals personally and by their names. In their individuality, the animals of a flock become subjects and in turn interaction partners, independent of religious interpretations. The owners may decide what happens with an individual animal from their flock, but they also have the feeling that they are beings that have their own will, that make their will felt as subjects, and that interact with human beings.

In turn, animal husbandry can also be described as an interaction between subjects from a religious point of view. The success and failure of stockbreeding is not only the result of human ability and action. Many Tyvans ascribe a crucial influence for the prosperity of their stock to the spirit masters, not only in the case of accidents, epidemics, animal theft, loss of animals, droughts, and meagre or rich pastures, but also in other respects. The spirit masters of the stocks, the corral, the pastures, the surrounding taiga or steppe, and the sacred places located nearby co-determine the life and economic success of pastoral nomads. Everything happening to humans and animals can be interpreted as the consequence of the interactions between humans and spirits.

The mixing and complementing of both models of world interpretation is part and parcel of the everyday life of most stockbreeders. The following example about the castration of young sheep and goats will demonstrate how the dominance and the interaction model can complement each other in a meaningful way. The annual castration of the young animals represents an intervention into the prosperity of the flock by its owners.

On 1 June 2005, in the spring camp of the herders Ajas Kara-oolovich Kyrgys and Chechena Mikhajlovna Ojun, at a place called Doora-Khovu located to the north of the Yenisei River, the lambs and kids were being castrated. To this end the owners of the animals sent for a veterinarian. The work took the whole day. The stockbreeders caught the male lambs and kids in the pen close to the camp. The children assisted in catching the animals. To the general amusement of onlookers they needed a long time to catch each goat or sheep.

Assisted by the herders, the veterinarian examined the animals and castrated them. The castration serves both the selection of fertile animals for breeding and a better utilisation of fodder. Castrated animals fatten faster than those that have not been castrated. The veterinarian used a long, pointed knife that he had whetted prior to the action. Each animal that was going to be castrated was laid on its back and its testicles were removed. The removed testicles were put in a bucket filled with milk and juniper in preparation for a feast in the evening.

Spittler's (1998) observations on the work of Kel Timia herders, a group of Tuareg living in the north of Niger, and his arguments about 'interactive work' (Spittler 2003), confirm my own observations of the playful skirmish between the boys and the lambs and kids. The catching of the young animals takes place interactively between the catcher and the animal, and both have their own will. The sons of professional herders clearly come to feel the will and the flight instinct of the young animals. This interaction becomes a trial of endurance between the boys and the animals that is amusing to the spectators. But the superior element in this 'play' that is not just a game is the human being. Moreover, the catching of the young animals follows a rational plan: namely, the animals will be castrated so that they will fatten and not reproduce.

Accordingly, it appears reasonable to situate the selection of the animals for castration, and the act of castration itself, within a model of human dominance over an environment that consists of exploited and therefore rather passive objects of human agency. The castration is an active, pragmatic, profit-oriented intervention in the fertility and reproduction of the flock. It follows the will of humans, not of animals, and – apart from the interests of the spirits in continuing human society – not that of spirits or other non-human subjects in the world of the Tyvans. The human owner of the flock and the colleagues he consults decide which animals will remain fertile for the purpose of breeding and which animals will lose their ability to reproduce. In the late 1960s and early 1970s, Erika Taube (1974b) found a stronger influence of the interaction model on animal castration among the Altai-Tyvans living in Mongolia. I, however, could not find any influence of the specifically Tyvan interaction model in relation to breeding. Only the resistance of the young animals and their struggle with the boys suggest an interaction between human and non-human subjects.

Nevertheless, the interaction model influenced the castration event in important ways. During the castration of lambs and kids, the stockbreeders used two elementary resources from the Tyvan version of the interaction model, namely milk and juniper. In doing so, they obviously did not only want to rely on their own competence alone but, instead, included religious resources to protect themselves from evil. In the interaction model, the prosperity of the flock does not only depend on the competence of the stockbreeder but also on the benevolence of the spirit masters and other natural subjects. As the stockbreeder told me, milk and juniper ensure ritual and religious purity. Both non-human subjects are used in all Tyvan rituals as well as in everyday life (on the use of milk, see Oelschlägel 2000). Milk and juniper make the wounds heal quickly, the flocks prosper, and ensure that the owners of the flock remain well and healthy.

The use of milk and juniper reveal several interactions. Firstly, we find an interaction between the stockbreeder, the flock, and the milk that is classified as pure and as contributing to religious and ritual purity. Secondly, there is an interaction between the human owner, the flock, the juniper and its purifying power, and the power of the wilderness in which the juniper grows. Finally, we can discover an interaction between people, the flock, and spirit masters who take much pleasure in milk and juniper and who safeguard the flock.

The concern in the procedure is primarily for ritual hygiene. The veterinarian did not explicitly disinfect the area to be cut, only wiping the knife on his trousers between cuts or dipping it into the mixture of milk and juniper. What the owners of the flock could not ensure themselves – the healthy prosperity of the flock – they ensured with the help of the spirit masters by using milk and juniper. Thus it seems that the most important property of Tyvan nomads, their herd, depends both on the self-determined action of the breeders and on a successful interaction between them, the flock, several subjects of nature (milk, juniper), and the spirit masters. During the castration, both models of world interpretation are mixed and complement each other. Furthermore, the example shows that the boundary between both models of world interpretation – which type of behaviour and what explanation belongs to either model of world interpretation – is neither absolute nor clear-cut. In the first instance and clearly visible from the outside, the human livestock owners personally decide about their animals in a dominant and purposeful intervention in the fertility of the flock. In castrating particular lambs and kids, they regulate the breeding on the one hand and the fattening of the flock on the other. According to the dominance model, we can allocate the prosperity of the flock to the human ability for stockbreeding. However, according to the interaction model, the herder's success depends on the invisible influences and control of the spirit masters. In the reflections of many Tyvans, a mix of both models is the most frequent. Depending on the situation and context, they interpret their success or failure in stockbreeding both according to the dominance as well as to the interaction model. Both models of world interpretation – in as far as they are different and contradictory – complement one another to form a meaningful whole that for many Tyvans is reasonable.

Context, Place, Time, and Counterpart as Reasons for Switching

A spontaneous switch from the dominance to the interaction model takes place in particular after negative or dramatic events. There are strokes of fate that nearly always provoke a switch to the interaction model. These include the death of a relative or acquaintance:

An unexpected catastrophe beset a family. A young relative of a friend died in June 2005. He was only 26.

When my friend forbade her 14-year-old daughter to attend the funeral, she justified her decision from the perspective of the interaction model. She had understood from a shamaness's divination that her daughter was highly sensitive to the spirits. Her conclusion was that her daughter ought to generally avoid contact with spirits. And the souls of the recently deceased were such spirits. Her daughter did not agree with her mother – she would have liked to have said goodbye to her cousin.

After the funeral, the daughter reported that she had seen the soul of her cousin walking through the flat during the day when she was fully awake. She saw only his face, which looked very much alive. Upon seeing him she had not been afraid, but had looked him sadly in the eye. In this way she could take leave of him, she explained. A little later she encountered him again. After that, he no longer appeared.

My friend's daughter was not the only one who had seen the deceased in the first 49 days after his death. During a get-together, another relative told us that she had been contacted by the deceased at night. She had suddenly woken up and seen him in a white shirt, the same he wore when he died. She explained to us that she had not wanted to be afraid of her younger 'brother' [Tyvans also call more distant relatives sisters and brothers]. They had looked sadly at each other, whereupon she said to him: 'Leave me now, everything is all right. Calm down and relax.' Then he disappeared. When similar things happened to others in the kin group, people said that the deceased, distraught about his unexpected death, had visited all relatives and friends.

Many Tyvans are convinced that the deceased wander through the world of humans until the forty-ninth day after their death. My interview partners explained to me that initially the deceased neither realise nor accept their death. Instead, they visit their relatives and friends, cherishing hopes that these will recognise them and in their behaviour suggest that the deceased is still alive. Moreover, people explained to me that the recently deceased are hungry and thirsty before they pass into the other world, which is why they ask their relatives for food in the first 49 days after their death. They furthermore ask for a light to help them find their way to the other world. Therefore nobody was surprised when recently deceased persons showed themselves to relatives.

This case shows that my friend's daughter became sensitive to the interaction model by her cousin's death and by her mother's prohibition to attend his funeral. The daughter changed her explanation of the events to fit with the interaction model, and saw the ghost of the deceased wandering through her flat.

Especially the use of the interaction model during such a personal crisis ensures that it remains present in people's minds. By contrast, there does not seem to be much reason to apply it in more pleasant situations. Something that has gone well does not need to be explained. It already appears optimal to the people involved. There is no need for a retrospective analysis of the event from an alternative perspective. A retrospective interpretation of favourable events from the perspective of the interaction model is therefore rare in Tyva.

Nevertheless, there are cases of immediate interpretation of positive events from the viewpoint of the interaction model. In such cases, people claim that they did not bring about favourable and successful situations on their own, but with the help of superior powers. I could observe such events when they were preceded by a ritual. Periods of time after regularly held annual rituals (e.g. the annual consecration of *ovaalar*) are typical. If a ritual was followed by a happy phase of life, then people regarded the ritual as particularly successful or the leader of the ritual (shaman or lama) and his or her local assistants as particularly talented. They were believed to be able to undertake a successful interaction with non-human subjects and to preserve and cultivate it over a longer period of time. The people concerned had contacted supernatural powers, negotiated with them successfully, found out what they wanted, complied with their will, and convinced the spirits to be favourable to them.

A ritual makes people sensitive to the interaction model. Even some time after the ritual the risks and opportunities of interactions between human and non-human subjects resonate in their consciousness. Regular rituals encourage the participants to use the interaction model more often as a guiding ideal for their interpretations, actions, and behaviour. Tyvans more often used the interaction model after rituals than at other moments. They ascribed their fortune, wealth, and success to the help of the powers and spirits with whom they had communicated during the rituals and with whose will they had aligned their actions and behaviour.

The following account is shaped by where the interview took place (the home of an important spirit master), when it took place (the period after the spring consecration of this spirit master's *ovaa*) and the narrator's counterpart (an anthropologist interested in the 'traditional Tyvan worldview'). The combination of place, time, and counterpart provoked my interview partner to interpret the narrated events as the consequence of a highly successful interaction with a spirit master. The conversation took place on a slope of the Udur Taiga, where the spirit master of the Toolajlyg Valley resides. My interview partner was a 50-year-old teacher and school director living in the Toolajlyg cooperative. I recorded the interview about the *ovaa* of the Orzhak clan on 28 August 2004:

> My father met the author Mongush Kenin-Lopsan, who told him: 'Where you live there is a forgotten *ovaa*, a sacred place. You should rebuild this *ovaa*.' When my father was seven, he has seen this *ovaa*. This was in 1931. Later the *ovaa* had been given up. Nothing was left of it. Since then seventy years have passed.
>
> In 2001, on the first of May, my father together with his children rebuilt the *ovaa*.
>
> When we rebuilt the *ovaa*, we invited a shaman from the shamans' association Drum [from Kyzyl]. We were more than seven persons and after rebuilding the *ovaa*, we consecrated it. In 2002, 2003, and 2004 we consecrated the *ovaa* again and again. The residents of the Toolajlyg cooperative were very happy with the reconstruction of our *ovaa*.
>
> In 2001 the shaman explained to us: 'The spirit master of the Toolajlyg resides on the Udur Taiga. He is a man and he said to you: "Thank you, my children, for rebuilding the *ovaa*. I will protect you, your livestock and your homeland!"'
>
> In 2002 another shaman visited us. He spoke like the first: 'The spirit master of the Toolajlyg is a man. He lives on the Udur Taiga. The spirit master said to me the following: "In the spring and the summer I will let it rain a lot. The grass will grow well."'

>We indeed had very rainy summers in 2002 and 2003. The grass was good. The livestock became fat. The kids and yak calves did not die. As the spirit master had promised, our lives improved in every respect. Now our pastoral nomads owned many fat animals.
>
>Another shaman from the shamans' association Nine Heavens in Kyzyl visited us in 2003. He said to us, just like the first and the second shaman: 'The spirit master came down from the Udur Taiga. His words were the following: "Your life has improved. There were no epidemics. The livestock is fat, healthy, and strong. Moreover no thieves came to steal."'
>
>Furthermore, my mother told me the following: 'Two generations ago our people in Toolajlyg saw a white-bearded old man on a white horse. People who met him became ill or died.'
>
>The spirit masters of places change. At that time this white-bearded old man was the spirit master of the land. Now we have another spirit master. After we rebuilt the sacred *ovaa* of Toolajlyg, the shamans saw another spirit master. This one is tall, strong, and a man in his prime. This spirit master is very quiet and warm-hearted (HG 16).

As a starting point for the narrative, the teacher mentioned his father's visit to Mongush Kenin-Lopsan. Kenin-Lopsan is the author of many books about shamanism that are well-known in Tyva. He is also a practising shaman. For these reasons, he was an authority on the interaction model for my interview partner's father.

Without a preceding accident – at least an accident was not mentioned – the two men had spoken about an old *ovaa* in the Toolajlyg Valley and concluded that it should be rebuilt and consecrated. *Ovaalar* are classified as places where Tyvans may contact the spirit masters of a particular region or clan and communicate with them. The initiative to contact the spirit master of the Toolajlyg came from Kenin-Lopsan and the father of my interview partner as well as from all persons assisting in rebuilding the *ovaa*. They invited and paid for a shaman to communicate with the spirit master of the Toolajlyg Valley.

The spirit master, in turn, accepted the offer to renew communication and interaction between him and the valley's residents. The herdsmen of the valley gave him a home and a place to receive offerings as well as the possibility to communicate with them. The spirit master reacted by disclosing his identity, by willingly accepting the offers, by positively co-determining the future of the valley, by bestowing fruitful grazing land and flocks on the people, and by diverting epidemics and thefts.

The reconstruction of the *ovaa* inspired the other residents of the valley to interact anew with the long forgotten spirit master who had been ignored in the Soviet period, hoping to benefit from the interaction. From then on, the desire to fulfil the duties of the interaction model seemed to rise anew every spring when the *ovaa* consecration took place. The periodical ritual continues to affect the Toolajlyg residents' thinking in the rest of the year. For example, they argue that success in stockbreeding, the absence of epidemics and periods of drought, as well as the good condition of the grazing land depend on the 'quiet and warm-hearted' spirit master of the territory and the successful interaction with him.

During my first visit to the valley in the summer of 1997, there had been an epidemic, killing whole herds of yaks. After renewed consecrations of the rebuilt *ovaa* and following the statements of the three shamans, my interview partner again became sensitive to the interaction model to explain events. He linked the positive economic developments to the consecration of the rebuilt *ovaa* and regarded these as the spirit master's reward to the valley's residents, expressing his gratefulness to them for again contacting him after a disruption of seventy years.

This case shows that after conducting a ritual, many Tyvans remain sensitive to the interaction model and tend to interpret events along its lines. Further examples show that the presence of Tyvans at a sacred place can provoke in them a switch from the dominance to the interaction model. These places include *ovaalar*, sacred trees, passes, mountains, springs, specific districts, and the wilderness in general. The behaviour of Tyvans changes visibly when they are in such places. In these sacred places, people turn from self-determined and superior persons to supplicant, thoughtful, careful and petitionary human beings.

Eye-catching for every visitor are the sacred places on the oft-travelled roads and tracks and along the paths that can only be used on horseback or on foot. All these roads and paths have their own sacred places, built at mountain passes or near dangerous passages. Such sacred places also include springs or sacred trees that Tyvans encounter on their way. In such places, drivers, riders, and pedestrians pause to conduct a small, spontaneous ritual for the spirit master of the site. Passersby circle the *ovaa* three times in a clockwise direction, leave stones on the *ovaa* or attach coloured ribbons to it, sacred trees, or bushes beside a sacred spring. It is considered beneficial to pause and rest at such places along the way, and to offer – prior to a meal – the first part of the food or drink to the master of the site. This practice should avert possible dangers along the way. Whether a passerby evades the dangers of travelling does not only depend on him or the physical condition of the road but on whether the spirit master protects him. The traveller asks for protection at the various sacred places designated to this end. There he contacts the spirit masters who are responsible for a particular stretch of the way. Not only a ritual to the spirit masters at the ritual sites, but also the observation of the norms and rules of the interaction model ensure the spirit masters' good will. A passerby will neither destroy nor pollute if he wants to avoid the spirit masters' wrath.

Protection during travel is very important for many Tyvans. Many roads are dangerous and unpaved, leading along steep slopes or through rivers. They connect villages and camp grounds in the loneliness of the taiga and the steppe, far away from human settlement. Damage to a vehicle, an accident, or the physical injury of a traveller or a horse may cause enormous problems. The physical dangers of the road and the fear connected with them are conceptually linked to the ritual places mentioned above based on interpretations based on the interaction model. At these sacred places this connection and the switch to the interaction model becomes apparent.

The sacred places along the roads and paths bring to mind again and again the rules, norms, and taboos of the interaction model. They keep the memory of the interaction model alive and make people sensitive to interpretations following the interaction model. In other words, if a human being during a journey encounters such a place, he tends to follow the perspective of the interaction model. He conducts a small ritual and bears in mind how to behave to please the spirit masters of the sacred places in the wilderness.

Not only particular places but also particular days in the course of a year may be connected to an interaction model and provoke a switch to it. For example, several Tyvans I talked with always or sometimes made use of a Buddhist interaction model by acting in accordance with a Buddhist astrological calendar. The calendar provided detailed information for each day of the year about favourable and unfavourable results of certain actions. Such actions included everyday tasks like shopping, cutting hair or nails, meeting friends, journeys, and other activities for which particular days could be suitable or not. Those Tyvans who regularly or sporadically followed the instructions of this Buddhist calendar saw their destiny and condition in direct dependency on their abidance of the calendar's instructions. For them a particular day demanded a specific kind of behaviour.

Certain days in the course of a year are reserved for annual festivals and rituals. In such cases the moment in time causes a change in the model of world interpretation. If the date of such an event comes closer, the interaction model becomes a dominant pattern of interpretation for everything affecting the people's lives.

As an example I want to point to the summer solstice, a festival that has Russian roots but has been enriched by Tyvan contents. On the night of 6 July 2005, I celebrated the midsummer celebrations together with friends. We went to a nice place on the Kaa-Khem River, a tributary of the Yenisei River at 11 o'clock in the evening. There we lit a fire, barbecued, ate, and drank. After midnight we went into the water, washed ourselves, and jumped over the fire.

On 7 July, the day after midsummer, I had several other experiences. On my way to the internet café I noticed how teenagers and children splashed passersby with water and threw water balloons at each other. My friends explained to me that on this day the water was cleansing, healthy, and beneficial for one's beauty. It was a part of the midsummer ritual. The ritual is called *prazdnik Ivana kupaly* (Ivan Kupala Day).

The explanation for this spectacle, in which mainly teenagers take part, is that the power of nature and water is at its peak at the summer solstice. Their power is connected to the stellar constellation at midsummer. My friends told me that water – especially during the night between 6 and 7 July – has the power to stimulate health and beauty. Such water transfers energies and natural powers extremely well. It is a medium. For this reason, humans should by all means take a bath on this night. One does not need to visit one of the many medical springs in Tyva because all water is at its maximal power at this moment. The subsequent leap over the fire has an additional cleansing effect.

The mutual pouring over with water follows the same principle. It is a special blessing and a present that people make to each other. By pouring water on each other, people bestow good health and beauty upon each other based in the power of water and nature. People use the power of nature by ensuring that they and others encounter it. Things that would usually provoke loud protest on other days are desirable at midsummer. Moreover, this ritual is a lot of fun.

This is how people interact with at least two non-human subjects during the summer solstice: the power and energy of nature and water.

Midsummer takes place only once a year. During the rest of the year Tyvans – both atheists and believers – frequent the many medical springs in Tyva, with or without a shaman. According to Tyvans, such springs are good for one's health, not on the basis of the minerals in the water but as a source of energy. Tyvans ascribe the strongest efficacy to those springs that are located in the wilderness, far away from human settlements. The energy of the wilderness increases with its remoteness to human settlement. In addition, Tyvans prefer to visit these springs in the autumn (September and October), the golden season of the year. Water only matures at particular periods of time. Like a fruit develops taste by ripening, springs develop their maximum healing power in the autumn. When this 'ripening' is complete, those Tyvans who regularly frequent medical springs, turn increasingly toward the interaction model.

Tyvans visiting a spring begin the interaction with a small offering in the course of which they name their ailments and ask the spirit master of the spring that they be cured. They offer food, hang coloured ribbons on the trees and bushes close to the spring, and finally douse themselves with spring water or drink it. The healing occurs on the one hand through the power and energy of nature, transferred by the water, on the other hand by the spirit master of the spring. Tyvans asking to be healed first need to placate the spirit master by conducting an offering. Only after the afflicted person has done so does the spirit master provide the spring's energies for healing the person. The spring's spirit master decides whether the therapy will be successful. But the willingness of the spring's spirit master also depends on the lifestyle and deeds of the person who wants to be healed. For this reason the visit to a medical spring by a Tyvan must be seen as an interaction between several human and non-human subjects. As the following example shows, a healing ritual at a medical spring can involve six parties: the patient, a shaman, the spirit master of the spring, the medium of water, the powers and energies of the place, and, finally, the moment of the 'ripening' of the water.

The following event was related by a 54-year-old shamaness and teacher who was living and working in Kyzyl on 1 November 2004. After she had described how she had healed a woman's left with a ritual spring consecration to explain to me the healing properties of water (see Y5 above), she added: '[Springs] flow below the ground and stream out of the earth. That is where the spring derives its power. Springs are also connected to the cosmos where it unites with it, that is, where it comes out of the earth. The spirit masters of springs are very strong and powerful' (Y5).

Apart from situation, place and time, counterparts such as conversation partners can also provoke a change in the model of world interpretation. This is especially apparent in the impression that shamans leave on religious laypeople.

So it happened during the journey with the four shaman siblings to Süt Khöl District in July 2004 that I described above. For several days, we visited the shaman sibling's relatives. At that time the men of the family and several acquaintances and relatives were concerned with building a wooden house and were planning to fell some trees. They only needed to go to the taiga nearby, cut the trees, and pull them with horses and a bit of labour a short distance from the woods. Then the shaman siblings became aware of their intentions.

After the shamans talked with the men of the family, the latter changed their plans. They postponed the cutting of the trees to conduct a complex offering and petitioning ritual to the spirit master of the taiga and to the trees to be cut. This took place on a rainy day in the taiga under the supervision of the shamans.

After the ritual, I inquired among the shamans' relatives to what extent they adhered to the rules of the interaction model in everyday life. I wanted to find out how self-evident it was for our hosts to conduct rituals to the masters of the taiga before cutting trees, collecting berries and herbs, or hunting. The result of my enquiry matched the experiences I made in other parts of Tyva. They explained that it was in no case self-evident for them to conduct a complex ritual before every intervention in nature. They rarely followed this norm of the interaction model. Nevertheless, they knew that in doing so they were behaving against their tradition and against the spirit masters.

During the conversation with our hosts I got the impression that to them it was important to find a reasonable balance in conducting their rituals. They did not think it was necessary to conduct a ritual before every economic activity. That would be too laborious and expensive. They regularly conducted rituals in the course of the year or after negative events, they told me. But economic activities in the yurt camp with the stock and the products of stockbreeding they saw pragmatically, following the dominance model. The success of stockbreeding depended on the persons practising it. To include spirits in this process was not necessary.

Although our hosts in Süt Khöl District told us many contemporary legends on the importance of respectful interaction between human and non-human subjects, they did not want to subordinate their whole lives to the norms and rules of the interaction model. Instead, they were looking for a reasonable compromise between dominance and interaction model. The demands of everyday work among Tyvan nomads do not allow them to be in permanent interaction with the spirits. Rituals do need to be conducted, but a few rituals in the course of the year suffice to live up to the interaction model's demands. Our hosts pointed out that they had conducted the offering and petitioning ritual mainly because the shaman siblings had been present.

Thus, the main role of the shaman siblings in the situation described above was to remind them of the need for respectful interaction and to bring about a switch to the interaction model. They explained to their relatives that they were not free to plunder the taiga without the agreement of its spirit master. If they did so, they would risk severe punishment by these guardians of nature. Our hosts followed the shamans' suggestion, even if they knew that after their departure they would abstain from further rituals. The presence of the shamans caused a change in model of world interpretation that our hosts followed although they did not find that this was absolute necessary.

Many Tyvans I met often preferred to ignore the interaction model. The dominance model allows them to complete all daily activities with a minimum of effort. To cut trees, Tyvans need a forest, tools, and experience in cutting, processing, and transporting the lumber. The question of whether trees are non-human subjects or if they have to see the cutting of trees in connection with the taiga's spirit masters is often not posed. In their busy everyday lives most Tyvans prefer to abstain from conducting complex rituals that cost additional effort. But when knowledgeable fellow human beings remind them of the punishments that threaten them if they do not obtain the spirit masters' permission to intervene in nature, the interaction model comes into focus and may become a guide for the interactive action of the people involved.

Hardship Resulting from the Spontaneous Switch to the Interaction Model

The dominance model entails difficulties that are often discussed in public. These include the heedless exploitation of nature, the destruction of the environment, or the abuse of animals. But the interaction model can also become a problem, especially when it causes interpersonal tension, psychical pressure, or social isolation.

In 1997 I met a young man in a Tyvan cooperative. He was regarded as a successful hunter and a talented diviner. But he was not accepted by his fellow men. Other members of the cooperative thought he was strange and crazy. They explained his abnormality with the energies of the wilderness to which he was permanently exposed during his hunting trips through the taiga. On the one hand, they said, he was a friend of the master of the taiga. That is why he was so successful in hunting. On the other hand, he was filled with the energy of the wilderness. His special skill in divination was a sign thereof. But he exaggerated with his hunting trips lasting several months. The dangerous energies of the wilderness had already clouded his mind and confused his senses. Other stockbreeders expressed their dislike of the young man by saying that he at times was completely unreliable. His social exclusion was strengthened by the fact that he – for the same reason – could not find a wife or start a family, and therefore did not own his own yurt and stock.

Sometime after our first meeting, he began to drink because he could not bear his social isolation, the disrespect of his fellow human beings, and their gossiping; and he became an alcoholic. He subsequently quit drinking and tried to become an accepted member of the community. He learned several trades and made an effort to serve the stockbreeders with this knowledge. In this way he tried to secure a place to stay during the winter months while continuing to hunt in the taiga for long periods during the summer. When I met him again in 2005, however, his efforts to integrate had barely improved his situation in the community.

The example of the lonely hunter shows how adherence to the interaction model can cause interpersonal tensions, social isolation, and even mobbing. The positive characteristics ascribed to the young man (a successful hunter and a talented oracle) were at the same time connected with his peculiarities. Their origin was to be found in his long sojourns in the taiga. As wilderness, the taiga is charged with energy. On the one hand, people need these energies to stay healthy and strong. But at the same time, too much can addle the mind. This was precisely what people noticed with the hunter. They excluded him from their community as an odd person and drove him to despair.

I was able to observe the exclusion of a person from his or her community because of a switch to the interaction model several times. The following example is especially instructive.

A Tyvan friend called Ina married when she was 24 (in the mid-1980s). She met her husband-to-be during her time at was then Leningrad State University. She had two children and was very happy. Ina had a friend from university, Aljona, who was not married but had children.

Suddenly the relationship between both women changed. One evening in the autumn of 2004, Ina invited her friend Aljona, her sister, and me for a visit. That evening Ina told Aljona that her sister's husband had been drafted as soldier and was being sent to Chechnya. Ina's sister reacted angrily. She snapped at Ina and said that Aljona did not need to know about her husband's problems. She refused to elaborate further about her reaction. The situation was all the more strange because in Tyva it is usual during such get-togethers and celebrations to say a toast for the lives and safe return of the soldiers. But they kept arguing until it was time to say goodbye.

In a later conversation with me, Aljona complained about the sister's behaviour. She said that Ina's sister suspected her of having caused the death of another friend's husband with her jealousy. This man had died in a traffic accident several years ago. For some time, her friends had talked about the fact that Aljona was bitter because she never married. Her friends alleged that Aljona was jealous of happy couples and especially of the couple where the husband had died. To Tyvans, jealousy can destroy that from which it arises. Accordingly, Aljona's jealousy had damaged the happiness of others. Ina's sister was thus afraid that Aljona's jealousy could bring her husband bad luck or even result in his death.

Aljona suffered from these allegations. She thus often asserted that she was happy with her life and had no reason to be jealous. She would never cast evil spells on people. Nobody had ever seen her try to cause damage upon others with the help of witchcraft or sorcery. Nevertheless, Aljona's situation among her friends increasingly changed for the worse. Ina's sister worried that something bad could happen to her husband. She spoke a lot about her fears and bit by bit seemed to convince Ina of the dangers of Aljona's jealousy. The gossip increased and Ina suddenly began to publicly accuse her best friend of being dangerously jealous. As a result of the increased gossiping, several friends broke off contact with Aljona. To protect themselves from Aljona's jealousy, her friends increasingly avoided her. If they met her in the street, Ina and other former friends refused to greet her.

Aljona felt helpless about the gossiping and unable to defend herself. Her social network was badly damaged. The situation had pulled the rug from under her feet and she found herself in a crisis. It was obvious that she was suffering.

This situation lasted several months. Then it seemed to relax. Aljona told me during a telephone call that she had again contacted her friends. She and Ina had talked things over and made peace. Soon they began to visit each other again regularly. But Aljona explained to me that she was often afraid that the reproaches about her allegedly dangerous jealousy could again become an issue for her friends.

In this case, Aljona was the victim of a rumour that her friends based on the interaction model, which aroused such strong emotions in several participants that they changed their behaviour towards her. The fear of her alleged jealousy, so strong that it could destroy happiness and even cause death, had led to a complete loss of trust in Aljona. Several friends broke off contact with her to protect themselves from possible danger. After some time, however, the tense and highly emotional situation under which Aljona suffered a great deal relaxed somewhat. After Ina and Aljona had talked things over, they seemed to return to their senses. The interaction model became less important, a return to 'normality' could be achieved and Aljona could return to her circle of friends.

This case clearly reveals the tragedy that can befall interpersonal relationships if individuals become the victim of negative interpretations of the interaction model. Of course, the reproaches made in such cases cannot be proven, but neither can they be disproven. The victims become the object of strong and emotional rumours and gossip. They are often associated with dangers, disrupting their social network and their relationships to their fellow human beings. The results are public ostracism, social exclusion, and isolation. The victims suffer from prejudices and often do not find a way out of these situations.

The Strategic Switch between the Models by Laypersons

It is difficult to say whether the switch between both models of world interpretation in the cases presented above occurred consciously or unconsciously. But it is also possible to identify conscious and strategic changes of world interpretation in the argumentation of many Tyvans. They appear during interpretations of experiences, during explanations of their own actions and during such action and behaviour itself.

Especially in 1995 and 1997, I noticed that many religious laypeople withheld information about the interaction model. During my first encounters with South-Siberian Tyvans, I found that many preferred to claim being atheists towards foreigners or – if they claimed any adherence to a religion – then only Buddhism. Especially when interpreting their experiences to foreigners they conformed to the dominance model. That means that they tried strategically to admit exclusively to the dominance model.

Without a doubt, experiences that all peoples of the Soviet Union have in common play a part in these cases (i.e. the devaluation of autochthonous religions and the persecution or even killing of religiously active persons). The Communist Party programme dictated a development from feudal society to a Soviet society in which differences of development between the nations as well as class society itself would be overcome. At least since Tyva's incorporation into the Soviet Union in 1944, propaganda emphasised the backwardness of animist and Buddhist beliefs that were allegedly linked to magic, superstition, and witchcraft.[72] Religion, even if folk religion, was presented as one of the most important hurdles on the way to a socialist and ultimately communist social system. Religion was supposed to stabilise and legitimate the differences between members of various social classes, the power of political and economic elites (including feudal rulers or clan leaders) and the powerlessness of the common people. In this period, the concept of *arat* became a political term in Tyva to denote representatives of the common people or the lowest class in nomadic society, who were oppressed and exploited by the feudal rulers. The politicised term *arat* was

---

[72] For further information see David (2001).

introduced in one of the first novels written in the Tyvan language: Salchak Toka's autobiographical book, translated into German as *Das Wort des Arat* (1951), which was awarded the Stalin Prize in 1950.

Even in 1995 and 1997, the rhetorical norms of the Communist Party were still noticeable in the arguments of my interview partners. Critique, persecution, education and years of re-education had produced a public denial of religious world interpretation among many Tyvans. If they remained true to the interaction model privately, Tyvans only admitted to it behind closed doors. In the Soviet period of Tyvan history a religious practice developed that I – following Streck (2007) – propose to call a 'silent religion'.[73]. It is hallmarked by shamanistic séances without drums and shamanist dress and it abstained from the public demarcation of sacred places. In this form, silent religion had the function to maintain interactions according to religious norms, and thus prevent the collapse of the network of human and non-human subjects. At the same time, silent religion protected religious persons from the grasp of state power. I argue that many Tyvans who were unable to dissociate themselves from religious thinking and action during the Soviet period consciously experienced the discrepancy between a public commitment to the dominance model and a privately practised interaction model.

Symbols of religion only returned to Tyvan public life after the turn of the millennium. In my first period of fieldwork in the South Siberian Republic of Tyva in 1995 I noticed increasing public religious activity. But only in 2004, was I permitted to record my research partners' voiced commitments to their religious world interpretation.

Just one example will suffice to illustrate this development. In 1997 I became acquainted with a woman in Mugur Aksy in whose household I lived for several months. At that time she presented herself to me as an atheist who thought of 'Tyvan tradition' as antiquated. Her convictions were so strong that she – despite my repeated requests – declined to correct the Tyvan texts I had collected on the interaction model. She argued that they were nonsense and not worth being collected or distributed. On the contrary, she was glad that her people had overcome this way of interpreting the world. But in 2004 her daughters told me about a true occurrence that she had handed down to them that showed how she had consciously denied her own religious convictions in 1997 and hid them from me.

The following true occurrence was told by the three daughters of the woman who may have experienced it. I recorded the story on 24 August 2004 in Mugur Aksy. The three daughters were a 34-year-old physician,

---

[73] See Streck (2013) and the edited volume *Die gezeigte und die verborgene Kultur* (Streck 2007) on the practice of concealing cultural elements.

living and working in Moscow, a merchant, aged 30 and living and working in Kyzyl and a systems administrator of 27 years living and working in Mugur Aksy.

> When – during the Soviet period – our mother was working in a library, an evaluation was to be done by the ministry from Kyzyl. Therefore a committee was due to arrive. The staff of the library felt the pending evaluation to be troublesome. They were annoyed by it. Our mother went with her colleagues to a wet river bank and began to pick flowers. After they had done so, the weather changed for the worse. It began to rain and a storm came up. As a result, the airplane could not land and the committee could not disembark. Because they had picked flowers, the spirit master of the Möngün Taiga had become angry (NA 12).

The story shows that interpretations and actions based on the interaction model did exist in Soviet times. It also addresses the anti-religious attitude and ideology of the communist elites. The irony is that the latter were defeated by weapons in which they did not believe. The ironic narrative was of the breaking of a taboo that helped the women prevent an evaluation by the committee. The librarians picked flowers and consciously and strategically broke the rules of the interaction model not to destroy anything in nature. In doing so they provoked the anger of the Möngün Taiga's spirit master. His revenge (bad weather) prevented the committee's airplane from landing. This secret victory over the superimposed communist dominance model founded in the interaction between human and non-human subjects was enthusiastically celebrated by the narrators and their audiences during each telling of 'true occurrences' that allude to events in the Soviet period.

The Professional Switch as a Tool for Shamans

Despite their commitment to the interaction model, shamans practise a permanent switching between both models as a consequence of their profession. Contemporary shamans *sell* their ability to mediate and in doing so their ability to interact with non-human subjects. The success of the market-oriented economic activities of contemporary shamans depends to a large extent on their managerial skills. Furthermore, a shaman's work is determined by the desire to earn an income and gain social prestige. Many shamans finance themselves and their families through their shamanistic activities. This new quality in the shaman's profession is so strongly marked by the dominance model that many laypeople see it as a contradiction to the interaction model. The case of the following shamanic clinic is exemplary.

In 2004 and 2005 most Tyvan shamans worked intermittently or permanently either in three shamanic clinics in Kyzyl or in a fourth such clinic in western Tyva (in Ak Dovurak). The three clinics in Kyzyl, connected to the already mentioned shamans' associations, are called Düngür, Tos Deer, and Adyg Eeren. In all of them, shamans treat clients for a fixed fee. In 1995 and 1997, most shamans shuttled between their home regions, where they also practised stockbreeding, and the shamanic clinic in Kyzyl, where they worked for several weeks or months a year earning the largest part of their income.

By 2004 and 2005 many more Tyvan shamans had settled in Kyzyl to devote themselves full time to this profitable activity, leaving their herds in the care of their relatives and neighbours.

A shamanic clinic can be compared to a medical centre. There is a receptionist who asks the clients about their complaints, assigns them to the appropriate shaman, and collects the fees. Before clients are admitted to the shaman, they take a seat in the waiting room. The shamans rent an office in the shamanic clinic where they conduct the requested consultations, treatments, and rituals. No allowances are made for an audience in the process, and neither clients nor shamans like to admit observers.

There are cheap and expensive shamans, depending on how many clients want to consult them. The shamans pay a fixed part of their income to the clinic staff and the owner of the building in which the clinic is housed.

This change in shamanistic practice is not received uncritically by laypeople. Historical sources and contemporary Tyvans agree that 'real' shamans work during the night, when the spirits are most active. But the opening hours of the shamanic clinics do not adhere to this fact. The success of a shamanic session is also dependent on the audience, which should participate emotionally in the session, but is excluded from the shamanic clinics. Lay Tyvans are also critical about certain strategies that are part of contemporary shamanism, such as advertising, international networking, modern management practices, and the production and selling of devotional objects. Everything that laypeople criticise seems to be marked by the dominance model, serving the financial gain that shamans derive from their work. That the potential profit is considerable can be seen in the fact that most contemporary shamans join a shamanic clinic to do their work in the lucrative business on a full time basis. Almost all shamans I met were able to sustain themselves and their families much more easily than many laypeople. The high prices that Tyvan shamans charge in comparison to other professions are seen critically. In marked contrast, oral traditions about historical shamans often describe them as very poor. Before 1944, shamans, like their clients, were often stockbreeders. During the day they had to work as pastoralists just like everyone else. It was their duty to put their shamanic abilities at the service of humans and spirits during the night. As a result, they often found themselves under much pressure. It was not in the shaman's interest to promote his craft, and clients often had to plea for a long time before the shamans agreed to treat them. The report of a 43-year-old anthropologist and folklorist living in Kyzyl is revealing on this issue. She said the following about contemporary shamans on 26 September 2004:

> Today shamans market themselves. They introduce themselves to the common people, promote themselves and announce: 'I am a shaman, I am able to perform and oracle with 41 stones, I can heal people, ritually cleanse the house of evil spirits and energies and conduct the ritual of the forty-ninth day after a person has died.' In the past we did not have this situation. Shamans did not publicly present themselves, they hid their talents and did not reveal themselves. People knew which shamans were real shamans. They went to a shaman on their own account. If necessary, they talked to him about their problems. They called the shaman for help. A real shaman does not immediately agree to help. You have to make plea with him, to persuade him. Only after pleaded long enough will he sometimes honour your request (SCHA 1).

Historically, shamans received little in exchange for their exhausting work. People compensated them with small presents, like a piece of cloth, some meat from a sacrificial animal, or other gifts that were largely symbolic. This kind of symbolic compensation had a religious meaning. For the shaman's gift to be effective, it required a countergift to be given in return.

The same interview partner had the following to say about contemporary shamans on 21 July 2004 in Kyzyl:

> Shamans and specialists of the oracle with 41 stones need necessarily to have their 'hands whitened' (Tyv. *kholun aktaar*). One can give them a small present, money, food, white food, and other gifts (e.g. books, souvenirs, earrings, a ring or similar jewellery, but nothing very expensive). We give so that the words and thoughts of the oracle specialist come true and bad oracle results are avoided. In the Tyvan language we say this kind of giving makes something well (SCHA 2).

Shamans, as religious laypeople remember them from the time before 1944, served the spirits. By fulfilling their duties they stayed psychically and physically healthy. If a shaman refused to fulfil his duties, he risked being afflicted with bad luck, illness, or even death at the hands of his own partner spirits. It was in the own interest of a shaman to ensure a good relationship with the partner spirits and not anger them, and to perform his role as a middleman between human and non-human subjects.

On closer inspection, however, the motivation of many shamans seems to have changed. Shamans continue to explain that their partner spirits oblige them to use their gifts and work regularly as a shaman. The partner spirits who awarded them the shamans' gifts watch over their activities. If doubts are raised about their motivation, shamans today react rather creatively with new explanations from the interaction model's point of view. Earning a living, one of the shaman's motives, is adapted to the old model. A shamaness explained to me that her high income is the result of her partner spirits' gratitude for her services. She also revealed to me that the size of her income shows that she has very powerful partner spirits and that her relationship to them is very good, thanks to her tireless work. If her partner spirits would not agree with her work in the shamanic clinic then she would not earn so much. In this way she did not leave any doubt that the activities of shamans and their earnings fit together.

Today no shaman is embarrassed to transform his talent into hard cash, advertise himself, and demand high prices. Phrases like, 'I need money. I should work again', can be heard, as can the defensive statement 'we need to live on something' with which shamans react to uninvited critique from laypeople.

Despite these secondary rationalisations, by means of which actual behaviour patterns of shamans are adapted to the historical interaction model, many aspects that today are part of the profession of shamans can also be linked to the dominance model. The acquisition and management of clients, payment in cash, the use of rooms in the shamanic clinic, self-organisation, and selling of devotional objects, among other things are marked by the dominance model and can be described as profit-oriented action. Many aspects of the dominance model seem to infuse and complement the interaction model in the activities of contemporary shamans.

The following example shows the change between the models of world interpretation, from the conclusion of an oral contract between a shaman and his client to their taking leave of each other.

On 3 October 2004 I attended a ritual in Mugur Aksy. It was the forty-ninth day after the death of an acquaintance. The ritual was led by a shaman, aged 57 and living in Kyzyl. His task was to feed the soul of the deceased and to convey her final words to her family.

In the ritual many relatives and neighbours took part. The deceased's family had already met a week before the ritual. Many arrangements were made, all motivated by the detailed requests and conditions the deceased had disclosed during the ritual on the seventh day after her death, which was held under the direction of the same shaman. The relatives of the deceased had gone shopping, cleaned the deceased's house, invited relatives and neighbours, slaughtered two sheep, and prepared the food for the guests and as sacrificial offerings. They had also invited the shaman to conduct the ritual.

Shortly before the ritual, the last preparations began, this time in the shaman's presence. Because he knew how to treat the souls of the deceased and what was necessary to succeed in contacting them, he gave the final instructions. On the appointed day, the participants in the ritual arrived. The sacrificial offerings, some food and the wood were packed before we set off in two cars to drive to a hillside below the burial ground. There, the participants built a fire and placed the sacrificial offerings on the firewood. The participants were very concentrated. Finally they sat down in a semicircle about three metres from the sacrificial hearth. The shaman drew a square around the hearth with his red-gripped whip, marking where the deceased's soul would be. He left one side open. As the shaman later explained, he had thus corralled the soul for the safety of the religious laypeople, leaving an opening so that he could himself access the fire. Laypeople were prohibited from sitting on the shaman's side of the hearth so that they would not run the risk of getting into contact with the soul which approaches the sacrificial fire from above and also leaves that way. The shaman crouched close to the hearth and began to concentrate. Then he lit the sacrificial fire with a branch of juniper. He took his ritual mirror and brought it to ring with a metal rod so as to call the soul of the deceased. After she had arrived, a long conversation followed between her and the shaman. He spoke to the deceased's relatives only intermittently, asking them about specific issues.

Again and again, the shaman offered the soul food and beverages. He let an assistant bring him what he wanted, and then he scattered it into the fire. In that time he asked the deceased questions and let her tell him what she wanted her relatives and friends know. The conversation lasted only as long as the fire was burning. When the fire went out, it was the sign that the soul was finished and wanted to leave. The shaman said goodbye and with his red-gripped whip closed the square around the fire. He then examined the burnt remains of the sacrificial offerings. He gathered from what he saw what and how much the deceased had consumed. From these he drew conclusions about her condition and future. Then he turned towards the audience and told them in detail what the deceased had disclosed to him. During the ritual, nobody had dared to speak without being asked. But now the atmosphere was more relaxed and the participants asked, discussed, and interpreted the deceased's words as the shaman had explained them. The participants began to eat and drink in honour of the deceased.

After returning from the ritual site to the house, the commemoration started. Before entering the house, the ritual participants washed their hands with milk and juniper. This form of ritual cleansing was necessary to eliminate the negative energies and impurities that come from a recently deceased person. During the feast all guests toasted the welfare of the deceased in her future life. The shaman stayed with the guests. Only when the guests left one after the other was the shaman also ready to leave. He made it clear in his farewell that he now wished to be compensated. The daughters gave him a very large amount of money for Tyvan standards. But the shaman was not satisfied. He did not express directly that the payment was too low for him, but he showed his discontent. When the shaman then left, the daughters said to me that they now feared that he would do them harm because of his anger. This subject dominated the discussions even on the next day.

The entire course of events on the forty-ninth day shows repeated switching between the dominance and the interaction model by both the shaman and the relatives. The preparations in the family can be understood as interactions between the soul of the deceased and her relatives. The deceased had asked her daughters to invite and cater for them during the first ritual on the seventh day after her death. Rituals and subsequent commemorations on the seventh and the forty-ninth day of death are a service to honour the deceased who dictates and observes their correct execution. Mistakes can be punished by the deceased's soul. Mortuary rituals not least serve to pacify the soul of the deceased, which cannot only be peaceful but also vengeful. Souls are led by the desire to take a close and beloved relative with them on their journey to the other world, which is what relatives need to avoid. Many Tyvans use this belief to explain the accumulation of deaths in a family within a short period of time.

At the same time, rituals for leave-taking from a deceased are the interest of the bereaved, who want to provide a final service to their departed relatives and to organise their feeding, reconciliation, and pacification. During the negotiations with the shaman invited to help, the deceased's daughters acted in accordance with their mother's wishes. They had to hire a shaman to meet their mother's demands, but also in their own interests. The shaman, by contrast, was selling his services. On the one hand, he was bound by his partner spirits to put his abilities at the service of humans and non-human subjects. That means that he had to act as a shaman when asked. On the other hand, he was not obliged to conduct this ritual specifically because he was not a member of the family's clan and did not come from the region, but from Kyzyl. Rather he was interested in the payment that a ritual like this brings. The decision to conduct the ritual or not (i.e. whether to accept the job offer) was his alone. He wanted to earn money and could have refused the job any time. For this reason, I argue that he acted mainly in accordance with the dominance model. After arriving in the house of the deceased, he began to organise the preparations. His knowledge came from his experience with similar events. This regards knowledge the spirits conveyed to him so that he could serve them. In the interaction model, the shaman is obliged to use his talent by committing his knowledge to the service of the spirits, souls, and other non-human subjects, and to avoid mistakes during the ritual's preparation. An incorrect preparation or execution of the ritual would anger not only the soul of the deceased but also the shaman's partner spirits. Not only would the relatives, but he himself, would face punishment.

While the deceased's relatives throughout the process based their interpretations and actions mainly on the interaction model, the shaman only adopted the interaction model with his arrival. He might have been the ritual specialist, but he was not the only actor in it. The entire process of the ritual on the hillside was governed by interactions between the shaman and the deceased. The latter had not only requested specific sacrificial foods and beverages, but also a book and the attendance of certain persons. The shaman had placed himself in the service of the soul and the family. He did not only have to answer her questions but also had to follower her last wishes and transfer her final words to the bereaved.[74] The duration of the ritual was also determined by the deceased. With the extinguishing of the sacrificial fire, the deceased was presumed to have left. The success of the interaction ultimately resulted from the collaboration of all involved parties: the partner spirits, the soul of the deceased, the shaman, and the entire kin-group. The subsequent celebration seemed to be a continuation of the interaction. It took place at the explicit request of the deceased. She had asked her daughters to host the guests at her final celebration and nobody wanted to save money or effort on the happy occasion. As far as I could observe, the first person to return to the dominance model was the shaman. He did so when deciding to leave the celebration and demand payment. Again the master of the situation, he was unhappy about the remuneration. His dissatisfaction clearly shows that today many shamans are no longer satisfied with the gifts of their clients, but have their own ideas about compensation. When a shaman expects a higher payment than his clients can afford, he becomes a professional manager of his own vocational activities. The price for the intermediary activities of a shaman does not seem to belong to the interactions with non-human subjects but becomes a pragmatic commercial interaction between humans. The shaman's work during a ritual

---

[74] For the conversation between the shaman and the deceased, see above ('The Pursuit of Stability in the Interaction Model', TO 1).

becomes a way to make money. The payment forms the complementing frame of the dominance model around the shaman's duties according to the interaction model. All actions connected to the forty-ninth day ritual, from the preparation to the leave-taking of the guests, are in accordance with the interaction model. But they also include elements that make it possible to argue for a mixing or complementing with the dominance model. This includes, in particular, the professional side of the contract between the shaman and the family of the deceased, but also the practice of slaughtering livestock, the preparation of food, the preparation of the tables and seating for the guests in the house and yard, as well as preceding shopping trips in Kyzyl.

Thus there were at least two contracts. The first was concluded between humans and the spirits. In this contract, the conditions were stipulated above all by the soul of the deceased and the partner spirits of the shaman. The entire process of the ritual was not only based on the will of the spirits and the soul of the deceased, but also on the interests of the people involved. In this way, the humans interacted with the non-human subjects involved.

The second contract was professional. It was concluded between humans, namely the bereaved and the shaman. This contract was based on the freedom of choice of both parties. The bereaved selected a shaman. The shaman decided to accept the job offer and to serve the bereaved. The latter in turn had to pay him for his services. This contract was drafted in accordance with the dominance model. Both contracts were honoured, but there was dissent about the latter being properly fulfilled.

It is possible to describe shamans as specialists with the skill to constantly and consciously switch between both models of world interpretation, to complement and to mix them. In doing so, shamans serve their own will and interest as well as the will and the interests of their clients.

On the one hand, they act for the well-being of religious laypeople by arbitrating between human and non-human subjects. On the other hand, they also act in their own interest to earn their livelihood. Both aspects together make up the professional switch of contemporary shamans that is characteristic for their work. In Tyva today, to be active as a shaman means having to combine work (a job based on the dominance model) and religious obligation (a responsibility based on the interaction model). Both sides, the shaman's profession (dominance model) and the shaman's mission (interaction model) have their own interpretations, behaviour, and strategies of action that shamans cleverly employ and apply. At the centre of attention in Tyva, therefore, is always the legitimation and credibility of the shamans, especially for religious laypeople. To preserve both, contemporary shamans have developed the ability to adapt new strategies deriving from the dominance model into the interaction model by using secondary rationalisations (see the next section). In doing so, they permanently adapt the historical interaction model to the present.

I would not argue that contemporary shamans are frauds, as some others do. They are responsive to the needs of their clients and fulfil their function in the interaction model. Even if they earn money on the religious market place, such a market exists. Up to the present day, the majority of Tyvans rely on the help of shamans and their mediating capabilities to help them live up to the demands of the interaction model. If shamans were to carry out their profession in a fraudulent way, they would quickly lose their credibility and therewith their clients. Conscious charlatanry would hardly remain unrevealed for long, and would not find acceptance among potential clients. Only the future can tell how well Tyvan shamans will be able to master the discrepancy between commerce (dominance model) and religious duties (interaction model) in their fundamentally contradictory profession.

Dealing with Change in the Interaction Model

Shamans are professionals confessing to the interaction model. They present themselves and their work from this perspective and derive their legitimacy from it. Shamans cannot deny the interaction model, or they would undermine their own status and role in Tyvan society. Thus they often react vehemently to doubts about the interaction model.

Contemporary shamans fight for more influence for this model in everyday life in Tyva. Their creative influence on the contents of the interaction model, their attempts to preserve it and make it applicable to the present, can be observed in this context. Practising shamans do not only create new rituals and ritual practises that they can offer to laypeople. They also create new interpretations, which they in turn use to advertise the interaction model. With their innovations they respond to contemporary needs in Tyva and in this way adapt the age-old tradition of shamanism to contemporary conditions.

The contents of the dominance model are changing quickly. Its development is accelerated by science, industrial development, and political and social changes, and is transferred by means of media, tourism, and education to the Tyvan people. Because modernity itself stands for a rapid and global development in all sectors of human life, the handling of the rapidly changing contents of the dominance model appears positive and natural. The adoption of new developments or insights in the interaction model, by contrast, seems to be more difficult and questionable. This is probably due to the fact that many Tyvans view the specifically Tyvan interaction model as their tradition. Related to the idea of 'tradition' is the question of 'authenticity'. From the Tyvan emic perspective, tradition is understood as the essence of culture, which lives on permanently and unchanged, handed down from the past. Nevertheless, the contents of the interaction model are also permanently renegotiated and adapted to contemporary developments. I have already pointed to this process of adaptation in the case of shamans who have to legitimate their financial motives to critical laypeople. But the development of the Tyvan interaction model also includes a discourse between various religions, showing changes in beliefs about souls based on Buddhist and Christian influences. In addition, reciprocal influences of shamanistic practices between the West and in Tyva contribute to changes in and the further development of Tyvan shamanism. Furthermore, New Age-ism, esotericism, and animism change the contents of the Tyvan interaction model.

In regard to the dominance model, many Tyvans adapt the influences from Western culture to which they are exposed, like scientific findings, the market economy, and new consumer goods, as well as modern living and working. They adapt new items and ideas to include them in their behaviour and argumentation if they promise to be advantageous.

In the interaction model new insights can also clash with traditional knowledge. If new ideas do not agree with the old ones, especially not with those of the interaction model, and people still want to insert them, they have to be made compatible. This takes place by responding to an innovation with a secondary rationalisation from the perspective of the interaction model, thus adapting and legitimating it. The following case illustrates this process.

In the Tyvan taiga and steppe, increasingly more 4x4 vehicles are appearing. The mainly professional drivers at their wheels, rarely stop at sacred places like *ovaalar* to perform a ritual for the spirit masters, as people on foot or horseback usually do. One explanation for this negligence was that the spirit masters do not expect cars to stop at each *ovaa*. In a car people drive safely and quickly. Only people on foot or horseback are at risk. Therefore the latter indeed take a break at a number of *ovaalar* and other sacred places to pay tribute to the spirit masters of the places. Cars, on the other hand, only pause at important sacred places, *ovaalar* at high mountain passes and those of the driver's clan.

In an all-terrain vehicle, Tyvans want to cover a long distance, preferably quickly and comfortably. A break at every *ovaa* – as the interaction model requires – would run counter to this desire. On a longer journey, travellers pass numerous sacred places. With increased speed, the dense network of sacred places becomes a handicap. The new practice not to stop at every *ovaa* does not conform with the interaction model. Tyvans wanting to make both ideals compatible look for a way to legitimate their behaviour according to the interaction model both towards themselves and others. The new rationalisation says that stops at *ovaalar* and other sacred places help ensure the traveller's safety, but that safety is more inherent to travel by 4x4 than to that on foot or horseback. Therefore, cars have no need to stop at each sacred site and the spirit masters do not demand this from them.

Shamans are masters in adapting Western influences or new developments to the interaction model because they have to permanently legitimate themselves to their clients. The following example concerns the shamanic clinic Nine Heavens in Kyzyl.

Ovaalar mark sacred places or ritual spaces for spirit masters. Tyvans build them at very wild and powerful sites, such as mountain passes or at the foot of specific mountains, preferably far from human settlement, to serve the spirit masters of such places and to participate in their power. When I first visited the shamanic clinic Nine Heavens, situated on the bank of the river Yenisei in the centre of the Tyvan capital Kyzyl, the *ovaa* built there immediately caught my eye. The space where the *ovaa* was situated fundamentally contradicted the rule mentioned above. In May 2005, I asked a shamaness (aged 55) about this *ovaa*. At the time she was working in the shamanic clinic to which the *ovaa* belonged. Without delay she conceded that an *ovaa* in the middle of a town is indeed unusual. She explained that when they founded the clinic and the shamans began to practise there, it soon became apparent that the master of the place with whom they had to permanently interact in their rituals had demanded an *ovaa* to serve and make sacrifices to him. Only under this condition had the spirit master agreed to support them in their work. I questioned why the spirit master had demanded his *ovaa* in the middle of the urban settlement of Kyzyl. As I later recorded in my notes, she replied:

> The master of the place where the clinic is situated is closely related to the master of the Yenisei. Through him he derives his power from the wilderness. The master of the Yenisei likes to linger here because the Yenisei originates here from the confluence of the Bij-Khem and Kaa-Khem rivers. These rivers only flow through wilderness and carry its power with them. The spirit master's power derives from that. But the shamans are obliged to follow the spirit master's instructions.

The shamaness's explanation is given from the perspective of the interaction model, seemingly without influence from the dominance model. She did not allow a discussion about a market-oriented strategy correlating with the dominance model that might also underlie her explanation. Tyvan laypeople at times ascribe commercial thinking to the shamans who built an *ovaa* in the middle of Kyzyl.

When I asked an acquaintance who had followed my conversation with the shamaness intensively about her opinion on the *ovaa* in Kyzyl, she replied that an *ovaa* does not belong in a town. She assumed that the shamans had installed the *ovaa* on the promenade close to the Yenisei because of its public appeal. The shamanic clinic Nine Heavens competes with two other shamanic clinics. All these institutions court clients on whom they depend for their survival. With this *ovaa,* Nine Heavens had a strategic advantage to attract financially strong clients, especially foreign tourists. She doubted whether these shamans were 'real shamans' and regarded them as charlatans who wanted solely to make money. When I pointed out that the spirit master wanted an *ovaa* she answered that if *ovaalar* had always been built outside of settlements, why should it suddenly be correct to do so now?

Here stands opinion against opinion. What remains is the assumption of many laypeople that the shamans of Nine Heavens found an explanation from the perspective of the interaction model for their market-oriented interests, namely to attract more clients. This explanation changes the contents of the interaction model and seems plausible. But it is not accepted by laypeople who abide by the old rules. Nevertheless, this explanation has enough persuasive power to legitimate the *ovaa* in Kyzyl against many sceptical laypeople, as the success of the shamanic clinic ultimately shows.

Summary

From the concept of 'plural world interpretations', the question arises if their flexible use follows certain rules and, if so, what these rules are. The following summary therefore describes the flexible use of both models of world interpretation and discusses the connections and rules, causes and consequences, as well as strategies for changing positions on the continuum between their extreme forms.

The dominance model is currently the most frequently used model of world interpretation in Tyva. Tyvans usually employ this model first when interpreting events, acting in, and reacting to them.

Spontaneous changes of the models of world interpretation therefore often take place in the following order: At first an interpretation or attempt to solve a problem according to the dominance model is applied and after some time the interaction model is drawn upon.

Often a complementing take place, that is, a shift in tendency from one model to the other model.

A shift from a first spontaneous application of the interaction model to the dominance model is much rarer.

Spontaneous switches from the dominance to the interaction model occur especially in problematic situations, especially after pragmatic and rational attempts to resolve the problem fail.

The switch to the interaction model usually accompanies a retrospective reflection on the event.

After a switch to the interaction model, a breach of rules of respectful interaction between human and non-human subjects is identified as the cause of negative situations.

Typical examples of such retrospective reflections from the perspective of the interaction model are so-called true occurrences, that is, reports of events, experiences, or adventures. Often they refer to a breach of norms by people and their subsequent punishment by non-human subjects, such as spirits.

After a spontaneous switch from the dominance to the interaction model, rituals of reconciliation are as typical follow-up actions.

These are followed by long-term behaviour modifications accompanied by the promise to follow the rules of the interaction model more consistently.

Especially accidents and strokes of fate cause a switch from the dominance model to the interaction model and ensure that the possibility to interpret events according to the interaction model is maintained.

In addition to the situation, there are further reasons for switching from the dominance to the interaction model. They include particular spaces (e.g. holy or ritual places), moments in time (e.g. days reserved for rituals), and counterparts (e.g. religious specialists or a researcher working on animism and shamanism).

Prompt interpretations of events based on the interaction model not preceded by a switch from the dominance to the interaction model can be found in periods after rituals. Rituals keep awake the interaction model in the people involved for a while after they are conducted.

Switches between the models of world interpretation can be carried out spontaneously or strategically. Strategic switches in both directions often take place if an individual or a group is not satisfied with the results of applying one of the models of world interpretation. Characteristic is the strategic use of the dominance model during Soviet times in order to hide personal religiosity.

The conscious strategic switch can often be observed in the case of shamans. Currently, shamans need to command several strategies in their business that are linked to the dominance model. These include networking, advertising, bookkeeping, opening and managing shamanic clinics, and the manufacture and sale of devotional objects.

In numerous statements made by Tyvan interview partners, a tendency to explain right and wrong behaviour and action can be found. Such a distinction is often accompanied by an effort to oppose both models of world interpretation as right and wrong and thus postulate the contradictory character of both models.

In so doing, many Tyvans created a narratively idealised pure form of one model of world interpretation. Interpretations of events and situations approximate the extreme forms of each model.

Despite the structural stability of both models of world interpretation, the post-Soviet period is characterised by an observable change in the contents of the two models.

The frequency of applying both models of world interpretation is also changeable. Currently, the dominance model is used more often than the interaction model, the use of which is limited to particular circumstances.

Epilogue: Plural World Interpretations, a Diversity of Views

In academia today, many of the humanities are marginalised as 'exotic'. Such accusations are misleading because the social sciences make a concrete and not to be underestimated contribution to the intellectual development of our society. By studying individual cultures and societies, anthropologists investigate problems that are central to our own society and their results should be applied to our own everyday lives. Anthropological research makes the detour around the non-native because the outside point of view on a foreign society reveals coherencies that for various reasons are difficult to observe in one's own society. On the one hand, it is harder to know one's self than to observe the case of another. On the other, the complexity of Western modernity makes it hard to view correlations on a deeper level. Social anthropology therefore follows the rule that all understanding of the self is preceded by an understanding of the foreign; an understanding of the foreign supports the understanding of the self. Both co-determine each other and thus cannot be separated. From this understanding accrues a sense of appreciation that we need so much in our Western society pervaded by pluralities: Western societies are multicultural; democracy is based on a multi-party system; Western populations are made up of social groups and social classes; our children are educated in a multi-tiered school system; the working environment is made up of many different professions, activities, and roles that must work together effectively; individual opinions are drawn from a plural market of views and positions. Little in our society is not affected by plurality. For this reason alone, we should broaden our approaches to studying our own complex societies so as to comprehend ourselves and each other.

The present study contributes to the theoretical understanding of the founding principle of democracy, namely freedom of speech and expression as codified among others in Article 19 of the Universal Declaration of Human Rights, adopted in 1948: 'Everyone has the right to freedom of opinion and expression; this right includes freedom to hold opinions without interference and to seek, receive and impart information and ideas through any media and regardless of frontiers'.[80]

The premise and consequence of this basic principle is the diversity of opinions and therewith the plurality of interpretation, understanding, argumentation, action, and behaviour. What is a diversity of opinion, how does it come into being, and how do we deal with it? The project outlined in this book provides part of an answer to this and related questions. Its results make it possible to become aware of the phenomenon of the plurality of opinions. The co-existence of different convictions and belief systems is a fundamental human characteristic. A better knowledge about their origins and how we live these every day can positively influence how we each deal with them in our very own personal lives. To understand the reasons behind diversities of opinion is to appreciate, promote, and defend them as a democratic value.

Human interpretation follows models. This means that it is geared to interpretation models that are predetermined by society, culture, and social context and to which we gain access through our socialisation. In order to understand the plurality of opinions, we need first to answer the question of how interpretation models come about and then to explain why we draw from a plurality of them. What I call interpretation models are what Peter L. Berger and Thomas Luckmann called 'realities' in their ground-breaking study *The Social Construction of Reality* (1966). These are 'social stocks of knowledge' that consist of 'recipes for the mastery of routine problems' (ibid. 43). As such these realities are also 'social constructions' (ibid. 55). Our creative handling of problems steadily enriches such realities with new content. By copying and repeating the recipes for routine problems, they become 'institutions' – common knowledge and a factual reality. As such, these stocks of knowledge force themselves upon us for use in everyday situations. Through socialisation processes we adopt them and transform them into subjective realities that we then follow voluntarily and to a large extent without question. This all can be seen as a cycle that takes place continuously in the wider field of our everyday social interactions.

As 'social constructions', interpretation models are also 'social realities'. They are realities that we recognise and acknowledge as such because we are inducted into them through socialisation by our peers and by authorities, and because we share them intersubjectively with others. If we see that others in a certain situation apply a certain interpretation model, we

---

[80] Article 19, Universal Declaration of Human Rights, as adopted by the General Assembly of the United Nations, 10 September 1948 (http://www.un.org/en/documents/udhr, last accessed 19 February 2015). See also, Constitution of the German Democratic Republic Article 5 [1].

gain the feeling that we would do right to do likewise. Thus, we draw our 'truths', including our opinions and beliefs, from these interpretation models. As archetypes and guidelines for interpreting events and situations as well as for understanding connections and directions of correct action and behaviour, they give us a sense of certainty that we are doing things properly when we apply them. In this way, social realities satisfy basic human needs, give us the assurance that we are acting meaningfully, and bring order into our lives.

To find one's way in a certain interpretation model is a lifelong learning process. On the one hand this is because every interpretation model has a high degree of complexity; on the other hand, the content of interpretation models is subject to a permanent renewal process. Again and again, new routines are added to existing ones. This can be witnessed in the rapid development of information technology shaping and changing everyday life around the world. Whether computers or consumer electronics, software or hardware, new products are constantly being introduced and increasingly co-determine our lives.

Human societies are far too complex to be based on only one interpretation model or social reality. All societies owe their plural world interpretations to a more or less strong differentiation into diverse interpretation models. Berger and Luckmann (1966) call this the 'social distribution of knowledge'. As they explained,

> I encounter knowledge in everyday life as socially distributed, that is, as possessed differently by different individuals and types of individuals. I do not share my knowledge equally with all my fellowmen, and there may be some knowledge that I share with no one. I share my professional expertise with colleagues, but not with my family.... The social distribution of knowledge of certain elements of everyday reality can become highly complex and even confusing to the outsider (Berger and Luckmann 1966: 46).

However, members of a society share a basic model, a common interpretation model that forms the basis of all further interpretation models (Schütz 1945: 533; Schütz 1971b: 394). The sociology of knowledge calls this 'everyday reality'. Humans adopt this basic model of interpretation during 'primary socialisation' in childhood, and we share it to a great degree with most members of society (Berger and Luckmann 1966: 129 ff.). This basic reality is the foundation of all interpretation, action, and behaviour in society, and all other interpretation models refer to it in some way. It forms the basis for all 'sub-models' or 'sub-worlds' that our culture and society offers us and which we only acquire selectively (ibid. 138). Sub-models are those interpretation models that include 'specialised knowledge' that help an individual to integrate into a particular social group and to handle institutions and routines that are part of group membership (ibid. 78).

While we have little choice in our socialisation into the everyday reality of our society in early childhood, and we learn the basic model of interpretation from our parents and others, we have much more influence in deciding which sub-worlds and sub-models we will access subsequently. We are, of course, subject to various social forces and influences, but we still have a say in deciding, for example, which profession we want to learn or what sport we want to practise.

Human beings orient themselves on the basic model of 'everyday reality' that all members of a society more or less share with each other. In addition, they draw on several sub-models in enclaves of their personal, private, and public lives that they share with smaller groups of people. These sub-models can be affected by family and relatives, professional life, religious affiliation, political interests and attitudes, hobbies, and other leisure activities. They all have their own routines of interpretation, argumentation, action, and behaviour. Humans must be inducted in each sub-model in a process of socialisation. They adopt it in a learning process. To do so, we rely in part on authorities or specialists, like a teacher, trainer, or pastor. But much can also be learned by observation, imitation, or study. That which is learned includes political attitudes; religious beliefs; moral values; knowledge of art, music, and literature; dress codes, and behaviour rules. Not all sub-models at our disposal are learned with the same intensity. We are more at home in some than in others; some we apply more often and more skilfully than others; and for some we have more sympathy and are more convinced of than for others. We desire access only to some sub-models. Others we refuse. Such desires or antipathies can be witnessed especially in matters of political or religious affiliation, which imply conscious decisions for a particular interpretation model. Not everyone wants to convert to Islam, and an ecologically-oriented politician will not want to argue from the sub-model of a conservative political party. Different interpretation models also provide us with different backgrounds for considering one and the same issue. A fisherman considers a river under other aspects than a worker in a hydroelectric station; a city dweller shopping in a supermarket has a different relationship to food than a farmer.

Interpretation models can be allocated to social groups and social specialisations. Social groups include kinship groups and circles of friends. Social specialisations include professions, religions, politics, and activities centred on leisure, culture, or art. How intensely various interpretation models differ from each other within one category, and how they influence our interpretation, argumentation, action, and behaviour towards varying forms of expression can be best demonstrated in a description of two professions that have each developed their own distinctive sub-model: natural science and theology. A natural scientist and a theologian interpret a common phenomenon in completely different ways and come to very different, essentially contradictory conclusions. A natural scientist follows the principles and methods of empiricism. Empiricism draws objective knowledge from sensual experience. In such a process, experience and observation alone are allowed as the basis for theory formation. Truth is based exclusively on experience, observation, and reproducible results. Only what can be observed can be proven. And only what can be proven can be true. In turn, only questions about truth are meaningful. All others are speculation or imagination.

Theology, on the other hand, is the study of the nature of God (for Christianity, Judaism, and Islam) or of gods (e.g. in antiquity). It is the study of faith, its sources (canonical writings), and practices (rituals, prayers, norms, and taboos). In cognitive processes realised in the context of religious interpretation models, phenomena that cannot be empirically proven can nevertheless be classified as true and fundamental. The influence of one or more intelligent non-human beings on the lives of human beings is not questioned. Nor are questions raised about the general validity of codified or canonical norms that circumscribe correct interpretation, action, and behaviour within a particular religious community.

In short, that which a natural scientist will declare to be natural law on the basis of empirical facts is attributed by a theologian to the will and work of God or gods.

The conflict between an ecologically-oriented and a conservative politician can be analysed in the same way. The first builds on the principle that we can only live secure and good lives if we protect the environment. The second, by contrast, argues that we can only live well if the economy keeps growing. Both develop different strategies and implement opposing policies. Despite their different interpretations, both have the same purpose in mind: the well-being of our society.

The fact that both political perspectives are based in a common political model does not prevent them from interpreting society and its development according to their individual sub-models (as presented in party statutes, resolutions and programmes) nor from enforcing their arguments in a competition of opinions and democratic elections. A parliamentary democracy is only possible when the existence of several political sub-models is permitted.

These two examples also show that two individuals can disagree about an issue and still both be right. That is, insights from different interpretation models can be of equal value, even if they contradict each other.

One reason behind this phenomenon is that the truth of an argument is only logically consistent within the interpretation model that was used to form it. The findings of a theologian can only be judged using theological criteria. The findings of a natural scientist can only be verified within the domain of the natural sciences. The strategies of politicians of various parties can be evaluated with reference to their common political model, but must also be understood in terms of their own sub-models.

All interpretation models, especially those founding theory, develop basic principles or premises for their use and methods for their implementation. Natural scientists, for example, follow the basic principle that only empiricism and repeatable experiments generate scientific knowledge. By contrast, Christian theologians rely on canonical knowledge of the Bible and apply it to all questions that need clarification. The results of the application of one interpretation model can be correct only when the basic principles of the interpretation model are included correctly in the argumentation and when the appropriate methods are applied in the right way.

Additional evidence for the equal value of different interpretations models is that the falsification of the insights of one interpretation model from the perspective of another are logically false. A natural scientist cannot empirically prove the non-existence of God because God eludes his detection. The natural scientist's instruments are not appropriate for such a demonstration. For him, the question of God's existence is not a meaningful question. In contrast, politicians from different parties have to comprehend each other's arguments in order to criticise them. Well-founded critique generally implies seeing things from the perspective of the other, retracing his arguments, and finding mistakes in his application of an interpretation model. The attempt to refute an interpretation model from the perspective of another interpretation model is pointless given the fact that all interpretation models are social constructions. This means that they are subject to the same imperfection and insufficiency of the human mind. To do so would be to play off one human construction against another. What is important is that these constructions are self-contained and consistent in themselves; this cannot necessarily be judged from the perspective of another construction. As human constructions, all interpretation models are equal. Nevertheless, an interpretation model can collapse when its preconditions and methods prove to be inconsistent. An interpretation model can also lose credibility when it becomes clear that its use has unwanted consequences, as in the case of the ideology of National Socialism.

In any case, human beings tend to permanently want to judge the quality of knowledge. This comparison of knowledge based in different interpretation models is based solely on individual decisions or social negotiations. In our personal decisions for or against an interpretation model, our socialisation helps us. In the short term, our decisions are determined by situation and context. Someone who has grown up in a Christian home will tend more often to refer to the Christian interpretation model in later life. They decide to do so. However, in certain situations and contexts, they will avoid doing so, for example when learning math or later when working in a context inconsistent with Christian interpretation models. In that case, situation and context (mathematics or profession) decide which interpretation model is applicable.

An individual deciding on an interpretation model may feel himself to be under greater or lesser social pressure because he desires credibility among fellow human beings. Such a desire quite often forces the use of a particular interpretation model considered suitable for a situation by a particular peer-group. Anyone who is nonconformist risks various forms of social exclusion.

In contrast to most other interpretation models, the natural sciences and theology have relatively well-defined and closed borders. The clarity of these borders should not be misleading. Most everyday sub-models are marked by smooth transitions in which fields of transdifference overlap. A person's application of one model of interpretation is only tendential because multiple models are often applied in mixed forms or complementarily.

The plural world interpretations that give this book its title emerge with the mixing and complementing of several interpretation models. Plural world interpretations, which include a diversity of opinions, concern not only society as a whole, but individuals as well. That is, we encounter different opinions among different people, but also within individuals, depending on the situation and context. How can individuals express such contradictory interpretations?

Society and culture provide individuals with innumerable sub-models. People deal with this variety of interpretations selectively.

On the one hand, people can adopt or reject a certain sub-model. On the other, sub-models are learned to differing degrees of intensity. While we do not adopt all sub-models but choose a few, we are acquainted with a larger number of them. This means that an individual can resort to a diversity of sub-models in everyday life. They all belong to our personal repertoire of interpretation, action, and behaviour. They may contradict or complement each other. They form in us a web of more or less overlapping subsets of routines and strategies. In the family, at work, and in leisure a multitude of interpretation models are used, influencing our view on all issues. Depending on the situation and context, we select some of these sub-models. We only rarely do so in a clear manner; more often we use the models in combination, in mixed or complementary forms. The multiplicity of sub-models available to us results in our own plurality of interpretations.

As Berger and Luckmann noted, interpretation models contain 'recipes for the mastery of routine problems' (1966: 43). For interpreting a situation or solving a problem, different models may provide different recipes.

Depending on the situation and context, people decide which interpretation model or which combination of interpretation models they prioritise. In doing so, they arrive at different interpretations, strategies, and solutions in different situations.

A mother sees a child from a different perspective than does a paediatrician or kindergarten teacher. In each of the three 'roles' (Goffman 1959), the adult sees the child from a particular sub-model and argues accordingly about the child's well-being. The paediatrician will consider the child's mental and physical development; the kindergarten teacher will be interested in his ability to integrate into and to behave in the kindergarten group; and the mother will see her beloved child as someone whom she wants to protect, care for, and nurture. The roles played by the adults determine their interpretation, action, and behaviour vis-à-vis the child. To a degree, all three will be able to understand the perspective of the others. Although a paediatrician or a kindergarten teacher might also be a mother, their choices of interpretation models in their professional roles will still determine situationally their interpretation, action, and behaviour.

I have tried to demonstrate the human plurality and flexibility of world interpretation by analysing two specifically Tyvan interpretation models of everyday life as well as of their flexible use by local actors in the South Siberian Republic of Tyva. I showed that the plurality of interpretations, and in turn the fundamentally democratic value of diversity of opinions, is an essential human characteristic. People – no matter the society in which they live – draw their interpretations of the world from various co-existing models that are of equal value. They create them to be plural and flexible. In addition, our appreciation of the plurality of interpretations and the diversity of opinions supports our willingness to change perspective and to take on and accept the perspective of others. Only in this way are we able to understand each other. The ability to change perspectives is followed directly by the ability to experience mutual empathy. We appreciate people more if we can understand their perspective. It follows that dictating an opinion by force is not only contrary to democratic values but also to human nature. For this reason alone, it should be our innermost desire to respect the opinions of others as much as our own.

Appendices

Краткое содержание: «Множественные интерпретации мира. Пример тувинцев Южной Сибири.»

Мы используем *множественные интерпретации мира* (англ. *plural world interpretations*) ежедневно и, в большинстве случаев, неосознанно. Осуществляется это за счёт одновременного и равноценного сосуществования различных моделей мировоззрения. Они являются продуктом творческой деятельностей человека и сосуществуют в качестве параллельных реальностей, дополняя и, одновременно, противореча друг другу. На примере тувинцев Южной Сибири данная книга знакомит с двумя моделями мировоззрения, а также с практикой их применения. Показывается, как локальные акторы гибко применяют две из существующего множества моделей: и для того, чтобы действовать в складывающихся ситуациях, и чтобы толковать их. Станет понятным, каким правилам при этом следуют тувинцы, какими мотивами руководствуются и какие это имеет последствия. Результатом явится картина современной культуры, которая будет отвечать имеющимся на данный момент запросам гибкости и многообразия в мировоззрении, действиях и поведении человека.

Введение

Название «*Множественные интерпретации мира*» отражает актуальную и наблюдаемую во всем мире множественность мировоззренческих моделей и человеческую способность гибко обращаться с ними. На примере тувинцев, живущих на юге Сибири, данное исследование представляет дополнение к тем гуманитарным работам, которые описывают культуры в категориях „традиции" и „современности". В центре данной работы находится не строгое проведение границ между традиционными и современными культурами и культурными элементами, а описание их сосуществования. Помимо этого, понятие *множественных мировоззрений* должно помочь нам занять необходимую для заданной цели более широкую позицию, которая представляет традицию и современность равноправно рядом друг с другом.

Термин „традиция" используется самими тувинцами в соответствии с „конвенциональным понятием традиции", как это определяют Хандлер и Линнекин (Handler и Linnekin 1984: 286), то есть как *непрерывная последовательность культурных основ:* «Превалирующая концепция традиции, как в общем смысле, так и в социальной теории, рисует ее изолированным телом или сердцевиной неизменяемых элементов, передаваемых по наследству из прошлого». Относительно такого натуралистического взгляда на традицию авторы высказывают мысль, что «традиция – это символический процесс [и] заданный смысл». Такое понимание термина базируется на взгляде, согласно которому «прошлое всегда конструируется в настоящем» (там же). В этом смысле мои собственные наблюдения в Туве также убеждают в том, что „традицию" нужно понимать „как изобретение" (см. также: Hobsbawm и Ranger 1992) Таким образом становится ясно, каким образом то, что мы в обиходе называем „традицией", постоянно видоизменяется и почему так сложно отделить исторические культурные элементы от недавних. Использование концептов „традиционности" и „современности" не только в языке российской повседневности, но отчасти и в языке науки упускает зачастую из виду тот факт, что как „традиционные", так и „современные" культурные элементы постоянно изменяются и подвергаются влияниям извне. Продолжающиеся дискуссии о терминах „традиция" и „современность" являются причинами неиспользования мною этих терминов в этой работе; вместо них я формулирую свои собственные, которые не столь нагружены с научной и бытовой точек зрения, и которые я вывожу лишь из структур представленных здесь моделей интерпретаций мира.

Новое понятие *множественных интерпретаций мира*, вводимое здесь в научный дискурс, позволяет осуществить такое описание современной культуры, которое на примере отдельных *акторов* охватывает множество параллельно существующих, равнозначных, но также и противоречащих друг другу моделей интерпретаций мира. В работе будет показано, как люди обращаются с ассортиментом различных моделей интерпретаций мира, насколько гибко их применяют с тем, чтобы реагировать на происходящие события или действовать в определенных ситуациях. Таким образом, я исследую существующее на данный момент множество моделей интерпретаций мира и способность человека свободно/гибко применять их в повседневной жизни.

После подробного введения в концепт *множественных интерпретаций мира* на примере тувинцев, чьими верованиями являются анимизм и шаманизм, будут показаны и описаны две модели таковых интерпретаций. С использованием терминов *модель доминирования* и *модель взаимодействия* будет осуществлен поиск стабильных структурных элементов, а также освещена изменчивость их содержания. Специфически тувинская *модель доминирования* основывается на современном понимании доминирования человека в природе, каковая состоит в основном из пассивных объектов человеческой деятельности. В противовес ей в повседневной жизни тувинцев присутствует особая тувинская *модель взаимодействия*. Она исходит из представления о взаимодействиях в мире, окружающем и включающем человека, и состоящем из человеческих и нечеловеческих субъектов.

Поскольку множество моделей интерпретаций мира является в равной мере неотъемлемой частью информационного, поведенческого, акционального репертуара локальных акторов, то данная работа уделяет большое внимание описанию свободного, гибкого обращения с ними. На основе большого числа примеров прослеживается, как отдельные тувинцы при толковании событий или при поведении в неких ситуациях осознано применяют две модели интерпретаций мира в зависимости от контекста или потребности, заменяя при этом одну другой или же смешивая их обе / дополняя одну другой. При этом анализируется то, какие правила регулируют гибкое использование этих моделей. Также рассматриваются причины и следствия смены моделей толкования, а также различие между спонтанной и стратегической их сменой у обывателей или же профессиональной у тувинских шаманов.

Теоретические основы

Используемое в данной работе понятие *множественные интерпретации мира* основывается на феноменологическо-конструктивистстих представлениях, согласно которым человек понимается как творец многообразных реальностей, которые определяют одновременно его толкования, а также основанные на этих толкованиях поведение и действия. Нижеприведенное определение проясняет употребление этого термина в данной работе: множественные интерпретации мира *обозначают толкования, и базирующиеся на этих толкованиях действия и поведение человека. Они основываются на гибком использовании различных одновременно существующих и равноценных моделей интерпретации мира. Будучи внутренне как содержательно, так и структурно непротиворечивыми, модели интерпретации мира, дополняя друг друга и одновременно друг другу противореча, относятся, таким образом, к репертуару знаний, поведения и действий человека.*

При моментальном толковании ситуаций и событий, а также при принятии решений о поведении и действии люди выбирают из множества моделей, которые в этой работе обозначаются как модели интерпретации мира. Употребление термина *модель* указывает на то, что для интерпретации конкретных ситуаций и событий акторы пользуются множеством „комплектов" с примерами или шаблонами, которые следует понимать, как логичные внутри себя системы, имеющие содержание и структуру. Большое число и многообразие моделей, а также гибкость в обращении людей с ними, подтверждают их модельный характер. В качестве моделей они не являются ни природной данностью, ни биологическим свойством человека, но лишь продуктом человеческого воображения. В данной работе они понимаются как *общественные конструкции* и, соответственно, как *общественный продукт* (Berger und Luckmann 2012 [1966]).

Используемые термины *интерпретация* или *толкование* не являются тождественными восприятию. *Интерпретация* и *толкование* подразумевают поведение человека, которое следует процессам его же человеческого восприятия. Воспринятая в конкретной ситуации информация впоследствии может быть интерпретирована по-разному. В этом случае тувинцы следуют тем *примерам* и *шаблонам*, которые обусловлены их культурой и которые обозначаются здесь как интерпретационные модели. Последующие же действия актор выстраивает также в соответствии с принятой моделью толкования.

Понятие *мир* – как составная часть понятий *множественные интерпретации мира* и *модели интерпретации мира* – основывается на конструктивистском понятии *жизненного мира* (англ. *life-world*), которое восходит к феноменологии Эдмунда Гуссерля (Husserl 1954 [1936]). Альфред Шютц (Schütz 1945: 533; Schütz и Luckmann 2003 [1975]) ввел его в форме *выдающаяся действительность* (англ. *paramount reality*) в социологический анализ. Позже это понятие развили Петер Бергер и Томас Лукман (Berger и Luckmann 2012 [1966]: 21-31), использовав его в виде термина *повседневный мир* (англ. *world of daily life*) или *повседневная действительность* (англ. *everyday social reality*).

Обе представленные в этой работе модели интерпретации мира – доминирования и взаимодействия – следует отнести к повседневной действительности. Они являются частью и одновременно основополагающим элементом социально конструированной „действительности повседневного мира" (Berger и Luckmann 2012 [1966]: 21-29).

Модели доминирования и взаимодействия можно представить как „хранилище знаний" (Berger и Luckmann 2012 [1966]: 43). Они состоят из „знания рецептов" (там же: 44) и служат для „решения рутинных проблем" (там же: 44). Будучи частью специфически тувинской повседневной реальности их можно смело расценивать как общие (интерсубъективные) для всех тувинцев.

В данном исследовании были рассмотрены две из множества существующих моделей интерпретации мира. Люди, живущие в индустриальном обществе, обычно ориентируются на модель мировоззрения, которую я в дальнейшем буду обозначать как *модель доминирования*. Это определение являет собой модель интерпретации мира, которая исходит из *доминирования человека над окружающей средой, состоящей скорее из пассивных объектов человеческого воздействия*. Эта модель характеризуется следующими чертами: (1) Она разделяет человека и окружающую его среду и противопоставляет их друг другу. (2) Она различает между активным действующим субъектом (человек) и скорее пассивными объектами человеческого воздействия (компоненты окружающей среды). Действие всегда исходит от субъекта – человека по направлению к как минимум одному объекту, который принадлежит к окружающей человека среде. (3) Активному человеку противопоставляется пассивная окружающая среда, которая следует законам природы, и которая поэтому может быть понята человеком, контролируема и подвержена его влиянию. (4) Взаимодействия возможны только между сознательными субъектами (людьми). Пограничными случаями являются инстинкты животных. Современному человеку они дают ощущение взаимодействия между человеком и животным. Тем не менее, инстинкты животных несравнимы с разумом и рассудком человека. (5) Осознанность, воля, разум и рассудок, как свойства человека, не являются свойствами окружающей его не-человеческой среды. Человек – единственный, кто способен осознанно работать над своей окружающей средой, однако законами природы ему поставлены границы. (6) При обустройстве жизни человек обустраивает и окружающую его среду. Лишь заблуждения и неверное понимание естественных взаимосвязей способны оттолкнуть человека от этого стремления.

Присутствие человека в мире с точки зрения *модели взаимодействия* выглядит иначе, чем в интерпретации согласно модели доминирования, хотя и не является его прямой противоположностью. Это понятие обозначает модель, которая исходит из *взаимодействий, происходящих в среде, окружающей и включающей в себя человека, и состоящей из человеческих и не-человеческих субъектов*. В его специфически тувинском выражении это определение имеет следующие свойства: (1) Человек является неотъемлемой частью мира. (2) Рядом с человеком существует множество не-человеческих субъектов (3) Между человеческими и не-человеческими партнерами или акторами происходит взаимодействие. Термин „взаимодействие между субъектами" не ограничивается людьми. (4) Наряду с человеком, в качестве активных субъектов рассматриваются все элементы окружающей среды. (4.1) К ним принадлежат духи и божества; животные и растения; но также предметы обихода – инструменты и машины, а также источники естественной энергии и сил; земля, небо, звезды, солнце и луна; элементы ландшафта, такие как вода, источники, реки и озера, горы и долины, леса, деревья, поляны и многое другое. Все названные элементы мира постоянно влияют на человеческую жизнь. (5) Разум, схожий с человеческим, приписывается не всем не-человеческим субъектам. (5.1) Однако нельзя представить себе духов и божества без способности мыслить, без рассудка и разума, без осознанных действий. (5.2) Субъекты модели взаимодействия подчиняются иерархии, которая ставит духов и богов на первое место, а людей на второе. Параллельно существуют энергии и силы, которые неосознанно и без определенной воли влияют на все компоненты мира. Дикие и домашние животные, растения, части ландшафта, инструменты и предметы обихода подчинены людям и духам, энергиям и силам. (5.3) Однако эта иерархия не является абсолютной. В зависимости от ситуации, в которой происходит взаимодействие, различные субъекты могут быть сильнее, равносильны или слабее друг друга. Например, если дерево не хочет быть спиленным человеком или животное не хочет быть убитым, то они устраивают на его пути препятствия.

В данной работе выявление структур модели доминирования и модели взаимодействия основывается на разделении структуры и содержания. Содержанием является то, что Щютц и Лукманн (Schütz и Luckmann 2003: 657) обозначают как „интерсубъективные символические значения", которые варьируют в зависимости и от культуры, и от исторического периода. Согласно формулировке Щютца и Лукманна (там же), они приводят к „невероятному множеству общественно-исторических форм". В то время как содержание какой-либо модели мировоззрения находится в процессе постоянного изменения и развития, структуры обеих интерпретационных моделей, напротив, кажутся по тенденции глобальными и стабильными во времени.

Концепт множественных интерпретаций мира

Целью предыдущей главы было введение в теорию и практику множественных интерпретаций мира на примере тувинцев Южной

Сибири. Данная работы сфокусирована на двух весьма распространенных в Туве моделях интерпретации мира и их гибком применении как отдельными персонами, так и группами людей. Это, с одной стороны, специфически тувинская *модель доминирования*, которую тувинцы охотно воспринимают как современное мировоззрение на основе русского влияния, и, с другой стороны, специфически тувинская *модель взаимодействия*, которую Тувинцы определяют как свою традиционную анимистско-шаманистическую картину мира. Наряду с еще одной моделью, специфически тувинской ламаистской картиной мира тибетского образца, все названные модели являются частью повседневной реальности тувинцев, которую они (модели) одновременно и формируют. Несмотря на то, что они зачастую противоречат друг другу, эти модели параллельно являются составляющими духовной культуры всех, с кем я общалась. Один и тот же тувинец может применить их и как вариант толкования чего-либо и как принцип выбора правильного действия и поведения.

1. Обе модели интерпретации мира, *модель взаимодействия* и *модель доминирования*, можно найти у тувинцев как существующие параллельно и со специфически тувинским содержанием.

2. Крайние проявления обеих моделей настолько принципиально противоречат друг другу, что интерпретация какой-нибудь ситуации с точки зрения одной модели выглядит условной, противоречивой и неприемлемой с точки зрения другой, и наоборот.

3. В высказываниях тувинцев обе модели интерпретации мира зачастую проявляются в *форме идеализированного нарратива*. Многие тувинцы охотно причисляют себя только к одной из двух моделей интерпретаций мира.

4. Мои собеседники различали оба вида интерпретаций и соотносили свои высказывания с эмическим понятиями „современности" или „традиции".

5. По своей структуре обе модели интерпретации мира представляются стабильными. Однако их конкретного содержания может быстро меняться. Причиной тому могут быть медиа, школьное или профессиональное образование, наука, путешествия, туризм, но также и эзотерика и нью-эйдж.

6. Ни одну из этих двух интерпретационных моделей нельзя приписать лишь „тувинцам": многие тувинцы чувствуют себя комфортно, пользуясь ими обеими, а также находясь между ними, в *трансдифферентном пространстве* (англ. *transdifference*).[7]

---

[7] Термин *transdifference* в англоязычной научной литературе обычно рассматривается в паре с дополняющим его (и одновременно контрастирующим с ним) термином

7. Наблюдения за действиями и поведением тувинцев, а также за их разговорами друг с другом позволяют увидеть толкования и интерпретации, которые используют обе интерпретационных модели, смешивая их или дополняя одну другой. При этом тувинцы в зависимости от потребности обращаются то к одной, то к другой крайности или же меняют свою позицию в континууме *трансдифферентного пространства* между этими моделями.

8. Сиюминутная интерпретация мира тувинцем зависит от его позиции в *трансдифферентном пространстве*, т.е. от той позиции, которую он занимает в определенный момент времени, в определенной ситуации и в определенном контексте в континууме, и от того, какой (позиции) он в данный момент желает следовать.

9. Из этого следует, что интерпретации мира у тувинцев подвержены постоянным изменениям не только с содержательной стороны, но также и структурно не являются *однозначными*, *одномерными* и *статичными*, а предстают скорее *гибкими*, *ситуативными* и *множественными*.

Этнография специфически тувинской модели взаимодействия

Для описания многообразных взаимодействий между субъектами человеческими и не-человеческими я использую примеры из тувинских народных верований (англ. folk religion), которые легли в основание данной работы в форме отчетов о событиях и пережитых ситуациях, интервью, записях ритуальных текстов, а также современных фольклорных текстов. В обобщенной форме выявляются следующие характерные черты:

1. Тувинцы не считают себя единственными разумными существами и действующими силами, живущими в мире. Они связаны *сетью* с нечеловеческими субъектами, с которыми они постоянно осознанно и неосознанно взаимодействуют. От успеха этих взаимодействий зависит благополучие человека, почему соблюдению правил и норм модели взаимодействия, а также осознанной осторожности при взаимодействии с нечеловеческими субъектами придается большое значение.

---

transculturality, и используется для обозначения феномена сосуществования (не обязательно множественных) контрастирующих объединений (аффилиаций) и признаков (атрибутирования), для указания тем самым на то, что́ остается после попытки распределения неких элементов по группам согласно логике включения/исключения.

2. Если судить по частоте упоминаний и взаимодействий с ними, то можно сказать, что *духи-хозяева* являются важнейшими нечеловеческими партнерами, взаимодействующими с людьми. Будучи истинными хозяевами, они защают все сущее, устанавливают правила и нормы обращения с ним, следят за их соблюдением и наказывают за проступки.

3. Любая деятельность человека может быть интерпретирована как *взаимодействие между людьми и духами-хозяевами*. В положительном смысле к этому относятся: принятие во внимание того, что *духи-хозяева* имеют власть над всем сущим; соблюдение требований этих духов и ими установленных правил и норм; проведение ритуалов благодарения, прошения и умиротворения; различные области духовной культуры, а также реализация талантов и способностей, данных духами-хозяевами. В негативном смысле любое нарушение правил и норм модели взаимодействия также следует понимать как взаимодействие между людьми и духами-хозяевами.

4. Толкование, поведение и действия многих тувинцев в соответствии с моделью взаимодействия поддерживается в настоящее время прежде всего за счёт устной традиции. К одному из важнейших жанров относятся так называемые *истинные случаи (*тув. *болган таварылгалар, современные предания*) (Oelschlägel 2013). Типичным их сюжетом является нарушение человеком правил уважительного взаимодействия между субъектами-людьми и нечеловеческими субъектами, и, как следствие, наказание (несчастье, болезнь, смерть). Популярны также рассказы, повествующие об удивительных награждениях тех, кто отличился особо корректным обращением с правилами и нормами модели взаимодействия.

5. Нарушение какой-либо нормы осознается людьми в основном лишь тогда, когда в их жизни происходит какое-то несчастье. *Исправление последствий нарушений этих норм* осуществляется поэтапно: толкование несчастья в соответствии с моделью взаимодействия; обращение к шаману с просьбой продумать ситуацию и выяснить, какие духи и каким образом связаны с ситуацией, и дать руководство к решению проблемы; проведение ритуалов умиротворения и прошения, обращенных к соответствующему духу (возможно под руководством шамана); обещание изменить свое поведение в плане более уважительного взаимодействия.

6. В связи с *духами-хозяевами* рассматриваются также *способности* людей. Способности не являются какими-то особенными врожденными качествами и не воспринимаются как награда одаренных. Способности – в понимании тувинцев – это обязательства.

Духи-хозяева различных талантов выбирают и обязывают людей служить какому-либо таланту, с тем, чтобы они занимались этим в мире людей. Человек, выбранный духом-хозяином какого-либо таланта, обязуется под угрозой наказания не скупиться на него, не злоупотреблять им, не создавать себе за счет этого таланта нечестных преимуществ и, что касается воплощения таланта, использовать максимум своих способностей.

7. Модель взаимодействия служит сохранению *гармонии, равновесия* и *стабильности* в сфере взаимной зависимости субъектов-людей и нечеловеческих субъектов. В случае если тувинец нарушает уравновешенное взаимодействие, то он подвергает себя опасности быть наказанным духами. Последствиями могут быть несчастные случаи, вызванные *духом-хозяином*. Духи могут так же нарушать стабильность уважительного взаимодействия. Например, опасность для отдельных людей могут представлять нападения заигравшихся или злых духов, которые считаются вредоносными.

8. Человек видит себя в постоянной зависимости от благосклонности различных духов. Однако, существование и благополучие духов рассматривается в зависимости от поведения и поступков людей. С одной стороны, человек зависит от того, что ему дают духи-хозяева. С другой стороны, неправильное обращение или даже разрушение данного ими ведет к негативным последствиям для самих *духов-хозяев*. Когда люди разрушают собственность какого-либо *духа-хозяина,* это значит, что они уничтожают его самого; неправильное обращение с собственностью духа-хозяина отнимает у него силы; неиспользование таланта и утеря знаний о том, как его использовать, ведет, вместе со своим исчезновением, к исчезновению самого *духа-хозяина*.

9. Одаренные духами *шаманы* также имеют свою функцию в модели взаимодействия. Они являются посредниками между субъектами-людьми и не-человеческими субъектами. При помощи *духов-помощников* они проясняют ситуацию, которая угрожает взаимодействию. В случае, если взаимодействие вышло из равновесия, они помогают снова восстановить состояние стабильности и гармонии. Их задача при этом – умиротворить духов-хозяев и побороть выходки вредоносных духов. Они руководят ритуалами умиротворения, прошения и благодарения и, в качестве предостерегающих советников, указывают людям путь уважительного взаимодействия с не-человеческими субъектами.

10. Таким образом, в тувинском восприятии человеческие и не-человеческие субъекты связаны между собой и зависят друг от друга при любых условиях.

Множественные интерпретации мира у тувинцев

Из изложенного выше концепта *множественных интерпретаций мира* возникает вопрос – на основе каких правил осуществляется гибкое обращение с ними. Именно поэтому основные пункты, приведенные ниже, посвящены теме гибкого обращения с обеими интерпретационными моделями и затрагивают связи и закономерности, причины и последствия, а также различные стратегии смены позиций в континууме между крайностями.

1. В качестве интерпретационной модели, *модель доминирования* чаще применяется в настоящее время. Она является в первую очередь руководящей линией для объяснения какого-либо события и реакции на него.

2. *Спонтанная смена* интерпретационных моделей часто происходит соответственно от первичного объяснения и решения проблемы согласно модели доминирования к последующему задействованию модели взаимодействия, однако с задержкой по времени.

3. Часто имеет место *дополнение*, т.е. смещение тенденции от одной модели к другой.

4. Реже и спонтанно применяется сначала модель взаимодействия, которая в последующем *сменяется* моделью доминирования.

5. *Неожиданная смена* модели доминирования на модель взаимодействия случается при проблемных ситуациях, в которых прагматичные и рациональные методы решения проблемы не действуют.

6. Переход к модели взаимодействия происходит часто как следствие *дополнительной рефлексии* относительно произошедших событий.

7. После перехода к модели взаимодействия, *причинами* негативной ситуации объявляются нарушения правил уважительного взаимодействия между человеческими и не-человеческими субъектами.

8. Типичными примерами таких дополнительных рефлексий, происходящих с точки зрения модели взаимодействия, являются так называемые *истинные случаи* (тув. *болган таварылгалар* или же *современные предания*). Они описывают зачастую нарушение людьми

норм и следующее за этим наказание, осуществляемое нечеловеческими субъектами, например, духами.

9. Типичным последствием внезапной смены модели доминирования на модель взаимодействия являются *ритуалы умиротворения*.

10. За ними вновь следует *долгосрочное изменение поведения*, которое сопровождается обещанием уважительнее выполнять предписания модели взаимодействия.

11. Возможность интерпретации ситуаций в соответствии с моделью взаимодействия поддерживается, прежде всего, *несчастными случаями* и *ударами судьбы,* которые в свою очередь, часто ведут к смене интерпретационной модели моделью взаимодействия.

12. Наряду с такими ситуациями, к замене модели доминирования на модель взаимодействия могут вести и иные причины: посещение определенных мест (к примеру, священных мест или мест отправления ритуалов), наступление определенного времени (напр., дни, отведенные под определенные ритуалы) и встречи с определенными людьми (напр., с религиозными специалистами).

13. Интерпретацию, осуществляемую вскоре после событий в соответствии с моделью взаимодействия, когда переход к ней от модели доминирования не является необходимым, можно наблюдать прежде всего *в период после ритуала.* Ритуалы поддерживают в их участниках идею модели взаимодействия еще некоторое время после их (ритуалов) проведения.

14. Смена интерпретационных моделей может осуществляться спонтанно или стратегически/намеренно. *Стратегические смены* (моделей) часто происходят в обоих направлениях в случаях, когда человек или группа людей недовольны результатами применения той или иной интерпретационной модели. Применение модели доминирования было характерно для советского периода с целью сокрытия собственной религиозности.

15. Осознанную *стратегическую смену* (модели) можно особенно часто и отчетливо наблюдать у шаманов. В настоящее время шаманы должны владеть различными стратегиями своего ремесла, чьи инструменты заимствованы из модели доминирования. К этому же относятся сетевой бизнес, реклама, бухучет, строительство и организация шаманских клиник, изготовление и продажа специальной атрибутики.

16. В многочисленных самопрезентациях тувинцев, у которых я брала интервью, прослеживается тенденция к объяснению (ситуаций) через правильное или неправильное поведение и действия. Такое

различие часто сопровождалось стремлением противопоставить друг другу обе модели как правильную и неправильную, и, таким образом, постулировать несовместимость обеих.

17. Таким путем можно получить модель, *имеющую нарративно идеализированную форму*. Толкование определенной ситуации или некоего события приближается в таком случае к экстремальному варианту модели.

18. В Туве, наряду со *структурной стабильностью* обеих интерпретационных моделей, бросается в глаза характерная для сегодняшнего времени ускоренная *изменчивость содержания* моделей доминирования и взаимодействия.

19. Изменчива также и частота применения обеих интерпретационных моделей. Модель доминирования применяется на сегодняшний день чаще, модель взаимодействия – реже, ограничиваясь при этом лишь определенными ситуациями.

Notes on the Author

Anett C. Oelschlaegel studied anthropology, Central Asian studies, and religious studies in Leipzig, Germany, where she completed her PhD in 2011. She is currently an associate of the Siberian Studies Centre of the Max Planck Institute for Social Anthropology. Her research focuses on the societies of Siberia and northern Central Asia. She has conducted fieldwork in the region since 1995 and spent a total of 18 months in the Republic of Tyva. Her research interests include plural world interpretations, the anthropology of religion (animism, historical and contemporary shamanism, and divination), oral tradition (contemporary legends), economic anthropology, postsocialist studies, and oral history.

Bibliography

Alekseev, N. A. 1987. *Schamanismus der Türken Sibiriens*. Hamburg: Reinhold Schletzer Verlag.

Allolio-Näcke, L., B. Kalscheuer, and A. Manzeschke (eds.). 2005. *Differenzen anders denken: Bausteine zu einer Kulturtheorie der Transdifferenz*. Frankfurt am Main: Campus Verlag.

Allolio-Näcke, L., and B. Kalscheuer. 2005. Wege der Transdifferenz. In L. Allolio-Näcke, B. Kalscheuer, and A. Manzeschke (eds.), *Differenzen anders denken: Bausteine zu einer Kulturtheorie der Transdifferenz*, pp. 15-25. Frankfurt am Main: Campus Verlag.

Alphen, J. van 1998. Einleitung. In J. van Alphen (ed.), *Schamanismus in Tuva*. pp. 8-13. Holzhausen/Wien: Museum für Völkerkunde Wien.

Arakchaa, K. K. 1995. *Slovo ob Arshaanakh Tyvy*. Moscow: PoliKom.

Arakchaa, T. 2009. *Household and Property Relations in Tuva*. M.A. thesis, Boise State University. Available online, http://scholarworks.boisestate.edu/cgi/viewcontent.cgi?article=1037&context=td.

Arapchor, A. D. 1995. *Tyva ulustung mifteri bolgash toolchurgu chugaalary*. Kyzyl: Tyvanyng nom ündürer cheri.

Bargatzky, T. 2007. *Mythos, Weg und Welthaus: Erfahrungsreligion als Kultus und Alltag*. Münster: LIT Verlag.

Belliger, A., and D. J. Krieger. 2006. Einführung in die Akteur-Netzwerk-Theorie. In A. Belliger, and D. J. Krieger (eds.), *ANThology. Ein einführendes Handbuch zur Akteur-Netzwerk-Theorie*, pp. 13-50. Bielefeld: Transcript Verlag.

Berger, P. L., and T. Luckmann. 1966. *The Social Construction of Reality: A Treatise in the Sociology of Knowledge*. New York: Doubleday.

Berger, P. L., and T. Luckmann. 2012 [1969]. *Die gesellschaftliche Konstruktion der Wirklichkeit: Eine Theorie der Wissenssoziologie*. Frankfurt am Main: Fischer.

Breinig, H., and K. Lösch. 2002. Introduction: Difference and Transdifference. In H. Breinig, J. Gebhardt, and K. Lösch (eds.), *Multiculturalism in Contemporary Societies: Perspectives on Difference and Transdifference*, pp. 11-36. Erlangen: Universitätsbund Erlangen.

———. 2006. Transdifference. *Journal for the Study of British Cultures* 13 (2): 105-122.

Budegechi, T. 1994. Mirovozzrencheskie osnovy tuvinskogo shamanstva. In T. Budegechi (ed.), *Shamanizm v Tuve: Materialy tuvinsko-amerikanskogo seminara uchenikh-shamanovedov i shamanov*, pp. 11-14. Kyzyl: Gosudarstvennyj Licej Respubliki Tyva.

Burn, L. 1993. *Griechische Mythen*. Stuttgart: Reclam.
Chevalier, J. F. 2010. Bilingualism and Literacy in the Republic of Tyva. *Sibirica* 9 (1): 1-22.
Cotterell, A. 1999. *Die Enzyklopädie der Mythologie*. Reichelsheim: Anness Publishing.
Cullen, B. 2003. Tradition, Moderne und interreligiöses Verstehen – Der Fall Nordirland. In M. Bongardt, R. Kampling, and M. Wörner (eds.), *Verstehen an der Grenze: Beiträge zur Hermeneutik interkultureller und interreligiöser Kommunikation*, pp. 210-24. Münster: Aschendorff.
David, L. 2001. *Stalinism and Empire: Soviet Policies in Tuva, 1921-1953*. Ph.D. dissertation. University of London.
Denaeghel, I. 1998. Der Schamanismus – zwischen Geheimnis und Postkommunismus. In J. van Alphen (ed.), *Schamanismus in Tuva*, pp. 14-23. Holzhausen/Wien: Museum für Völkerkunde Wien.
Deusen, K. van. 2004. *Singing Story, Healing Drum: Shamans and Storytellers of Turkic Siberia*. Seattle: University of Washington Press.
Devlet, M. A. 1998. Die alten Heiligtümer von Tuva und der Ursprung des Schamanismus. In J. van Alphen (ed.), *Schamanismus in Tuva*. pp. 36-51. Holzhausen/Wien: Museum für Völkerkunde Wien.
Diószegi, V. 1962. Tuva Shamanism: Intraethnic Differences and Interethnic Analogies. *Acta Ethnographica Academiae Scientiarum Hungaricae* 11 (2): 143-190.
——. (ed.). 1963. *Glaubenswelt und Folklore der sibirischen Völker*. Budapest: Akadémiai Kiado.
——. 1978. Der Werdegang zum Schamanen bei den nordöstlichen Sojoten. *Acta Ethnographica Academiae Scientiarum Hungaricae* 8 (3-4): 269-292.
Diószegi, V., and M. Hoppál (eds.). 1996. *Shamanism in Siberia: Selected Reprints*. Budapest: Akadémiai Kiadó.
Divaev, A. A. 1896. Etnograficheskie materialy ... sobrannye i perevedennye. In A. A. Divaev (ed.), *Sbornik materialov dlja statistiki Syr-Dar'inskoj oblasti*, pp. 1-96. Tashkent: t.V.
Donahoe, B. 2002. Hey, You! Get Offa My Taiga! Comparing the Sense of Property Rights Among the Tofa and Tozhu-Tyva. *Working Paper* 38. Halle: Max Planck Institute for Social Anthropology.
——. 2003a. The Troubled Taiga: Survival on the Move for the Last Nomadic Reindeer Herders of South Siberia, Mongolia, and China. *Cultural Survival Quarterly* 27 (1): 12-18.

———. 2003b. Hunting for a Solution: Tozhu Wild Animal Resources Threatened. *Cultural Survival Quarterly* 27 (1): 48-52.
———. 2004. *A Line in the Sayans: History and Divergent Perceptions of Property among the Tozhu and Tofa of South Siberia.* Ph.D. dissertation, Indiana University.
———. 2005. Southern Siberia. In *The Indigenous World 2005*, pp. 56-63. Copenhagen: International Work Group for Indigenous Affairs (IWGIA).
———. 2006a. Who Owns the Taiga? Inclusive vs. Exclusive Senses of Property among the Tozhu and Tofa of Southern Siberia. *Sibirica* 5 (1): 87-116.
———. 2006b. Olenevodstvo Tuvincev-Todzhincev segodnja. *Voprosy izuchenija istorii i kul'tury narodov central'noj Azii i sopredel'nykh regionov*, pp. 121-132. Kyzyl: Nacional'nyj muzej imeni Aldan-Maadyr.
———. 2008. Tuvincy-Todzhincy: Ocherk sovremennoj kul'tury. In D. A. Funk, and N. A. Alekseev (eds.), *Turkskie narody vostochnoj Sibiri*, pp. 186-204. Moscow: Izdatel'stvo Nauka.
———. 2009. Comparative Analysis of Property Rights among the Tofa and Tozhu of Southern Siberia. In S. Namsaraeva, Ni Ma, and Wang Yudeng (eds.), *Makesi Pulangke shehui renleixue yanjiusuo: Xibolia huigu*, pp. 2-22. Beijing: Minzu chubanshe.
Donahoe, B., J. O. Habeck, A. Halemba, and I. Santha. 2008. Size and Place in the Construction of Indigeneity in the Russian Federation. *Current Anthropology* 49 (6): 993-1020.
D'yakonova, V. P. 1975. *Pogrebal'nyj obrjad tuvincev kak istoriko-etnograficheskij istochnik.* Leningrad: Izdatel'stvo Nauka.
———. 1976. Religioznye predstavlenija altajcev i tuvincev o prirode i cheloveke. In V. I. Stefanovich (ed.), *Priroda i chelovek v religioznykh predstavlenijakh narodov Sibiri i Severa*, pp. 268-291. Leningrad: Izdatel'stvo Nauka.
———. 1977. Religioznye kul'ty tuvincev. In *Pamjatniki kul'tury narodov Sibiri i Severa*, pp. 172-216. Leningrad: Izdatel'stvo Nauka.
———. 1981. Materialien zum Schamanentum der südlichen Tuwiner. *Jahrbuch des Museums für Völkerkunde zu Leipzig* 33: 36-42.
———. 1996. The Vestments and Paraphernalia of a Tuva Shamaness. In V. Diószegi, and M. Hoppál (eds.), *Shamanism in Siberia: Selected Reprints*, pp. 152-166. Budapest: Akadémiai Kiadó.
———. 2005. Das Schamanentum bei den Süd-Tuwinern. In A. C. Oelschlägel, I. Nentwig, and J. Taube (eds.), *'Roter Altai, gib Dein*

Echo!' Festschrift für Erika Taube zum 65. Geburtstag, pp. 67-77. Leipzig: Leipziger Universitätsverlag.
Evans-Pritchard, E. E. 1937. *Witchcraft, Oracles and Magic among the Azande*. Oxford: Clarendon Press.
Funk, D. A. 2005. *Worlds of Shamans and Storytellers* (A Study of Teleut and Shors Materials). http://www.iea.ras.ru/cntnt/levoe_meny/struktura/fotogalere/funk.html.
Funk, D. A., and L. Sillanpää (eds.). 1999. *The Small Indigenous Nations of Northern Russia: A Guide for Researchers*. Vaasa: Social Science Research Unit 29, Åbo Akademi University.
Furst, P. T. 1998. Die Wurzeln des Schamanismus in Asien und Amerika. In J. van Alphen (ed.), *Schamanismus in Tuva*, pp. 24-35. Holzhausen/Wien: Museum für Völkerkunde Wien.
Goffman, E. 1959. *The Presentation of Self in Everyday Life*. New York: Doubleday & Company.
Grünwedel, H. 2008. Schamanenbiographien zwischen Sibirien und Deutschland. Gegenwärtige Wanderbewegungen von Ritualen im Raum Dazwischen. *Journal-Ethnologie.de*. http://www.journal-ethnologie.de/Deutsch/Schwerpunktthemen/Schwerpunktthemen_2008/Rituale_heute/Schamanenbiografien_zwischen_Sibirien_und_Deutschland/index.phtml.
——. 2010. Shamanic Rituals from Siberia to Europe: Cultural Exchanges between Indigenous Healing Traditions of the Tyva and Neo-Shamans in Germany. In A. Michaels et al. (eds.), *Ritual Dynamics and the Science of Ritual*, Vol. 5: Transfer and Spaces. Wiesbaden: Harrassowitz.
——. 2012. *Schamanismus zwischen Sibirien und Deutschland: Kulturelle Austauschprozesse in globalen religiösen Diskursfeldern*. Bielefeld: Transcript.
Halemba, A. 2002. *Power in Places and Politics in Altai*. Paper presented at the Fourth Nordic Conference on the Anthropology of Post-Socialism, Copenhagen, April 2002. Available online, http://www.anthrobase.com/Txt/H/Halemba_A_01.html.
——. 2006. *The Telengits of Southern Siberia: Landscape, Religion and Knowledge in motion*. London: Routledge.
Handler, R., and J. Linnekin. 1984. Tradition, Genuine or Spurious? *Journal of American Folklore* 97 (385): 273-290.
Harva, U. 1938. *Die religiösen Vorstellungen der Altaischen Völker*. Helsinki: Suomalainen tiedeakatemia.
Hobsbawm, E., and T. Ranger (eds.). 1992. *The Invention of Tradition*. Cambridge: Cambridge University Press.

Hoppál, M. 1994. *Schamanen und Schamanismus*. Augsburg: Pattloch Verlag.
Hoppe, T. 1998. *Die ethnischen Gruppen Xinjangs: Kulturunterschiede und interethnische Beziehungen*. Hamburg: Deutsches Überseeinstitut.
Humphrey, C. 1980. Introduction: Nomadism and the State. In S. Vajnshtejn (ed.), *Nomads of South Siberia: The Pastoral Economies of Tuva*, pp. 1-33. Cambridge: Cambridge University Press.
———. 1989. Perestroika and the Pastoralists: The Example of Mongun Taiga in the Tuva ASSR. *Anthropology Today* 5 (3): 6-10.
———. 1998. *Marx Went Away, but Karl Stayed Behind*. Ann Arbor: University of Michigan Press.
———. 1999. Shamans in the City. *Anthropology Today* 15 (3): 3-11.
Humphrey, C., M. Mongush, and B. Telengit. 1993. Attitudes to Nature in Mongolia and Tuva. A Preliminary Report. *Nomadic People* 33: 1-12.
Husserl, E. 1970. *The Crisis of European Sciences and Transcendental Phenomenology: An Introduction to Phenomenological Philosophy*. Evanston: Northwestern University Press.
———. 1954 [1936]. *Die Krisis der europäischen Wissenschaften und die transzendentale Phänomenologie*. Den Haag: Nijhoff (Husserliana Band VI).
Ingold, T. 1986. *The Appropriation of Nature: Essays on Human Ecology and Social Relations*. Manchester: Manchester University Press.
———. 1994. Tool-use, Sociality, and Intelligence. In K. Gibson, and T. Ingold (eds.), *Tools, Language, and Cognition in Human Evolution*, pp. 429-445. Cambridge: Cambridge University Press.
———. 1996. Hunting and Gathering as Ways of Perceiving the Environment. In R. Ellen, and K. Fukui et al. (eds.), *Redefining Nature: Ecology, Culture and Domestication*, pp. 117-155. Oxford: Berg.
———. 2000. *The Perception of the Environment: Essays in Livelihood, Dwelling and Skill*. London: Routledge.
———. 2002. Jagen und Sammeln als Wahrnehmungsformen der Umwelt. In A. Gingrich et al. (eds.), *Metamorphosen der Natur: Sozialanthropologische Untersuchungen zum Verhältnis von Weltbild und natürlicher Umwelt*, pp. 69-102. Wien: Böhlau Verlag.
James, W. 1890. *The Principles of Psychology*. 2 vols. New York: Holt.
Johansen, U. 1961. Neues archäologisches und ethnologisches Material aus Tuva. *Ural-Altaische Jahrbücher* 38: 283-285.
———. 1967. Zur Methodik der Erforschung des Schamanismus. Der tuvanische Schamanismus in den Untersuchungen von V. Diószegi. *Ural-Altaische Jahrbücher* 39 (3-4): 208-229.

——. 1992. The Transmission of the Shaman's Position in South Siberia. In M. Hoppal (ed.), *Shamanism*, pp. 501-507. Budapest: Akadémiai Kiadó.
——. 1998. The Universe of a Tuva Shamaness: Representations of the Shaman's Spirits. *Ural-Altaische Jahrbücher* 15: 202-210.
——. 2001. Shamanism and Neoshamanism: What Is the Difference? In H. P. Francfort, and R. N. Hamayon (eds.), *The Concept of Shamanism: Uses and Abuses*, pp. 297-303. Budapest: Akademiai Kiado.
——. 2003. Shamanistic Philosophy: Soul - A Changing Concept in Tyva. *Shaman: Journal of the International Society for Shamanistic Research* 11 (1-2): 29-49.
——. 2004. Vom Schamanismus zum Neoschamanismus in Sibirien und Zentralasien. *Jahrbuch des Museums für Völkerkunde Leipzig* XLII: 65-76.
Kastan'e, I. 1912. Iz oblasti kirgizskikh verovanij. *Vestnik Orenburgskago uchebnogo okruga* 3: 71-93.
——. 1913. Iz oblasti kirgizskikh verovanij. *Vestnik Orenburgskago uchebnogo okruga* 5: 149-166.
Kaziev, B. 1983. Skazitel' Agol. In B. Kaziev (ed.), *V strane skazok*, pp. 100-103. Alma-Ata.
Kazyrykpaj, B. O. 2000. *Bodaldar*. Kyzyl: Tyvanyng nom ündürer cheri.
Keitel, Ch., and L. Allolio-Näcke. 2005. Erfahrung der Transdifferenz. In L. Allolio-Näcke, B. Kalscheuer, and A. Manzeschke (eds.), *Differenzen anders denken: Bausteine zu einer Kulturtheorie der Transdifferenz*, pp. 104-117. Frankfurt am Main: Campus Verlag.
Kenin-Lopsan, M. B. (also spelled Lopsang). 1987. *Obrjadovaja praktika i fol'klor tuvinskogo shamanstva*. Novosibirsk: Izdatel'stvo Nauka.
——. 1993. *Magija tuvinskikh shamanov*. Kyzyl: Novosti Tuvy.
——. 1994a. Koordinaty dushi u Tuvincev. In T. Budegechi (ed.), *Shamanizm v Tuve*, pp. 17-27. Kyzyl: Gosudarstvennyj Licej Respubliki Tyva.
——. 1994b. *Tyva chonnung burungu uzhurlary*. Kyzyl: Novosti Tuvy.
——. 1994c. Whereabouts of the Soul among Tuvans. In T. Budegechi (ed.), *Shamanizm v Tuve*, pp. 27-37. Kyzyl: Gosudarstvennyj Licej Respubliki Tyva.
——. 1995. *Tyva khamnarnyng algyshtary: Algyshi tuvinskikh shamanov*. Kyzyl: Novosti Tuvy.
——. 1996. The Funeral Rites of Tuva Shamans. In V. Diószegi, and M. Hoppál (eds.), *Shamanism in Siberia: Selected Reprints*, pp. 144-151. Budapest: Akadémiai Kiadó.

———. 1997. *Shamanic Songs and Myths of Tuva*. (ed. M. Hoppál). Budapest: Akadémiai Kiadó.
———. 1998. Die mythischen Wurzeln des tuvinischen Schamanismus. In J. van Alphen (ed.), *Schamanismus in Tuva*, pp. 68-91. Holzhausen/Wien: Museum für Völkerkunde Wien.
———. 1999. *Tyva changchyl: Tyva chonnung changchyldary*. Moscow: Trojka.
———. 2002. *Mify tuvinskikh shamanov: Tyva khamnarnyng torulgalary*. Kyzyl: Novosti Tuvy.
———. 2003. *Koordinaty dushi u tuvincev // Rodina shamanizma – Tuva*, pp. 12-21. Kyzyl.
———. 2005. 'Chernoe nebo': Mifologicheskie materialy. In *Muzej v XXI veke: problemy i perspektivy*, pp. 21-32. Kyzyl: Nacional'nyj muzej Aldan Maadyr.
———. 2009. *Tuvinskie shamany*. Kyzyl: IPC Maska.
———. 2011. *Schamanengeschichten aus Tuwa*. Göttingen: Lamuv.
Kim, T., and M. Hoppál (eds.). 1995. *Shamanism in Performing Arts*. Budapest: Akadémiai Kiadó.
Kurbatskij, G. N. 2001. *Tuvincy v svoem fol'klore*. Kyzyl: Tuvinskoe knizhnoe izdatel'stvo.
Kuular, D. S. 1959. O tuvinskikh legendakh i predanijakh. *Uchenye zapiski*, pp. 134-142. Kyzyl.
Latour, B. 1987. *Science in Action: How to Follow Scientists and Engineers through Society*. Milton Keynes: Open University Press.
———. 1996. On Actor-Network Theory: A Few Clarifications. *Soziale Welt* 47 (4): 369–382.
———. 2005. *Reassembling the Social: An Introduction to Actor-Network-Theory*. Oxford: Oxford University Press.
———. 2007. *Eine neue Soziologie für eine neue Gesellschaft: Einführung in die Akteur-Netzwerk-Theorie*. (trans. Gustav Roßler). Frankfurt am Main: Suhrkamp.
Law, J., and J. Hassard (eds.). 1999. *Actor Network Theory and After*. Oxford: Wiley-Blackwell.
Leenhardt, M. 1984 [1947]. *Do Kamo: Die Person und der Mythos in der melanesischen Welt*. Frankfurt am Main: Ullstein.
Leimbach, W. K. 1936. *Landeskunde von Tuwa, das Gebiet des Jenissei-Oberlaufes*. Gotha: Perthes.
Levin, T. C., and V. Süzükei. 2006. *Where Rivers and Mountains Sing: Sound, Music, and Nomadism in Tuva and Beyond*. Bloomington: Indiana University Press.

Lösch, K. 2005. Begriff und Phänomen der Transdifferenz: Zur Infragestellung binärer Differenzkonstrukte. In L. Allolio-Näcke, B. Kalscheuer, and A. Manzeschke (eds.), *Differenzen anders denken. Bausteine zu einer Kulturtheorie der Transdifferenz*, pp. 26-49. Frankfurt am Main: Campus Verlag.

Mänchen-Helfen, O. 1931. *Reise ins asiatische Tuwa*. Berlin: Verlag der Bücherkreis.

——. 1992. *Journey to Tuva: An Eye-Witness Account of Tannu-Tuva in 1929*. Los Angeles: University of Southern California Ethnographics Press.

Mannaj-ool, M. Ch. 2004. *Tuvincy proiskhozhdenie i formirovanie ètnosa*. Novosibirsk: Izdatel'stvo Nauka.

Miropiev, M. 1888. Demonologicheskie razskazy kirgizov. *Zapiski imperatorskago russkogo geograficheskogo obshchestva po otdelu ètnografii*, 3rd ed. St. Peterburg.

Mongush, M. V. 1992. *Lamaizm v Tuve*. Kyzyl: Tuvinskoe knizhnoe izdatel'stvo.

——. 1994. Tuvincy v Kitae: Problemy istorii, jazyka i kultury. *Uchenye zapiski: Seria istoricheskaja* 38: 30-56.

——. 2001. *Istorija Buddizma v Tyve*. Novosibirsk: Izdatel'stvo Nauka.

Oelschlägel, A. C. (also spelled Oelschlaegel). 2000. Der Weg der Milch: Zur Produktion und Bedeutung von Milchprodukten bei den West-Tyva Südsibiriens. *Tribus – Jahrbuch des Linden-Museums Stuttgart* 49: 155-171.

——. 2004a. *Der Weiße Weg: Naturreligion und Divination bei den West-Tyva im Süden Sibiriens*. Leipzig: Leipziger Universitätsverlag.

——. 2004b. Religion des Alltags. Zur Naturreligion der Tyva im Süden Sibiriens. *Tribus – Jahrbuch des Linden-Museums Stuttgart* 53: 69-97.

——. 2005a. Deutung und Wahrheit: Zwei Divinationspraktiken bei den Tyva im Süden Sibiriens. In A. C. Oelschlägel, I. Nentwig, and J. Taube (eds.), *'Roter Altai, gib Dein Echo!' Festschrift für Erika Taube zum 65. Geburtstag*, pp. 377-400. Leipzig: Leipziger Universitätsverlag.

——. 2006. Tuvinskoe gadanie *khuvaanak* – voprosy k prirode. In *Muzej v XXI veke: problemy i perspektivy*, pp. 89-95. Kyzyl: Nacional'nyj muzej Aldan Maadyr.

——. 2010. Plurale Weltinterpretationen und Transdifferenz: Dominanz- und Interaktionsmodell in der alltäglichen Praxis der West-Tyva in Süd-Sibirien. *Zeitschrift für Ethnologie* 135 (2): 305-336.

——. 2013a. *Plurale Weltinterpretationen: Das Beispiel der Tyva Südsibiriens*. Fürstenberg/ Havel: Kulturstiftung Sibirien.
——. 2013b. *Der Taigageist: Berichte und Geschichten von Menschen und Geistern aus Tuwa. Zeitgenössische Sagen und andere Folkloretexte* (in German, Russian and Tyvan). Marburg: Tectum Verlag.
Ottinger, U. 1993. *Taiga*. Berlin: Nishen.
Peters, L. 1993. In the Land of Eagles: Experiences on the Shamanic Path in Tuva. *Shaman's Drum: A Journal of Experiential Shamanism* 33: 42-49.
Pimenova, K. V. 2009. The Emergence of a New Social Identity: Trajectories and Life Stories of Post-Soviet Shamans in the Republic of Tuva. In H. Beach, D. A. Funk, L. Sillanpää, and A. Yu. Vakhrushev (eds.), *Post-Soviet Transformations*, pp. 161-185. Uppsala: Uppsala University.
Potanin, G. N. 1883. *Ocherki severo-zapadnoj Mongilii*. St. Petersburg: Bezobrazov.
Potapov, L. P. 1960. Materialy po etnografii tuvincev rajonov Mongun-Tajgi i Kara-Cholja. In *Trudy Tuvinskoj kompleksnoj arkheologo-etnograficheskoj ekspedicii* I. *Materialy po arkheologii i etnografii zapadnoj Tuvy*, pp. 171-237. Moscow-Leningrad: Izdatel'stvo Nauka.
——. 1963. Die Schamanentrommel bei den altaischen Völkerschaften. In V. Diószegi (ed.), *Glaubenswelt und Folklore der sibirischen Völker*, pp. 223-256. Budapest: Akadémiai Kiado.
——. 1969. *Ocherki narodnogo byta tuvincev*. Moskva: Izdatel'stvo Nauka.
——. 1975. Über den Pferdekult bei den turksprachigen Völkern des Sajan-Altai-Gebirges. *Abhandlungen und Berichte des staatlichen Museums für Völkerkunde Dresden* 34: 473-487.
——. 1996. The Shaman Drum as a Source of Ethnographical History. In V. Diószegi, and M. Hoppál (eds.), *Shamanism in Siberia: Selected Reprints*, pp. 107-117. Budapest: Akadémiai Kiadó.
Potapov, L. P., Yu. L. Aranchyn, L. B. Grebnev et al. (eds.). 1966. *Tyvanyng Töögyzy*. Kyzyl: Tyvanyng nom ündürer cheri.
Purzycki, B. G. 2010. Spirit Masters, Ritual Cairns, and the Adaptive Religious System in Tyva. *Sibirica* 9 (1): 21-47.
Radloff, W. 1960 [1893-1911]. *Versuch eines Wörterbuches der Türk-Dialecte*, 4 vols. The Hague: Mouton.
Reid, A. 2002. *The Shaman's Coat: A Native History of Siberia*. New York: Walker and Co.
Schenk, A., and G. Tschinag. 1999. *Im Land der zornigen Winde*. Zürich: Unionsverlag.

Schütz, A. 1945. On Multiple Realities. In *Philosophy and Phenomenological Research* 5 (4) (June 1945): 533-576.
———. 1955. Symbol, Reality, and Society. In L. Bryson et al. (eds.), *Symbols and Society*, pp. 135-202. New York: Harper.
———. 1971a. Über die mannigfaltigen Wirklichkeiten. In A. Schütz, *Gesammelte Aufsätze*, 1: *Das Problem der sozialen Wirklichkeit*, pp. 237-298. Den Haag: Martinus Nijhoff.
———. 1971b. Symbol, Wirklichkeit und Gesellschaft. In A. Schütz, *Gesammelte Aufsätze*, 1: *Das Problem der sozialen Wirklichkeit*, pp. 331-411. Den Haag: Martinus Nijhoff.
Schütz, A., and T. Luckmann. 2003 [1975]. *Strukturen der Lebenswelt*. (trans. Monika Reif-Hülser). Konstanz: UVK Verlagsgesellschaft.
———. 1973-89. *The Structures of the Life-World*. 2 vols. Evanston, IL: Northwestern University Press.
Schwab, G. 1977. *Die schönsten Sagen des klassischen Altertums*. Leipzig: Insel-Verlag.
Seiwert, H. 2005. Kodifizierte Normen, soziale Normen und Praxis – am Beispiel des chinesischen Buddhismus. In P. Schalk et al. (eds.), *Im Dickicht der Gebote: Studien zur Dialektik von Norm und Praxis in der Buddhismusgeschichte Asiens*, pp. 15-38. Uppsala: Acta Universitatis Upsaliensis.
Spittler, G. 1998. *Hirtenarbeit: Die Welt der Kamelhirten und Ziegenhirten von Timia*. Köln: Rüdiger Köppe Verlag.
———. 2003. Work – Transformation of Objects or Interaction Between Subjects? In B. Benzing, and B. Herrmann (eds.), *Exploitation and Overexploitation in Societies Past and Present*, pp. 327-338. Münster: LIT Verlag.
Streck, B. (ed.). 2007. *Die gezeigte und die verborgene Kultur*. Wiesbaden: Harrassowitz.
———. 2013. *Sterbendes Heidentum: Die Rekonstruktion der ersten Weltreligion*. Leipzig: Eudora Verlag.
Taube, E. 1972. Die Widerspiegelung religiöser Vorstellungen im Alltagsbrauchtum der Tuwiner der Westmongolei. In *Traditions religieuses et para-religieuses des peuples altaïques: Communications présentées au XIIIe Congrès de la "Permanent international altaistic conference"*, (Strasbourg, 25-30 juin 1970), pp. 119-138. Paris: Presses Universitaires de France.
———. 1974a. Zum Problem der Ersatzwörter im Tuwinischen des Cèngèlsum. In G. Hazai, and P. Zieme (eds.), *Sprache, Geschichte und Kultur der Altaischen Völker: Protokollband der 12. Tagung der*

Permanent International Altaistic Conference 1969 in Berlin, pp. 589-607. Berlin: Akademie-Verlag.
——. 1974b. Das Kastrierfest bei den Tuwinern des Cengel-sum. In *Asien in Vergangenheit und Gegenwart: Beiträge der Asienwissenschaftler der DDR zum 29. Internationalen Orientalistenkongress 1973 in Paris*, pp. 443-457. Berlin: Akademie-Verlag.
——. 1977a. Zur Jagd bei den Tuwinern im Cengel-sum in der Westmongolei. *Jahrbuch des Museums für Völkerkunde zu Leipzig* 31: 37-59.
——. 1977b. *Das leopardenscheckige Pferd*. Berlin: Kinderbuchverlag.
——. 1978. *Tuwinische Volksmärchen*. Berlin: Akademie-Verlag.
——. 1981a. Notizen zum Schamanismus bei den Tuwinern des Cengel-sum (Westmongolei). *Jahrbuch des Museums für Völkerkunde zu Leipzig* 33: 43-69.
——. 1981b. Die Tuwiner im Altai. *Veröffentlichungen des Museums für Völkerkunde Dresden* 4: 34-40. Berlin: Akademie-Verlag.
——. 1981c. Anfänge der Seßhaftwerdung bei den Tuwinern im Westen der Mongolischen Volksrepublik. In R. Krusche (ed.), *Nomaden in Geschichte und Gegenwart: Beiträge zu einem internationalen Nomadismus-Symposium am 11. und 12. Dezember 1975 im Museum für Völkerkunde Leipzig*, pp. 97-108. Berlin: Akademie-Verlag.
——. 1990. Ein Quell für Fragen zu Folkloretradition und Glaubensvorstellungen nicht nur der Sibe-Mandschuren. *Orientalistische Literaturzeitung* 85: 261-271.
——. 1991. Ālajanīj – ālanīj – ā. Die Einleitungsformel eines altaituwinischen Erzählers als ethnographische Quelle. In *Varia Eurasiatica: Festschrift für Professor András Róna-Tas*, pp. 183-193. Szeged: Department of Altaic Studies.
——. 1992. Zur ursprünglich magischen Funktion von Volksdichtung. *Ural-Altaische Jahrbücher* 11: 112-124.
——. 1994a. Bezeichnungswirrwarr um ein kleines Türkvolk. In K. Röhrborn, and W. Veenker (eds.), *Memoriae Munusculum: Gedenkband für Annemarie von Gabain*, pp. 131-38. Wiesbaden: Harrassowitz.
——. 1994b. *Skazki i predanija altajskikh tuvincev*. Moscow: Vostochnaja Literatura.
——. 1995. Überlieferungen zur Geschichte der Tuwiner im Altai. In D. Schorkowitz (ed.), *Ethnohistorische Wege und Lehrjahre eines Philosophen: Festschrift für Lawrence Krader zum 75. Geburtstag*, pp. 279-292. Frankfurt am Main: Peter Lang.

——. 1996a. Sterben und Tod bei den Tuwinern im Altai. In R. E. Emmerick et al. (eds.), *Turfan, Khotan und Dunhuang: Vorträge der Tagung 'Annemarie v. Gabain und die Turfanforschung'*, pp. 317-325. Berlin: Akademie-Verlag.

——. 1996b. Zur gegenwärtigen Situation der Tuwiner im westmongolischen Altai. In Á. Berta et al. (eds.), *Symbolae Turcologicae: Studies in Honour of Lars Johanson on his Sixtieth Birthday 8 March 1996*, pp. 213-225. Stockholm: Swedish Research Institute in Istanbul.

——. 1997. Warum erzählen Erzähler manchmal nicht? Vom Erzählen und seiner Beziehung zum Numinosen. In Á. Berta (ed.), *Historical and Linguistic Interaction between Inner-Asia and Europe: Proceedings of the 39. Permanent International Altaistic Conference, Szeged, Hungary, June 16-21, 1996*, pp. 351-63. Szeged: Department of Altaic Studies.

——. 1998. Von den Märchen der Mongolen. *Mongolische Notizen* 7: 42-49.

——. 2000. Märchenerzählen und Übergangsbräuche. *Märchenspiegel: Zeitschrift für internationale Märchenforschung und Märchenkunde* 11 (4): 122-124.

——. 2004. Glaubensäußerungen zentralasiatischer Nomaden in ihren Märchen und Erzählungen. *Märchenspiegel: Zeitschrift für internationale Märchenforschung und Märchenkunde* 15 (4): 3-9.

——. 2007. Die Verse in der erzählenden Volksdichtung der altaischen Tuwiner. In H. Boeschoten, and H. Stein (eds.), *Einheit und Vielfalt in der türkischen Welt: Materialien der 5. Deutschen Turkologenkonferenz, Universität Mainz, 4.-7. Oktober 2002*, pp. 298-309. Wiesbaden: Harrassowitz.

——. 2008. *Tuwinische Folkloretexte aus dem Altai (Cengel/ Westmongolei): Kleine Formen*. Wiesbaden: Harrassowitz.

Taube, J. 2008. *Albasty – Kindbettdämonin und Vamp bei den Kasachen; allgemeiner Teil*. Huy-Neinstedt: Wortraum-Edition.

Toka, S. K. 1951. *Das Wort des Arat*. (trans. G. Tanewa). Berlin: Verlag Kultur und Fortschritt.

Tryjarski, E. 2001. *Bestattungssitten türkischer Völker auf dem Hintergrund ihrer Glaubensvorstellungen*. (trans. Reinhold Schletzer). Berlin: Reinhold Schletzer Verlag.

Vajnshtejn, S. I. (also spelled Vajnštejn, Weinshtein). 1961. *Tuvincy-Todzhincy. Istoriko-ètnograficheskie ocherki*. Moscow: Izdatel'stvo vostochnoj literatury.

——. 1963. Die Schamanentrommel der Tuwa und die Zeremonie ihrer 'Belebung'. In V. Diószegi (ed.), *Glaubenswelt und Folklore der sibirischen Völker*, pp. 359-368. Budapest: Akadémiai Kiado.
——. 1964. *Tuvinskoe shamanstvo*. Moscow: Izdatel'stvo Nauka.
——. 1972. *Istoricheskaja ėtnografija tuvincev*. Moscow: Izdatel'stvo Nauka.
——. 1977. Eine Schamanen-Séance bei den östlichen Tuwinern: Bericht über meine Begegnung mit dem Schamanen Šončur am Ufer des Tere-Chol im Sommer 1963. *Jahrbuch des Museums für Völkerkunde zu Leipzig* 31: 27-35.
——. 1980. *Nomads of South Siberia: The Pastoral Economies of Tuva*. (ed. Caroline Humphrey, trans. M. Colenso). Cambridge: Cambridge University Press.
——. 1984. Shamanism in Tuva at the Turn of the 20th Century. In M. Hoppál (ed.), *Shamanism in Eurasia*, part 2, pp. 353-373. Göttingen: Edition Herodot.
——. 1996a. The ērens in Tuva Shamanism. In V. Diószegi, and M. Hoppál (eds.), *Shamanism in Siberia: Selected Reprints*, pp. 167-177. Budapest: Akadémiai Kiadó.
——. 1996b. *Die Welt der Nomaden im Zentrum Asiens*. (trans. Reinhold Schletzer). Berlin: Reinhold Schletzer Verlag.
——. 2001. *Istorija Tuvy*, 2 vols. Novosibirsk: Nauka.
——. 2005. *Geheimnisvolles Tuva: Expedition ins Herz Asiens*. (trans. Sew'jan I Weinshtein et al.). Oststeinbek: Alouette Verlag.
Vitebsky, P. 2001a. *Schamanismus. Reisen der Seele, magische Kräfte, Ekstase und Heilung*. Köln: Taschen.
——. 2001b [1995]. *The Shaman: Voyages of the Soul: Trance, Ecstasy and Healing from Siberia to the Amazon*. London: Duncan Baird Publishers.
Voss, E. 2008. Von Schamanen und schamanisch Tätigen: Peinlichkeit und ihre Vermeidung im Kontext des modernen westlichen Schamanismus. In M. Münzel, and B. Streck (eds.), *Ethnologische Religionsästhetik: Beiträge eines Workshops auf der Tagung der Deutschen Gesellschaft für Völkerkunde in Halle (Saale) 2005*, pp. 111-122. Marburg: Curupira.
——. 2011. *Mediales Heilen in Deutschland: Eine Ethnographie*. Berlin: Dietrich Reimer Verlag.
Znamenski, A. A. 2007. *The Beauty of the Primitive: Shamanism and the Western Imagination*. Oxford: Oxford University Press.

Zorbas, K. 2007. *Agents of Evil: Curse Accusations and Shamanic Retaliation in Post-Soviet Tuva (Siberia)*. Ph.D. dissertation, University of Cambridge.

Index

action; as interaction 103, 124, 140; follow-up a 215; in the dominance model 48-9, 165-216 *passim*; in the interaction model 17, 20, 39-43, 77-144 *passim*, 182, 203, 209-10; patterns of 43, 49, 54; purposeful 56, 141, 188, 194, 198, 206, *see also* behaviour
actor; as subject 50; human ix, 39-40, 42, 49, 50, 54-8, 77, 100, 124, 140, 209; individual (Tyvan) ix, 39, 54-8, 77, 224; non-human 49-50, 77, 124, 140
actor network theory (ANT) 39, 56, 77, *see also* Latour
Adyg Eeren (Bear Spirit; shamanic clinic) 20, 180, 204; *see also Düngür*; Kenin-Lopsan; *Tos Deer*
agency, *see* human agency
Ak Bashtyg Mountain 82, 101
ak chem (food made from milk) 41, 83, *see also* white food
Ak-Oj River 87, 92, 118, 121, 184
albys (evil spirit) 17, 90-1, 118, 121-3, 176
albystaar (madness) 91, 109, 111, *see also* shaman illness
alcohol 14, 83, 84, 92, 176-7, *see also araka*; *khoitpak*; milk brandy, vodka
alcoholism 11, 14, 176, 199, *see also* drunkenness
Alekseev, N. A. 51n, 78n, 90n, 109n, 241
algysh (invocation) 17, 81-2, 113, 246, *see also* blessing
Altai, Republic 82
Altai-Dyva 7-8, 20, 114, *see also* Taube, E.
Altai-Tyvans 115, 187
ancestor 1, 87-8, 95, 109-10, 129, 137-8
animate 97, 100, 117, *see also* soul(s); spirit(s)

animism 18, 52, 56-8, 78, 110, 165, 212, 215, 240; or shamanism 56, *see also* traditional worldview
animistic-shamanistic worldview 58, 77, 172-3, *see also* interaction model, specific Tyvan
anthropology xi, 3, 217, 240; anthropological quest 168; anthropological research 217
araka (milk brandy, distilled *khoitpak*) 92, 128n, *see also* white food
artefact 41, 45, 53, 87
artysh (juniper) 83, *see* juniper
aryg (pure, clean) 17, 136, *see also* purity
arzhaan (healing spring) 41, 138
asbestos 10, 98n, 165
atheism 18; atheist 174, 195, 201-2
axis mundi 81
aza (evil spirit) 17, 90-2, 96, 109n, 121-4, 174-6
aza-buk (evil spirit) 121, 123
aza-chetker (evil spirit) 91, 121, 123

Baj Taiga (administrative region) 168
baj yjash (rich tree) 85-6, 107, 132, 138
balance 1-4, 99, 124-5, 138-9, 141, 143, 197; balanced interactions 136; human quest for 1-4; unbalanced energy 139, unbalanced interactions 141, 143, *see also* human quest for balance
Bargatzky, Th. 48, 241
baza (cooperative centre) 12, 135
behaviour 17, 20, 39-43; correct (or proper) 49, 53, 110, 134, 141-2, 175; incorrect 83-4, 90, 110, 115, 121, 141, 167, 178, 216, 219; modified 193, 206, 215, *see also* action; misbehaviour

belief 2, 3, 18, 20, 98, 103, 123, 201, 208, 212, 218-20, *see also* soul(s); spirit(s)
Belliger and Krieger 39, 56, 77
Berger and Luckmann 44, 51, 54-5, 218-9, 224, 230, 241
Bij Khem (river) 213
birth 45, 106, 132, *see also* rebirth
blessing 11, 17, 19, 21, 78, 81-2, 101, 114, 124, 128, 132-6, 175, 195, *see also algysh*; offering
Breinig and Lösch 47-8, 175, 241
Buddhism 18, 52, 58, 194, 201, 212
Budegechi, T. 20n, 42n, 51n, 78n, 79n, 241
buk (evil spirit) 121, 123
burkhan (Tyv. god) 78
Buryatia 7, 11n
butter; clarified 102, 117, 132

Callon, M. 39, *see also* actor-network theory (ANT)
Cartesian dualism 48, *see also* Descartes; *res cogitans*; *res extensa*
castration 186-8
category 40, 48, 220
cattle 8, 80, 94, 106, 114, 122, *see also* stockbreeders
celebration 19, 82-4, 109, 120, 127, 195, 199, 209
chalama (sacrificial ribbon) 81, 86
change; of behaviour 177, 181, 183, 190, 193, 200; between models of world interpretation 52, 59, 172, 177, 182-3, 190, 193-4, 196, 198, 201, 206; in perspective 57-8, 167, 224; in the (interaction) model 41, 50, 59, 204, 206, 211-6, *see also* shift; switch
charlatan 211, 214; charlatanry 211
chetker (evil spirit) 17, 90, 91, 94, 121, 123, 176
childlessness 85, 182, *see also* fertility, infertility

children 11-4, 80-6, 92, 106, 111, 121, 127-8; fear for 123-4
Christian 52, 212, 221-3; Christianity 221
class 11, 201, 217
clinic, *see* shaman association/ clinic
codified (norm) 43n, 167, 217, 221
collectivisation 9, 11-2
communication 43, 80, 83-4, 104, 117, 172, 186, 192
communist 171-3, 201-3, *see also* dominance model, Soviet
compromise xv, 3, 143, 197
conflict; between models of world interpretation 1, 171-2, 221; between people and spirits 93, 130, 141; internal 172; social 85, 102, 170, 172, 182
consecration 81-6, 99, 132, 190-3, 196; consecrate 17, 99, 101-2, 108, 135, 137
construction; economic 87; human 55; of meaning 47; social 54-5, 218, 222
contemporary legends xi, 1, 16-7, 19, 21, 98-9, 109, 113, 125, 132, 140-1, 172, 178, 197, 240, *see also* 'true occurrences'
content and structure of models of world interpretation 39-40, 51-5, 58-9, 167, 240
content; of models of world interpretation 29, 39, 51-5, 58-9, 83, 167, 195, 208, 211-2, 214, 216, 218-9; of Tyvan animism 18, 83, 126; of Tyvan dominance model 211; of Tyvan interaction model 53, 58-9, 195, 211-2, 214, *see also* definition, of models of world interpretation; interaction model, specific Tyvan; structure of models of world interpretation
continuum ix, 52-3; between extreme points 53, 166, 182, 214; between models of world interpretation ix,

52-3, 58-9, 166, 175; of transdifference 52, 59, 166, 175
cooperative 11-2, 198; Toolajlyg 88, 135, 191
cosmos 85-6, 95, 129, 138, 196; cosmic energies 85
countergift 205
creation 1-2, 114, *see also* construction
crime 11, 14

damage 1, 91, 124, 131, 142, 174-5, 178, 180-4, 194, 200
death 3, 79, 88, 93, 96-9, 109-13, 117, 120, 126, 129, 130, 142, 171n, 177, 182, 189-90, 199-200, 205-6, 208; deceased 93-5, 113, 125-30, 177-8, 189-90, 206-10
definition; of contemporary legends 17n; of models of world interpretation 39-40, 43, 48-55, *see also* structure of models of world interpretation
deities 78, 79, 95; as protectors 78, *see also* god(s); spirit(s)
Descartes, R. 48, *see* Cartesian dualism; *res cogitans*; *res externa*
development 2, 3, 9-11, 15-6, 44, 51, 58, 193, 201-2, 211-3, 217, 219, 224, *see also* progress
diireng (evil spirit) 17, 90, 94-5, 176
Diószegi, v. 20n, 41n, 109n, 241
divination 1, 19, 110-1, 125-6, 139, 141, 169-70, 189; diviner 198, 240, *see also khuvaanak*
divine 1, 170
dominance model/ model of human dominance ix, 39, 44, 48-59, 98, 165-216 *passim*; human dominance over the environment/ nature ix, 4, 44, 168, 187; Soviet/ communist dominance model 168, 172-3, 202-3, 215, *see also* change; interaction model;

model(s) of world interpretation; shift; switch
Donahoe, B. xi, 9, 20n, 41n, 242-3
drunkenness 14, 177; as a pact with evil spirits 176; drunk 105, 111, 128, 176, *see also* alcoholism
dualism, *see* Cartesian dualism
Düngür (Drum, shamans' association or clinic) 19-20, 95, 191, 204, *see also Adyg Eeren*; Kenin-Lopsan; shaman clinic; *Tos Deer*
Dyva, *see* Altai-Dyva; Altai-Tyvans
D'yakonova, V. P. 20n, 42n, 51n, 78n, 79n, 90n, 110n, 243

economy; market 212, 221; planned 9-10; subsistence 13, 41; Tyvan 10-2, 145-64
education 59, 79, 202, 211; political 10, 18; professional 13, 59
ee (pl. *eeler*) (spirit master) 17, 79n, 81, 87, 96, 100, 104, 113, 135, 169, 184-5, *see also* spirit master
emic, *see* method
Enlightenment 2; enlightened 43
environment 1-4, 14, 16, 43-4, 49, 53, 56, 97, 102-3, 121, 138, 141, 169-70, 185, 187, 198, 217, 221; environmentalism 97, 102, 103, 121, 138, 141; overexploitation 98n
esoteric movement 15-6, 19-20, 52, 59, 212, *see also* neo-shamanism; New Age
etic, *see* method
Evans-Pritchard, E. 3-4, 244
everyday reality 51, 54-5, 58, 219-20
evil spirits, *see* spirits, evil
exchange xi, 13, 15, 16, 125, 205
externalisation 54, *see also* Berger and Luckmann; internalisation; objectification

factual state 43, 52, 167-8, *see also* ideal state
fairy tales 21, 114-7, *see also* legend
father sky 78, 120, *see also* mother earth
fear; for punishment 1, 49, 92-3, 112; of shamans 111-2, 172, 208; of spirits 49, 92-3, 112, 121, 123, 129; spirits having fear 123
feast 187, 208, *see also* festival
fermented milk (*khoitpak*) 92, 105, 108, 117, 128, *see also araka*; white food
fertility 79, 85; infertility 130; lower fertility 139; of the flock 187-8, *see also* childlessness
festival 16, 84, 120, 128, 137, 194-5, *see also* Naadym festival
folklore 16, 19n, 140, 171; folklorist 87, 94, 100, 110-1, 113, 120, 123, 205
fortune 2, 83, 102-8, 114, 127, 139-41, 179, 191, *see also* misfortune
fortune telling 19, *see also* divination; oracle
funeral 112, 130, 177, 189-90
Funk, D. A. xi, 9, 117n, 244, 249

gifted persons, *see* talented or gifted persons
glasnost 10
god (s) 1, 2, 50, 78-9, 95, 120, 221-2; god of heaven 95, 120, *see also burkhan*; deities; spirit(s); theology
Goffman, E. 224, 244
Grünwedel, H. 15, 19-20, 20n, 42n, 52, 109

Habeck, J. O. xi, 243
Halemba, A. 138, 243-4
Harva, U. 20, 42n, 51n, 78n, 79n, 244
healer 80, 84, 106, 117n

healing 86, 110, 113, 188, 196, 205; spring (*arzhaan*) 41, 84, 99, 132, 135-6, 138, 195-6
health 79, 83, 85, 99, 112, 125, 135, 139-40, 171, 173, 184, 192, 195, 199, 205, *see also* illness
health care system 11
heaven 95, 192, 213-4; heavenly 95
herb(s) 101-2, 129, 140, 197
Hobsbawm and Ranger 41, 228, 244
Hoppál, M. 20n, 41n, 109n, 242-3, 245
human ability ix, 55, 110, 186, 189
human agency ix, 39, 44, 48-9, 56, 98, 169, 187
human and non-human subjects, *see* subjects; *see also* interaction model; spirit(s); spirit master
human behaviour, *see* behaviour
human beings 1-3, 43, 45, 49, 53-4, 56-7, 77-8, 80, 84-5, 87, 89, 90ff.; as active subjects 49-50, 56, 175, *see also* subjects
human dominance, *see* dominance model
human quest for balance 1-3
human subjects, *see* subjects
Humphrey, C. 11n, 20n, 41n, 245
hunter 8, 9, 13, 50, 89-91, 95, 97, 101, 104-5, 108, 110-3, 118-20, 137, 178, 198-9
husbandry 185-6
Husserl, E. 54, 230, 245, *see also* life-world; phenomenology; Schütz and Luckmann

ideal state 43n, 52-3, 167-8, 175, 177, see also factual state
illness 84, 90, 91, 102, 109, 111, 120-1, 127-9, 141-2, 176, 184, 205, *see also* shaman's illness (*albystaar*); health
Ingold, T. 77, 245
instinct ('self-will') 49, 186-7

interaction model 4, 16-20, 39, 44, 48-53, 55-9, 77-144 *passim*, 165-94 *passim*, 196-8, 200-3, 206, 208-16; contravention against rules and norms of 78, 115, 130; counteraction against rules and norms of 183, 185; disrespectful interaction 84, 104, 112; narratively idealised pure form 51-2, 58-9, 167, 172-5, 185, 216; respectful interaction 19, 45, 49, 83, 87, 90, 98-104, 125, 129-31, 141-3, 165, 181, 183, 186, 192, 215, 225; rules and norms of 41, 43, 49, 53, 78, 98, 100, 105, 107, 130, 134-5, 141-2, 167, 169, 176, 183, 194, 197, 202, 215, 221; specific Tyvan 16, 44, 50, 53, 56, 78; taboo in the 98, 105, 138, 194, 203, 221, *see also* animistic-shamanistic worldview; change; dominance model; ideal state; model(s) of world interpretation; shift; switch
'interactive work' 39, 56, 186-7, *see also* Spittler
internalisation 54, *see also* Berger and Luckmann; externalisation, objectification
'internalized' insight 51, *see* Berger and Luckmann
intersubjectivity 43n, 45-7, 50-5, 218
Islam 220-1

James, W. 3, 39, 45, 52, 57, 245, *see also* multiple realities; paramount reality; sub-universa; Schütz
Johansen, U. 19, 20n, 42n, 52, 110n, 245-6
juniper (*artysh*) 83, 126; and milk 187-8, 208; offering of 83-4, 102, 117, 132, 207; purifying smoke 117, 123; ritual cleanser 174-5

Kaa Khem (river) 195, 213
Kaziev, B. 117, 246
Keitel and Allolio-Näcke 47-8, 246
Kenin-Lopsan, M. 19, 20n, 42n, 78n, 79n, 191-2, 246, *see also* Düngür
kham 85-7, *see* shaman, shamaness
kham yjash (shaman tree) 85-6
Khandagajty (village) 111, 171
kharagan (shrub) 94, 123
khoitpak (fermented milk) 92, 105, 108, 117, 128, *see also araka*; white food
khuvaanak (oracle) 139, *see also* divination
Kierkegaard, S. 46, 57
kinship 13-4, 220
kolkhoz 9, 11n, 12
Kyzyl (capital) 8-9, 13, 15-6, 20, 85-8, 90, 94-5, 100ff.
Kyzyl Taiga 104, 106, 111, 118

Lake Baikal 7
lama (*kheling*) 10, 83, 92, 101, 106, 127n, 178, 185, 190
landscape 18, 41, 50, 80, 85, 87, 133, 140, 166
Latour, B. 39, 77, *see also* actor-network theory (ANT)
Law, J. 39, *see also* actor-network theory (ANT); Law and Hasard
Law and Hasard 39, 247
laws of nature 56; natural law 221; Russian law 10
laypeople 15-6, 18-9, 83, 94, 113, 173, 178, 196, 201-7, 210-2, 214
Leenhardt, M. 3-4, 247
legend, *see* contemporary legends; 'true occurrences'
libation 85, 88, 100, 102, 136, 165, *see also* offering; sacrifice
life-world 54, 230, *see also* Husserl, Schütz and Luckmann
Lösch, K. 47-8, 175, 241, 248, *see also* Breinig and Lösch

Luckmann, T., *see* Berger and Luckmann; Schütz, and Luckmann

madness (*albystaar*) 45, 122, *see also* shaman, illness
Mänchen-Helfen, O. 20, 79n, 109n, 114, 248
magic 3, 18, 201, *see also* superstition; witchcraft
Marx, K. 11n, 173, 245
'masters of knowledge' 115, *see* Taube, E.
media 15, 59, 125, 211, 218
mediate 203, 211
medicine 120, 127, 184
medium 40, 195-6
medpunkt (medical care) 12
method 16, 20; comparative 42; emic 40, 53, 59, 77, 140, 167, 175, 182, 185-6, 192-3, 207, 212; empirical 42, 53, 167, 175, 221; empiricism 2, 221-2; etic 48, 167, 170; native 19, 123-4, 140, 222; qualitative 53, 57-8
milk 8, 80, 187-8; brandy (*araka*) 83, 92, 105, 108, 117, 128n; breast 127-8; fermented (*khoitpak*) 92, 105, 108, 117, 128; and juniper 187-8, 208; milking 80, 184; products (*ak chem*) 11-2, 41, 83, 86, 139; spirits 95; tea 79, 83, 88, 102, 108, 132, 165; white food 41, 83, 128, 136, *see also ak chem.*; *araka*; juniper; *khoitpak*
misbehaviour 90, 121, 178
misfortune 2, 23, 99, 103-8, 112, 120-4, 130-1, 141, 175, 183, *see also* fortune
model(s); of world interpretation 17-20, 39, 40, 43, 44, 47-59, 77-8, 166-8, 171-2, 174-5, 181-2, 184, 186, 188-9, 194, 196, 198, 201, 206, 210, 214-6; co-existence of ix, 3, 44, 218, 224, 244; complementing 40, 166, 175, 186, 210, 214, 223-4; contradicting ix, 2, 39-44, 48, 53-4, 56-9, 141, 165-70, 173, 182, 189, 203, 216, 221-3; dominance 39, 44, 48, 50-2, 55-9, 98, 166-70, 172-6, 178-9, 181-7, 189, 193, 197-8, 201-4, 206, 208-16; flexible use of 4, 17-8, 44, 54-6, 58-9, 166, 184, 214, 224; global 51-2, 58, 211; interaction 4, 16-20, 39, 44, 48-52, 55-9, 98, 99, 107, 108, 110-3, 116, 118, 120, 124-5, 130-2, 134-5, 137, 140-3, 165-94 *passim*, 196-8, 200-3, 206, 208-16; substituting 4, 177, 184-9, *see also* change; parallel realities; shift; switch,
model of human dominance, *see* model(s), dominance
model of interaction, *see* model(s), interaction
modern 7, 15, 39-44, 51, 204, 212; influences 58, 175; models 48; worldview 56, 58, 168
modernity ix, 40-4, 50, 52, 59, 77-8, 167, 211, 217, *see also* progress; tradition
Möngün Taiga (Silver Taiga) 82, 88, 101, 121, 123, 168, 178, 203
Moscow 11, 13, 101, 126, 132, 178, 203
mother earth 78, 98, 120, 165, *see also* father sky
mountain, *see* Ak Bashtyg Mountain; Möngün Taiga
Mugur Aksy (village and centre of Möngün Taiga district) 79-84, 89-95, 98, 101, 105-8, 121-3, 126-7, 133-9, 174-8, 202-3, 206
multiple realities 39, 44-7, 54, 57, 250, *see also* James, W.; parallel realities; plurality; Schütz, A.
murder 10, 14
music 16, 84, 110, 115, 118-20, 133, 220, *see also* New Age; singing

myth 1, 3-4, 21, 45; mythical thinking 3-4, *see also* rational thinking
mythology 2n, 45

Naadym festival 120, 137
narration 19, 110, 115-6
narrative 1, 2, 16, 17n, 19, 52-3, 58-9, 89, 104-5, 107, 109-12, 115-8, 142, 167, 175, 178, 184-5, 192, 203, 216, *see also* interaction model, narratively idealised pure form
narrator 19, 96, 109, 191, 203
nature 17, 79-80, 100, 108, 195-8; dominance over 168; natural resources 9-10, 13, 97, 100; overexploitation of 98n, 198; and pollution 107, 121; protection of 2; relation to 110, 121, 138-9
Neolithic domestication 51
neo-shamanism 15, 19, 52, 244
network 11, 14, 39-40, 56, 77, 97, 99, 140, 142, 169, 173, 200-2, 204, 212; networking 14, 204, 215, *see also* actor-networking theory
New Age 20, 52, 59, 212, *see also* esoteric movement
nomad(s) 7-9, 12-5, 19, 41, 101-2, 139-42, 168-9, 186-8, 192, 197, 201
non-human beings 1, 172, 221, *see also* human beings; spirit(s)
non-human subjects, *see* subjects
norms of the interaction model, *see* interaction model

objectification 54, 221, *see also* externalisation; internalization
objects in the dominance model ix, 44-6, 48-50, 56, 77, 169-70, 187, 201, 204, 206, 216, *see also* human agency; subjects

Oelschlägel [Oelschlaegel], A. C. ix, 8, 16, 17n, 20n, 21, 78n, 79n, 90n, 125, 140, 165, 170, 188, 235, 240
offering 79, 83-8, 99-102, 107, 117, 118, 120, 129-132, 138, 177, 183, 192, 197, 207; of oral tradition 118, 132, 136, 179; ribbon 99-102, 107, 135; smoke 83-8, 99-102, 107, 117, 135-8, 185, *see also* blessing; libation; ritual; sacrifice
oracle 3, 95, 112, 139, 169-70, 199, 205, *see also* divination; *khuvaanak*
oral tradition 20, 100, 115, 118, 133, 142, 204, 212, 240, *see also* contemporary legends; 'true occurences'
ovaa (ritual site) 18, 80-4, 101, 107, 120, 129, 136-9, 177, 191-3, 212-4; consecration of 81-3, 190-3
overtone singing (*khöömej*) 15-6, 110, 120

parallel realities 58
paramount reality 45, 52, 54-5, 230, *see also* James, W.
partner spirit(s), *see* spirit(s)
passive objects, *see* objects in the dominance model
perestroika 10, 19, 126, 167, 172
phenomena 40, 47, 77, 172-3, 221
phenomenology 54
plural world interpretations ix, 3-4, 17-8, 39-40, 43-4, 52-4, 58-9, 141, 165, 167, 214, 217, 219, 223, 227, 240, *see also* content, and structure of models of world interpretation; dominance model; interaction model; model(s) of world interpretation
plurality 39-40, 43-4, 57, 217-8, 224, *see also* James, W.; multiple realities; parallel realities; Schütz, A.

poem 17, 21; folk poetry 114; poet 81; poetry 110, 114, 120, 133-4, *see also* oral tradition
police 13, 109, 170-3
politician 220-2
Potanin, G. N. 7n, 20, 249
Potapov, L. P. 20n, 42n, 51n, 79n, 98n, 249
poverty 11, 12-4, 85, 130, 139, 182
power; energy and 50, 78, 83-5, 117, 137, 139, 179, 199; human 1-2, 56, 92, 94; of non-human beings 1, 49, 84-6, 108, 117-8, 132, 136, 138-40, 188, 190, 195-6; powerful places 83, 213; religious 78; shaman's 117, 172-3, 179-80; of spirits 80, 82, 84, 88, 95, 100, 117, 124, 134, 137-40, 185, 206, 213
progress 1-4, 10, 173, 184, *see also* change; development
protection 1, 2; against evil spirits 123-4, 194; of nature 2; religious 19, 102-3, 140, 185, *see also* deities; god(s); punishment; spirit(s)
psychology 3, 45
puk/ puktar (evil spirit) 17, 87-8, 90, 93, 109n, 121
punishment; by shamans 171; by spirits 1, 98, 105, 112-3, 120-4, 134, 141-3, 167, 171, 176, 178, 197-8, 209, 219, *see also* protection
purity 117, 123, 138, 188; impure 47, 208; 'pure ground' (wilderness) 17, 136-40; pure places 108, 137; purifying 117, 123, 188; religiously pure 139, 188

Radloff, W. 10, 249
rational thinking 3-4, *see also* myth, mythical thinking
rebirth 130; reborn 125-30
religion(s) 1, 19, 44-5, 137, 173, 201, 212, 220, 240; folk 140, 166, 201, 234; as 'opium' for the people 173; 'realities of religion' 52; 'silent religion' 202
res cogitans 48, *see also* Descartes
res extensa 48, *see also* Descartes
ritual 15, 19, 83-9, 108, 113, 117, 125-7, 129-33, 138-41, 142-3, 179-80, 190-3, 206-10; annual or seasonal 99, 102, 120, 190, 195; assistant 83, 190; healing 196-8; purity 188, 205; reconciliation 130-1, 141-3, 180-3, 208, 215; site (*ovaa*) 18, 41, 80-2, 177, 208, 212-5, *see also* libation; offering; sacrifice
rules and norms of the interaction model, *see* interaction model

sacred (*ydyktyg/ ydyk*) 17, 18, 41, 53, 80, 84-6, 99, 103, 107-10, 132, 136-9, 165, 186, 191-4, 202, 212-3; fire 103; people 110; place (*ydyktyg cher*) 17, 53, 80, 86, 99, 107-8, 132, 136-9, 186, 192-4, 202, 212-3; power 85; spring 18, 165, 193; tree (*ydyktyg yjash*) 17-8, 41, 80, 84-6, 107, 193, *see also* healing, spring; ritual, site (*ovaa*); shaman, larch; *tel yjash*; *ydyktyg/ ydyk*
sacrifice 79-81, 87, 107-8, 113, 115, 126, 135-8, 213; smoke/fire 81, 83, 107-8, 135, *see also* libation; offering; ritual
Schütz [Schuetz], A. 39, 44-7, 52, 54, 57, 59, 219, 230, 250; and Luckmann 39, 46-7, 51, 54, 57, 230, 232, 250, *see also* James, W.; life-world; multiple realities
shaman, shamaness (*kham*); association or clinic 15, 19-20, 95, 179-81, 191-2, 203-4, 206, 213-4, 216; dress 117, 171, 202; drum 114, 117, 128, 135, 171, 202; gift or talent 108-13, 117,

141-2; grandmother 95; illness (*albystaar*) 91, 109, 111; larch (*kham dyt*) 85-6, 108; as mediator 82-4, 86-8, 91, 93-4, 104-5, 109-10, 126-36, 142-3, 172, 191-2, 197; Mountain (Khamnar Tej) 87, 92, 121, 184; persecution 171, 201-2; power 92, 94, 117, 143, 171-2, 179-80; practice 114, 180, 193, 202, 204-6, 210, 212; professional 113-4, 178-89, 203-16; and punishment 112; 'real' or 'proper' and 'false' 113-4, 204-6, 211, 214; and ritual/ séance 7n, 15, 82-4, 86-8, 91, 93, 102, 125-32, 135-6, 142-3, 171, 183, 191-2, 196, 202, 206-11, 253; siblings/ sisters 101, 177-9, 181, 196-7; and spirit masters 100, 102, 117, 122, 141; and switch 178-89, 203-16; tree (*kham yjash*) 85-6, 98-100, 108, 132, 138; utensils 171; Western shamans 15, 212, *see also Adyg Eeren* (Bear Spirit); *Düngür* (Drum); partner spirit(s); ritual; *Tos Deer* (Nine Heavens)
shamanism 15, 19, 52, 56, 76, 108-10, 114, 171-2, 192, 204, 211-2, 215, 240; modelled on Tyvan 15; neo-shamanism 15, 19, 52; show 15; Western 15, 212, *see also* animistic-shamanistic worldview
shift; between models 181, 214-5; between 'provinces of meaning' 57; from emic to etic 167; from interaction model to dominance model 170-1, 181, 215; of perspective 77; from rational to mythical thinking 3-4, 46, 53, 57; from shamanism to neo-shamanism 52, *see also* change; switch
shock 14, 46, 57, 112, 178, *see also* Schütz, A.
shulbus (evil spirit) 17, 121, 123, 176
sickness, *see albystaar*; madness

'silent religion' 202, *see also* Streck, B.
Silver Taiga (Möngün Taiga) 8, 82, 108, 136
singing 15-6, 84, 96, 110-2, 118-20, *see also* overtone singing; throat singing
socialisation 55, 98, 218-20, 223
socialism 9-12, 167, 172, 201, 223
soul(s); of animals and plants 95; of children 123; of humans 2, 91-3, 97, 109, 122, 125-6, 130, 189, 206-10; as *puktar* 93; white soul 127, *see also* spirit(s)
Soviet 9-14, 18-20, 98-9, 166, 168, 171-2, 175, 193, 201-3, 215-6, *see also* dominance model
Sovietisation 9, 166
specific Tyvan interaction model, *see* interaction model, specific Tyvan
spirit(s); enjoy talents 119; evil 1, 17, 49-50, 53, 77-8, 80, 87-8, 90, 100, 109n, 118, 120-4, 136, 140-3, 165, 171-3, 176, 180-4, 204-6, 210, 215; fire 102-4, 135, 138; partner 95-6, 109, 114, 117, 122, 136, 141-3, 171n, 180-4, 189, 205-10; possession 45, 53, 79, 116, 122-3, 169; protecting 88, 90-1, 93-6, 99, 109, 112; steal human souls 122-3; 'time of the spirits' 177, *see also albys*; animism; *aza*; *buk*; *diireng*; drunkenness; *ee*; *puk*; *shulbus*; spirit master; subjects
spirit master (*ee*, pl. *eeler*) [*Herrengeist*] 41, 79-89, 96, 99-124, 131-43, 166, 168-70, 176, 185; of a body of water 105-7, 110, 135, 138; of a camp, a yurt, a stock, a corral 138, 184-5; of a fire (*ot eezi*) 87-8, 102, 135; of a flat 131; of a healing spring 135, 196; of a powerful place 137-8; as protectors 80, 87, 140; of the shaman's homeland 179; of a shaman larch 108; of the Silver

Taiga (Möngün Taiga) 108, 136; of the taiga 97, 100, 104-5, 117, 197, 203; of talents 110-1, 115-9, *see also ovaa*
Spittler, G. 39, 56, 77, 186-7, 250, *see also* 'interactive work'
spring (season) 4, 82-3, 120, 191, 193
spring (source) 18, 80, 84, 193; consecration 81-3, 120, 132, 191, 196; healing (*arzhaan*) 41, 84, 99, 135-8; medical 195-6; mineral 79, 80, 84; sacred 18, 165
stability 1-3, 51, 58, 124-6, 130-2, 135, 143, 216, *see also* balance; change; progress
stockbreeders 7-13, 97, 140, 169-70, 184-8, 198-9, 204, *see also* nomad(s)
Streck, B. xi, 202, 202n, 250, *see also* 'silent religion'
structure of models of world interpretation 39-40, 51-5, 58-9, 240, *see also* content, of models of world interpretation; definition, of models of world interpretation
subjects; human 49, 56; human and non-human ix, 19, 44, 49-50, 53 56-8, 77-144 *passim*, 165, 168, 175, 188, 191, 196-7, 202-3, 205, 208, 210, 215; non-human ix, 4, 19, 44, 49-50, 53, 56-8, 77-144 *passim*, 172-3, 176, 182-4, 187-8, 190-1, 195, 198, 203, 210, 215, *see also* dominance model; human beings; interaction model; spirit(s); spirit master
subsistence 9, 12, 14, 41, 102
sub-universa 3, 45, 52, *see* James, W.
Süt Khöl (village) 87, 92, 94-5, 100, 103-4, 106, 112, 123, 184, 196-7
suicide 11, 14
summer solstice 195
supernatural 45, 97, 172-3, 190
superstition 18, 174, 201, *see also* magic; witchcraft

switch ix, 4, 17-8, 45-6, 53, 57, 166-7, 172; professional 203-11; situational and contextual 43, 166, 184-9, 224; spontaneous 176-82, 182-4, 189, 193, 198-201, 215; strategic 201-3, 215, *see also* change; shift

taiga 8, 12, 14-5, 80-2, 91, 95, 101, 137, 139; charged with energy and power 117, 179, 199; spirit masters of the taiga 97, 100-1, 104-7, 112-3, 117-9, 136, 178-9, 186, 194, 197-8, *see also* Baj Taiga; Kyzyl Taiga; Möngün Taiga (Silver Taiga); Toolajlyg Taiga
talented or gifted persons 88, 91-5, 100, 106, 108-20, 140-3, 198-9, 205-6, 209, *see also* shaman, shamaness; spirit master, of talents
Taube, E. xi, 7n, 8, 20, 20n, 42n, 78n, 79n, 90n, 101n, 112, 114-6, 187, 244, 248, 250-2
Taube, J. 109n, 122n, 243, 248, 252
tel yjash (forked tree) 85-86, *see also* sacred, tree
theft; as breach of interaction model 169; of human lives 105; of human soul 91; of stock animals 168-70, 181, 186
theology 221, 223
thieves of livestock 99, 169-70, 182, 192
throat singing (*kargyraa*) 16, 96, 110-1, 120
Toolajlyg (valley and cooperative) 88-91, 101, 103-5, 118, 121, 129, 135, 191-3; Toolajlyg Taiga 89
Tos Deer (Nine Heavens, shamanic clinic) 20, 192, 204, 213-4, *see also Adyg Eeren*; *Düngür*; shaman, association or clinic

tradition ix, 18, 40-4, 50-1, 56, 59, 167, 212, *see also* interaction model, specific Tyvan; modernity; oral tradition
traditional; animism 18, 58; culture 15, 18, 19, 48, 77; singing 15; Tyvan interaction model/ world interpretation 19, 48-9, 140, 167, 172, 197, 211-2, *see also* interaction model, specific Tyvan
traditional worldview 40-4, 51, 56, 173, 175, 191; based on Tyvan animism or shamanism 56-7, 172, *see also* animism; interaction model, specific Tyvan
transdifference; concept of 39, 47-8, 52, 59, 166, 175, 223, *see also* Breinig and Lösch; continuum
transition 46, 126, 223
tree, *see baj yjash* (rich tree); sacred, tree (*ydyktyg yjash*); shaman, larch (*kham dyt*); shaman, tree (*kham yjash*); *tel yjash* (forked tree)
'true occurrences' (*bolgan tavarylgalar*) 17, 19, 98, 106, 125, 132, 142, 171, 202-3, 215, *see also* contemporary legends
Tyva; Republic of Tuva 9; Republic of Tyva ix, 7-11, 15-16, 18ff.; Tannu Tyva 9, 175, 248; Tozhu-Tyva 8-9, 81n, 98n, 242-3; Tuvinian Autonomous Territory 9, *see also* Altai-Dyva; Altai-Tyvans
Tyvan animism or shamanism 18, 56-7, 172
Tyvan interaction model 53, 58-9, 77-144 *passim*, 165-95 *passim*, 211-2, 214, *see also* interaction model, specific Tyvan

Ulug Khem (Yenisei River) 97, 106
universe 3, 142, 173; sub-universe 3, 45, 52, *see also* James, W.; Schütz, A.; sub-universa

Vajnshtejn [Vajnštejn, Weinshtein], S. I. 8, 20n, 42n, 51n, 58n, 78n, 79n, 90n, 109n, 245, 253
Vitebsky, P. 109, 110n, 253
vodka 95, 128, 129n, 165, 177, *see also araka*; milk, brandy

water 79, 80, 84, 86, 94-5, 99, 100, 105-6, 110, 121, 128, 135, 138-9, 195-6, *see also* spring (source)
Weinshtein, *see* Vajnshtejn
Western scholars 16, 20
Western shamans 15, 212
Western society/ societies 52, 217
whip (red-gripped) 91-2, 121-3, 207
white food 41, 83-4, 128, 136, 205; *ak chem* 41, 83-4; *araka* 128, 128n, *see also khoitpak* (fermented milk); milk
White Headed Mountain (Ak Bashtyg) 82n, 83, 108, 136
wilderness 17, 53, 95, 100, 102, 118, 136, 138-40, 179-81, 188, 193-5, 198, 199, 213, *see also* purity, pure ground
witchcraft 3, 200, 201
world interpretation, *see* dominance model; interaction model; model(s) of world interpretation
worldview 39-40, 51, 56, 58, 168, 173, 175, 191; Buddhist 58; Tyvan 51, 56
wrestling 84, 110, 120

ydyktyg/ ydyk 17, 80
ydyktyg cher (sacred place) 17, 53, 80, 86, 99, 107-8, 132, 136-9, 186, 192-4, 202, 212-3
ydyktyg yjash (sacred tree) 17-8, 41, 80, 84-6, 107, 136-8, 193
Yenisei River 105, 187, 195, 213-4, *see* Ulug Khem
yurt 15, 19, 41, 80, 87ff.; camp 87, 92, 102, 105-6, 121, 197

Halle Studies in the Anthropology of Eurasia

1 Hann, Chris, and the "Property Relations" Group, 2003: *The Postsocialist Agrarian Question. Property Relations and the Rural Condition.*

2 Grandits, Hannes, and Patrick Heady (eds.), 2004: *Distinct Inheritances. Property, Family and Community in a Changing Europe.*

3 Torsello, David, 2004: *Trust, Property and Social Change in a Southern Slovakian Village.*

4 Pine, Frances, Deema Kaneff, and Haldis Haukanes (eds.), 2004: *Memory, Politics and Religion. The Past Meets the Present in Europe.*

5 Habeck, Joachim Otto, 2005: *What it Means to be a Herdsman. The Practice and Image of Reindeer Husbandry among the Komi of Northern Russia.*

6 Stammler, Florian, 2009: *Reindeer Nomads Meet the Market. Culture, Property and Globalisation at the 'End of the Land'* (2 editions).

7 Ventsel, Aimar, 2006: *Reindeer,* Rodina *and Reciprocity. Kinship and Property Relations in a Siberian Village.*

8 Hann, Chris, Mihály Sárkány, and Peter Skalník (eds.), 2005: *Studying Peoples in the People's Democracies. Socialist Era Anthropology in East-Central Europe.*

9 Leutloff-Grandits, Caroline, 2006: *Claiming Ownership in Postwar Croatia. The Dynamics of Property Relations and Ethnic Conflict in the Knin Region.*

10 Hann, Chris, 2006: *"Not the Horse We Wanted!" Postsocialism, Neoliberalism, and Eurasia.*

11 Hann, Chris, and the "Civil Religion" Group, 2006: *The Postsocialist Religious Question. Faith and Power in Central Asia and East-Central Europe.*

12 Heintz, Monica, 2006: *"Be European, Recycle Yourself!" The Changing Work Ethic in Romania.*

13 Grant, Bruce, and Lale Yalçın-Heckmann (eds.), 2007: *Caucasus Paradigms. Anthropologies, Histories and the Making of a World Area.*

14 Buzalka, Juraj, 2007: *Nation and Religion. The Politics of Commemoration in South-East Poland.*

15 Naumescu, Vlad, 2007: *Modes of Religiosity in Eastern Christianity. Religious Processes and Social Change in Ukraine.*

16 Mahieu, Stéphanie, and Vlad Naumescu (eds.), 2008: *Churches Inbetween. Greek Catholic Churches in Postsocialist Europe.*

17 Mihăilescu, Vintilă, Ilia Iliev, and Slobodan Naumović (eds.), 2008: *Studying Peoples in the People's Democracies II. Socialist Era Anthropology in South-East Europe.*

18 Kehl-Bodrogi, Krisztina, 2008: *"Religion is not so strong here". Muslim Religious Life in Khorezm after Socialism.*

19 Light, Nathan, 2008: *Intimate Heritage. Creating Uyghur Muqam Song in Xinjiang.*

20 Schröder, Ingo W., and Asta Vonderau (eds.), 2008: *Changing Economies and Changing Identities in Postsocialist Eastern Europe.*

21 László, Fosztó, 2009: *Ritual Revitalisation after Socialism: Community, Personhood, and Conversion among Roma in a Transylvanian Village.*

22 Hilgers, Irene, 2009: *Why Do Uzbeks have to be Muslims? Exploring religiosity in the Ferghana Valley.*

23 Trevisani, Tommaso, 2010: *Land and Power in Khorezm. Farmers, Communities, and the State in Uzbekistan's Decollectivisation.*

24 Yalçın-Heckmann, Lale, 2010: *The Return of Private Property. Rural Life after the Agrarian Reform in the Republic of Azerbaijan.*

25 Mühlfried, Florian, and Sergey Sokolovskiy (eds.), 2011. *Exploring the Edge of Empire: Soviet Era Anthropology in the Caucasus and Central Asia.*

26 Cash, Jennifer R., 2011: *Villages on Stage. Folklore and Nationalism in the Republic of Moldova.*

27 Köllner, Tobias, 2012: *Practising Without Belonging? Entrepreneurship, Morality, and Religion in Contemporary Russia.*

28 Bethmann, Carla, 2013: *"Clean, Friendly, Profitable?" Tourism and the Tourism Industry in Varna, Bulgaria.*

29 Bošković, Aleksandar, and Chris Hann (eds.), 2013: *The Anthropological Field on the Margins of Europe, 1945-1991.*

30 Holzlehner, Tobias, 2014: *Shadow Networks. Border Economies, Informal Markets and Organised Crime in the Russian Far East.*

31 Bellér-Hann, Ildikó, 2015: *Negotiating Identities: Work, Religion, Gender, and the Mobilisation of Tradition among the Uyghur in the 1990s.*